Ministering Spiritually to Families

William Jeynes • Enedina Martinez
Editors

Ministering Spiritually to Families

Springer

Editors
William Jeynes
California State University
Long Beach
California
USA

Enedina Martinez
Department of Education
Point Loma Nazarene University
San Diego
California
USA

ISBN 978-3-319-13301-0 ISBN 978-3-319-13302-7 (eBook)
DOI 10.1007/978-3-319-13302-7

Library of Congress Control Number: 2014960145

Springer Cham Heidelberg New York Dordrecht London

Printed on acid-free paper

Springer is part of Springer Science+Business Media (www.springer.com)

Preface

Ministering Spiritually to Families is designed to serve as an academic textbook and counseling resource book that draws together writers that have served as specialists, usually both as academics and practitioners, in helping families thrive. The role of spirituality in strengthening families is one of the most understudied aspects of counseling. As a result, many psychologists and family counselors have little understanding of the place of faith in strengthening families. Moreover, they often possess stereotypes about religious people. This is especially true of counselors who are not people of faith themselves. Some family therapists view people of faith as too idealist, overly focused on right and wrong, and even as prudes.

For counselors that are Christian or of another faith, *Ministering Spiritually to Families* will help them substantially enhance his or her effectiveness in helping families across a number of different age groups and situations. For those others who are not faith-oriented, it will help them to understand, respect, and guide those who are believers. Recent Gallup polls indicate that the vast majority of Americans identify themselves as Christian and most of them view their faith as quite important in their lives. With these statistics in mind, it is of utmost importance for counselors to be able to relate with these individuals.

There are certain books that deal with the issue of ministering spiritually to families. Nearly all of them, however, suffer from one of three weaknesses. First, often they are dated. Second, they do not look at the issue of ministering spiritually to families in a way that combines the academic and the practical, that is so important to maximize the efficacy of a book. Third, they examine families at a very narrow and specific level. Regarding the final shortcoming, most books examine families with a focus either at the pre-marital timeframe, or address marital quality, or raising children. Almost none of them address all three spheres. *Ministering Spiritually to* Families is designed to help families at all stages of the life-course.

- In addition, few books offer the perspective of how children influence parents and that what constitutes an effective parent changes over the life course. Not only do the writers and editors who put together this book intend to use it in their university classrooms, but they also expect that academics, those in ministry, and families will desire to draw from the knowledge and wisdom contained in its pages.

All in all, the book, Ministering Spiritually to Families, is a source that can aid in the development of family ties over a large span of the life-course. It will be a tremendous resource for academics and practitioners desiring to help people believe for the right future spouse, during the process of marriage, and during the rather long span of time that they are raising children. It is a book that covers a wide range of topics, many of which are scarcely ever addressed in one volume with any real depth. In this way, this book functions to help families everywhere apply the deep but simple truths of the Bible that will make families healthier and happier.

Acknowledgments

We are very thankful to many individuals who played a large role in making this work possible. We want to thank numerous people in the academic world at Harvard University and the University of Chicago for helping Bill give birth to this project and in guiding Bill through the early stages of writing many of these chapters. We also want to thank several dear friends whose encouragement with respect to this project touched Bill deeply. Among these dear friends are Wayne Ruhland, Jean Donohue, Charles & Marion Patterson, Dan Johnston, Larry & Vada DeWerd, Sung Wu, Tim & Sarah Kim, Jessica Choi, Sylva & Peter Lee, and Randi Johnson. We want to thank Pablo Martinez, Enedina's father, for his endless encouragement and prayer support. We want to thank Enedina's nieces Sherry and Sheila and her sister Becky Salimi for their patience and love. We want to give special thanks to Azucena Solis, Enedina's prayer partner and teacher friend for over 25 years, and her loving church family from Shadow Mountain Community Church.

We also want to thank the presidential administrations of George W. Bush and Barack Obama for allowing Bill to share these principles in speeches in Washington D.C. at various government departments and the White House. Bill is incredibly blessed to have been married 29 years to his wife Hyelee, whose support has been exemplary. Without her prayers and support, this work never could have been completed. Bill is blessed and honored to have three wonderful boys, whom we thank for their love and inspiration. We also what to thank God for giving us the strength and providence to complete this project. We are very grateful for His encouragement and strength. To God be all the glory, for we are merely His servants

William Jeynes and Enedina Martinez, Editors

Introduction to *Ministering Spiritually to Families*

William Jeynes writes an important overview of the potential for ministering spiritually to families in the most general sense, in Chap. 1 entitled, "The Powerful Role of Faith In Family Ministry." Dr. Jeynes asserts that marriage can be a much more joyful experience than it is for most people. The chapter lays out a narrative that explains how faith can have a vital role to play in family ministry and help the joys of marriage become restored in many relationships. Individual faith tends to spawn many of the qualities necessary to make it possible for a thriving marriage to emerge. The chapter examines how counseling that is largely devoid of religious considerations, as well as similar emphases within broader society, have stifled many expressions and advantages of faith that were once deeply rooted in marriage and society. The chapter contains many insights that will enhance one's family life.

William Jeynes and Ralph Winter write Chap. 2, "Why Families Do Or Don't Breakdown," that is based on biblical principles and solid research that examines what divides and unifies families. Dr. Jeynes and Dr. Winter divide the factors into four distinct categories, based on the four combinations of two sets of factors, i.e., whether the factors are internal or external to the family and whether it has a positive or negative influence on the overall spiritual and psychological health of the family. The chapter is designed to strengthen families, due to an enhanced awareness of the forces at work both inside and outside the family that can serve to influence its members. **Lou Selzer writes the next chapter,** "Spiritual Mentoring For Healthy Family Development." This chapter presents a mentoring model that as proven effective in fostering healthy family development. It examines how dependent spirituality, one which responds to the Spirit, undergirds the effectiveness of an integrated strategy for mentoring family heads. His writing is immensely practical.

Gary Rieben writes the fourth chapter, which is quite touching entitled, "The Power of a Husband's Delight in his Wife." Dr. Rieben asserts that if husbands would redirect their devotion toward their wives and children, we would see a profound and positive effect that would transform the character of our nation. **William Jeynes** writes the fifth chapter entitled, "Preparing For Your Future Spouse." The chapter provides guidance for those contemplating the very important decision of anticipating- and pursuing- the decision of preparing for one's future spouse. The author provides principles that young adults can apply to each stage of the preparation process, including building the right personal foundation for making this event possible, how to believe for the right person, and what actions to take once one thinks he or she might have met that person. The chapter provides a great deal of wisdom that will enhance the chances of premarital and marital success.

Joe Wilmoth writes a solid research based piece called, "Marriage Preparation: A Ministry with Lasting Benefits." Dr. Wilmoth declares that With the vast majority of marriage preparation provided in a religious setting, churches are uniquely positioned to help couples improve marital quality and stability by providing research-based and biblically sound premarital counseling. This chapter discusses the importance of church-based premarital counseling and gives tools for developing an effective ministry. The chapter includes background information about clergy involvement in premarital counseling; best practices for marriage preparation; and the attitudes and behaviors of U.S. clergy related to this ministry that we have discovered in our research.

Dick M. Carpenter writes the next chapter named, "Worldview, Christian Maturity, and Young Adulthood: The What, When, Where, and How of Education after High School." Dr. Carpenter insightfully argues that the years directly following high school graduation play a significant part in the realization of Christian maturity. During this time, children begin to take ownership over most aspects of their life, including their spirituality. For many, this process unfolds simultaneously with post-secondary education in colleges or universities that can strengthen the faith system of the student's childhood or divert her/his attention to a different pursuit. Consequently, children in their late teens need the guidance of parents to help them find the environment that will best enable them to grow in their Christian maturity, develop a Christ-centered worldview, and acquire the skills necessary to succeed personally and professionally.

In "Scriptural Views Of Parenting" William Jeynes presents biblical principles that are designed to help mothers and fathers be more effective parents. The chapter first examines a real centerpiece of faith-filled parenting, which is living by what is true and yet demonstrating loving sensitivity. Balance along a number of dimensions is a real emphasis of the chapter. Dr. Jeynes also examines the notion that one can be demonstrate better parenting skills for children of certain ages versus others and how the parent can adjust to become a more effective parent at some of the ages that are more challenging.

In "The Impact of Family Religiosity for Latina/o Youth: Building a Case for Personal and Academic Enhancement through Faith," **René Antrop-González, Tomás Garrett,** and **William Vélez** describe the dual role of religiosity and its impact on academic achievement according to the experiences of 10 poor Puerto Rican students. They also discuss the implications of their findings in relation to families in the hopes that people can encourage schools to seriously look to faith communities and places of worship as important partners in the educative process.

In "Christian Principles For Ministering To Families With Children With Disabilities," **Mary Poplin** convincingly notes that the principles of Judeo-Christian help people value and love those who have disabilities much more than one commonly sees in the world. It begins with a view of the human person's highest and most real identity, which goes far beyond our disabilities and the utilitarian abilities valued by our secular culture. This view from "above" offers us God's perspective, which is larger, greater and more creative than current law, theory and/or practice admits. It begins with a view of the "disabled", first and foremost, as a beloved and essential member of God's very diverse family. Dr. Poplin's thoughtful perspective will touch, encourage, and challenge the reader.

"Laying a Strong Foundation in the Family: The Power of Storytelling" is an intriguing chapter by **Roger Friend**. Dr. Friend asserts that spiritual counselors and leaders can strengthen families if they are able to convey various spiritual truths regarding the family and character via storytelling. The author states that one can reach family members of all ages, particularly children using this technique. The chapter gives a variety of examples of teaching spiritual truths via this vast, relatively underutilized, means of communicating truth.

Together these chapters provide the reader a very comprehensive view of what it means to effectively minister spiritually to families.

Contents

Contributors

René Antrop-González School of Education, Dalton State College, Dalton, GA, USA

Dick M. Carpenter II Dept of Education, University of Colorado, Colorado Springs, CO, USA

Roger Friend Vista Christian Fellowship, Vista, CA, USA

Tomás Garrett College of Letters and Science, University of Wisconsin-Milwaukee, Milwaukee, WI, USA

William Jeynes Witherspoon Institute, Princeton, NJ, USA

California State University, Long Beach, CA, USA

Mary Poplin Graduate School of Education, Claremont Graduate University, Claremont, CA, USA

Gary Rieben Give Me That Book, La Quinta, CA, USA

Lou Selzer Christian Trinity Church, Eastpointe, MI, USA

William Vélez College of Letters and Science, University of Wisconsin-Milwaukee, Milwaukee, WI, USA

Joe D. Wilmoth Mississippi State University, Mississippi, MS, USA

Ralph Winter U.S. Center for World Missions, Pasadena, CA, USA

Editors Biography

Bill (William) Jeynes (Senior Editor) has served in counseling ministry for over 34 years and in academics for 23 years. He and his wife have counseled thousands of families over the years and he has three degrees in Psychology and Counseling and a fourth in a related field. He is a Professor at California State University, Long Beach and a Senior Fellow on the Family at the Witherspoon Institute in Princeton, New Jersey. He graduated first in his class at Harvard University and also graduated from the University of Chicago, where he received the Rosenberger Award for the most outstanding student in his cohort. Bill has ministered in churches in every inhabited continent and in nearly every state in the country. He has spoken a number of times at Yoido Full Gospel Church in Korea, the largest church in the world. He has spoken on family and faith issues for the White House, the U.S. Department of Justice, the U.S. Department of Education, and the U.S. Department of Health & Human Services. He has spoken for both the G. W. Bush and Obama administrations. He has spoken for foreign and UN leaders, Harvard University, Cambridge University, Oxford University, Columbia University, Duke University, Notre Dame University, and the Harvard Family Research Project. His 4-point family and economic proposal given to the Acting President of Korea was passed and became the foundation for their economic and family policy to arise from the Asian Economic Crisis of 1997–1998. He has about 140 academic publications, including 12 books on family and faith issues.

Dr. Jeynes has been interviewed or quoted by the Washington Post, the Los Angeles Times, The Wall Street Journal, the New York Times, the London Times, the Associated Press (AP), CBS, NBC, ABC, FOX, public radio, Al Jazeera and many other news sources. His work has been cited and quoted numerous times by the U.S. Congress, the British Parliament, the EU, and many State Supreme Courts across the United States. Dr. Jeynes has been listed in *Who's Who in the World* for each of the last nine years and received a Distinguished Scholar Award the California State Senate, the California State Assembly, and his university. He formerly taught at USC and the University of Chicago. Bill has been married for over 28 years and has three wonderful children.

Enedina Martinez (Assistant Editor) is a former Roman Catholic nun, who taught in private and public schools for 25 years. She is an evangelical Christian, professor of education, liberal studies program coordinator in the School of Education at Point Loma Nazarene University, and a Wesleyan Center Scholar. She has been a member on the advisory board of the Wesleyan Center for Twenty-first Century Studies for the past 6 years. Dr. Martinez has taught a wide array of courses at the university level. She has three graduate school degrees including an Ed.D. from Northern Arizona State University and MA degrees from Point Loma Nazarene University and Bethel Theological Seminary.

The Powerful Role of Faith in Family Ministry

William Jeynes

Abstract The author asserts that marriage can be a much more joyful experience than it is for most people. The chapter lays out a narrative that explains how faith can have a vital role to play in family ministry and help the joys of marriage become restored in many relationships. Individual faith tends to spawn many of the qualities necessary to make it possible for a thriving marriage to emerge. The chapter examines how counseling that is largely devoid of religious considerations, as well as similar emphases within broader society, have stifled many expressions and advantages of faith that were once deeply rooted in marriage and society. The author suggests that acknowledging that strength that faith can provide can help create an atmosphere of love in a marriage such that there are far fewer fights and a spirit of thankfulness rather than one of entitlement. The chapter delineates truths that will help counselors and families increase the chances of helping couples disagree rather than fight, be thankful rather than feel entitled, love rather than hold back, and enter in to the full joy of marriage.

Keywords Family · Marriage · Ministry · Faith · Spirituality · Religion · Christian · Counseling

The Joys of Marriage

The joys of marriage often fall short of what they can be because couples frequently take their eyes off of Christ's example and instead focus on the examples set by other people (Piper 2011). This is especially problematic in contemporary society, because the moral standards established in recent decades have been in steady decline (Allen and Atkins 2012; Jeynes 2010a). What many individuals have sometimes

W. Jeynes (✉)
Witherspoon Institute, Princeton, NJ, USA
e-mail: whjharvard@post.harvard.edu

California State University, Long Beach, 6572 Red Coach Drive Huntington Beach, CA 92647, USA

W. Jeynes, E. Martinez (eds.), *Ministering Spiritually to Families*,
DOI 10.1007/978-3-319-13302-7_1

overlooked is that as these standards have declined, so have the interpersonal goals in a marriage (Fine and Harvey 2006; Selvaggio and Meath 2008). In past generations, churches and even wider society taught that married couples should sacrifice for one another and that arguments were to be avoided. Now terms like "delayed gratification" are viewed almost like curse words (Craker 2011). Moreover, a large number of marital counselors assert that arguing is actually good or, at the minimum is to be accepted as an unavoidable component of married life (Bach and Wyden 1998; Coulson 1983; Doinick 1998).

If one uses the Bible as one's guide, God views marriage entirely differently. Moreover, if the willingness to sacrifice and avoid arguments is absent from a marriage, what replaces it is a relationship dominated by the formidable force of entitlement and an atmosphere that fosters hurt and these forces form a foundation that is the very antithesis of what is needed for a successful marriage (Lamb 1997; McDonald and Robinson 2009; McLanahan et al. 2013; Selvaggio and Meath 2008).

Lowered Standards for Marriage & A Spirit of Entitlement

Recently, there was a pastor giving a talk on relationships, who uttered a startling statement that was a reminder of the extent to which standards of character have declined in recent decades. He claimed that Christians needed to reject the standards of holiness once promulgated as the ideals of daily Christian living. Believers were not transparent enough, he argued. And indeed, that part is true. But he followed-up on that statement by declaring that one should readily admit his or her faults and that if a person could not admit to either lusting or getting very angry in the last 2 days, that such a person was either deceived or a liar. Now perhaps if the speaker had used the timeframe of 10 years rather than 2 days, some consensus could have been reached. But the timeframe was mind-boggling to many. Clearly, many wondered about the quality of the pastor's relational life and indeed he shared that there were many strains. The virtually non-existent moral standards made one wonder how a marriage and family could thrive with the absence of even the most basic scruples.

This lack of a reasonable moral compass has played a large role in producing an epidemic of marital failure throughout the nation (Jeynes 2006c; Selvaggio and Meath 2008). Without this compass a pervasive attitude of entitlement reigns in a marriage and chips way at the foundation of that relationship (Block 2013). And few things do more damage to relationships, of any nature including marriage, than an attitude of entitlement. That is, an attitude one carries of, "You owe me" and "I deserve this from you." The reality of the matter is that in any relationship people are owed either nothing or much less than they think. This planet and this life owe people nothing. God owes His creation nothing. In intimate relationships much less is owed than people tend to think (Block 2013).

In a marriage, to the extent that there are vows and Bible-based promises, there are clearly certain expectations that one should have of a marital partner. But ultimately, acts of love should be appreciated in a blessed attitude of thankfulness and humility (Clinton and Ohischlager 2002; Kostenberger and Jones 2004). These two qualities are at the very antithesis of an attitude of entitlement. Entitlement assumes deservedness and in reality, before God, people deserve nothing (Block 2013; Piper 2011). This same spirit also asserts that there is little that merits one's thankfulness, because of the de facto pride that concludes that a person is somehow entitled to acts of sacrifice and kindness by others. It is this lack of appreciation that is at the very heart of many peoples' rejection of the significance of the sacrifice of Jesus Christ. And it is this same lack of appreciation that causes the deterioration of many marriages (Kindlon 2001). With each expression of appreciation and thankfulness a marriage grows stronger (Post 2000). In contrast, with each expression of entitlement a relationship becomes weaker and slowly begins to debilitate.

To understand why an attitude of entitlement is so destructive, one does not have to look far for a parallel. Myriad people have argued that many Americans have a spirit of entitlement (Block 2013; Ehrensaft 1997; Kindlon 2001; Sigman 2009). The former group points to record numbers of able-bodied Americans on the welfare rolls, receiving food stamps, and the attitude of many young people in the United States. Numerous historians, social scientists, and other leaders believe that the increasing incidence of this attitude is contributing to the decline of the United States to the status of having a second rate standard of living. Economists increasingly point to the fact that the 50 % of Americans receiving entitlements is creating an untenable burden on the American middle class (Block 2013; McDonald and Robinson 2009; Sigman 2009).

Creating an Atmosphere of Peace

For any civilization to thrive for an extended period of time, there needs to be extended periods of peace; and warfare should be minimized (Cahill 1994; Johnson 1997). The same may be said of constructing a strong marriage. Disagreements in a marriage should be kept to a minimum (DeMuth 2006; Vangelisti 2004). Some of them can be valuable for cultivating a higher level of mutual understanding in the long run. To the extent to that is true, some disagreements are necessary. What this means, however, is that husbands and wives should attempt to limit their disagreements to those that are absolutely necessary.

Most disagreements are unnecessary. Most disagreements result from one of several phenomena or a combination of them (Arnold 2007; Kruschwitz 2001). First, sometimes the speaker does not talk clearly. This can create certain misunderstandings. Second, sometimes the hearer does not listen particularly closely. Third, numerous times the two people are generally in agreement, but are simply expressing very similar ideas in two different ways (Arnold 2007; Kruschwitz 2001). Fourth, the two misunderstand each other because of semantics or some other language-based reason (Jeynes and Littell 2000).

One way that these unnecessary disagreements can be minimized is to first acknowledge these and other reasons. Husbands and wives should acknowledge that sometimes one does not communicate clearly (Arnold 2007; Jeynes 2005; Kruschwitz 2001). I recall a man who was constantly getting in arguments with his spouse (and other people as well) because when there was a misunderstanding he consistently insisted to his wife, "You're not listening." Never once did he confess to the possibility that he could have been more lucid in his communication. Rather, it was always the other person's fault. And this caused a plethora of conflict in his life. To insist that he always speaks clearly and if there is any misunderstanding it is the fault of the listener virtually guarantees eventual conflict. No one is perfect. The reality is there are many times over the course of time when a person can be clearer (Arnold 2007; Kruschwitz 2001). There are copious reasons why a person's sentence might be unclear and all it takes is one of these reasons to make a statement more nebulous than the speaker intended. Some of the reasons include that a communicator may be tired, assume the listener understands more than he or she does, be in a hurry, be ill, not care that much about the subject, be unfamiliar with the subject, or be dealing with intricate subject matter.

If a husband and wife both understand that a dearth of clarity in a sentence can spawn misunderstandings and consequently can also produce disagreements, then they can minimize them by deliberately making an effort to speak more clearly and when a disagreement is beginning to arise, checking to see if a lack of clarity in speech was the cause. The person who spoke needs to ask, "Could I have delineated the gist of the sentence in a clearer way?"

It is equally true that the failure to listen closely might also cause a misunderstanding (Arnold 2007; Kruschwitz 2001). Once again, there are a variety of reasons why a person may not listen as carefully as he or she should. Among these reasons are a person may be simultaneously watching or listening to something else, have his or her mind on another matter, have something worrying him or her, be tired, be relatively unconcerned or uninterested in what the other person is saying, be ill, have a competing noise that makes it difficult to discern what is being said, and a host of other reasons. Once again, to avoid miscommunications resulting from listening, it is key that one ask if he or she could have done a better job of listening (Jeynes 2002b).

It is also amazing the frequency with which people who disagree are largely in unity on the propounded issue, but are expressing their ideas in different ways. On the one hand, this happens so frequently that it is actually quite humorous. But on the other hand, the regularity of these events also testifies to the extent to which miscommunication so easily takes place in a marriage.

Learning How to Disagree

One of the primary problems that married couples have is that they often do not know how to disagree with one another in a way that serves to reinforce the strength of the marital relationship as opposed to weakening the union. It should be noted at this juncture that although some disagreements between a husband and wife are by definition good, they usually are not constructive and in these cases are generally harmful to the relationship. Hence, this chapter has already examined how to limit the number of disagreements. Clearly, this fact contributes to the strength of a marriage (Hetzendorfer 2009; Tessina 2008; Vangelisti 2004). But a second step one should take in dealing with differences between a man and wife is to learn how to disagree (Kruschwitz 2001). That is, there are ways of disagreeing that increases the chances that good can emerge out of the disagreements and minimizes the chances that the differences in views will lead to arguments.

If a couple is to desire divine disagreements, then they must learn to develop the discipline of committing their disagreements to God. When a husband and wife sense a major disagreement commencing, the first step they should take is to pray and commit the time that is about to transpire to God. To some, even to suggest such a discipline may seem mind-boggling. But the reality is that not only is it possible to develop this degree of spiritual self-discipline, but it a major key to having a truly Christ-centered marriage. There are a number of very important benefits to this practice. First, it commits the marriage to God. Second, it commits the conversation to God. With this deliberate decision to be aware of God, the husband and wife tend to be much more careful about what they say to each other and before God. As a result, far fewer hurtful statements are spoken.

When a husband and wife sense a major disagreement beginning, the second step they should take is to attempt to recall all the loving acts their marriage partner had done. This takes a prodigious amount of self-discipline. When one's spouse has committed a wrong against oneself, it is only natural to think of a host of other similar transgressions that one's marriage partner has committed (Jeynes 2009a). As natural as this inclination may be, few personal habits can eat away at a marriage faster. The reason why this propensity is so deleterious is because when a misunderstanding or argument develops over one particular incident, its significance is quite limited. However, when a person brings up the past suddenly the conflict broadens to something much more than a particular event, but rather becomes topical or even comprehensive or all-encompassing, depending on the extent to which old infractions are brought up. The more broadly defined the dispute becomes, the more dangerous it is to the very relationship itself. As this takes place, the argument becomes less and less about an event and more and more about personhood.

Such an increase in intensity and scope in a dispute is also dangerous because everyone wants to feel that past wrongs, if they have been genuinely repented of, have been forgiven by one's marriage partner. But when these old skeletons are resurrected, one is inclined to conclude that these other wrongs were never forgiven in the first place (Kruschwitz 2001). Instead, when one's spouse revisits these supposedly forgiven issues again, the question that come to one's mind is, "Huh, where did that come from?"

The Unfortunate Acceptance of Fighting as the Norm

It is unfortunate that people's definition of a "normal" marriage has become diluted over the last several decades (Jeynes 2003a, b). Fifty- to sixty- years ago fights in a marriage were regarded as generally unhealthy and should be limited as much as possible. As time has passed, however, marital fights have become more accepted and even regarded as healthy in a relationship. This went far beyond simply asserting that disagreements were a regular and healthy part of a marriage, but that the actual fights were healthy (Bach and Wyden 1998; Coulson 1983; Doinick 1998). Consequently, Americans, as a whole, and even those in the church have lowered their definition of what the ideal marriage is all about (Jeynes 2011a, b). Ultimately, when the ideal is lowered, the quality of many marriages declines.

One reason why the number of combative spouses is increasing is because the percentage of people who view themselves as fighters has been on a major upswing. I recall speaking with a university student of mine, who was frequently having conflicts with other people. I asked her why it was that she was constantly having disputes with other people. She replied that the reason was that her mother had always taught her to be a fighter and that if she wanted anything in life, she had to fight for it. I shared with my student that if someone was *against* her, I could understand to some degree why she would want to fight that person. But I then asked her how on earth she could ever want to fight those that were *for* her. The young lady was clearly stunned and then shared, "*My goodness,* I never thought of that." Although she adamantly reaffirmed that she needed to fight anyone who was even in the slightest bit against her, she nodded her head pensively and uttered that she would really have to rethink some of her views on life.

The reality is, however, that there are a variety of statistics that suggest that there are a lot of angry people out in the world who have the attitude that they are going to fight just about anybody, if that is necessary (Fauteux 2011). As much as such an attitude often creates the same hurt and animosity that caused *the fighter* to be so pugnacious, the fighter is often either oblivious to this fact or pretends to be oblivious and tends to leave a trail of conflict, unnecessary wounds, and distrust wherever he or she tends to go (Fauteux 2011). And sadly, when a person enters a marriage with this kind of an attitude, instead of that relationship being a source of healing, restoration, and comfort, the home becomes yet another site of tension and battle. And indeed this is especially unfortunate because life is filled with a plethora of battles and challenges and to have one's marital life filled with such conflict is often so totally unnecessary. Moreover, it is disconcerting when this takes place, because it is God's plan for matrimony to be one of a person's greatest sources of strength. And when the reverse it actually the case, the grand potential for marriage goes largely unrealized (Meyer 2002; Minith 2004; Montague 2011; Murray 2001).

Few activities drain unnecessary strength out of people more than fighting those who are for you. I Corinthians 9:26 (*Holy Bible*, NIV 1979) states:

Therefore I do not run like a man running aimlessly: I do not fight like a man beating the air.

The declaration of the previous verse (*Holy Bible*, NIV, I Corinthians 9:25 1979) is that the goal of any race is to win and verse 26 builds on this assertion. That is, if one wants to win a race, he does not "run aimlessly" or "fight like a man beating the air." When people fight those that are for them, they do, in fact, "fight like a man beating the air." In other words, they waste a phenomenal amount of energy fighting needlessly and with no positive effect. It is analogous in some sense to Don Quixote's famous or rather infamous battle with windmills in a book that bears his name. Don Quixote was no doubt convinced that his encounter with these windmills would yield some positive effect. But in the end he was fighting wind (air) and the means of wind production (Cervantes 2006). There is a certain degree of irony that both I Corinthians 9:26 and this section of Don Quixote involve taking on wind (Montague 2011). In one sense those who engage in such warfare are battling nothingness with clearly no gain or advantage to such activity. That is one spiritual truth that arises out of both of these encounters.

It is nevertheless true, however, that even a deeper treasure radiates from both of these sets of experiences. That is, when one embarks in a battle against the wind, one engages in combat against a force that can potentially push from behind him or her and yield victory. Wind, whether it is directly from the air or from windmills, is a source of power that, when it is surging from behind one's back or from another power source, like a windmill, can produce great effects. Might the benefit of these effects potentially be exaggerated? There is no doubt that this is so. Nevertheless, it is indisputable that if one has a tailwind, or runs a "wind assisted" 100 m race, or benefits from the power of a windmill or turbine engine, life's participants can prevail with regularity to the extent that they choose to utilize the power of the wind. Wind, then, can generate the precise energy that is necessary to be victorious. And this being the case, how foolish does one have to be to not only fail to harness this energy, but actually become its enemy by refusing to access its energy and succor, which are so patent and available. And yet as foolish as this clearly is, countless people fight their spouses who are that wind personified and can be a source of such great power and the "wind beneath one's wings" (Jeynes 2006a).

In Galatians 3:1 (*Holy Bible*, NIV 1979) the apostle Paul uses the phrase, "Oh foolish Galatians" and although the topic of his exhortation is different than the one being discussed here, the essence of Paul's concern is still the same. People are capable of such utter acts of stupidity without God. And indeed, one of the wisest perceptions an individual can make is to fathom the divine extent to which human beings are capable of the most inane beliefs and actions without God and yet have the potential to be exemplars of God's wisdom and ethereal intelligence with God. It is nothing short of astounding the frequency with which people fight their spouses, when their marriage partners are in fact the very resource God has provided to yield ultimate triumph. To continue to engage in this activity is an act of supreme idiocy. When one apprehends this principle, then one understands that fighting the air is not only aimless and an incredible waste of time, but is rather also like a deep sea diver attacking his or her air tanks and a survivor of a jetliner crash in an ocean seeking to puncture his or her life jacket. And as imprudent as such behavior appears, it becomes clear how frequently it is done when one understands that billions in the world wrestle and resist Jesus Christ, the very individual who has offered to save their soul. And indeed, frequently battling a spouse who is generally very supportive often reflects a person's deeper illogical wrestling match with God Himself.

Allowing God to Develop a Marriage that has Almost no Arguments

When discussing arguments in a marriage, it is important to distinguish between arguments and disagreements. There will always be periodic disagreements between a husband and wife. In fact, a disagreement once in awhile is healthy for a marriage. Both members of the team ought to feel free to be themselves. While there is always that goal of oneness between the husband and wife, it should not be something that is forced. Nor should it be a state of affairs that in any way diminishes the unique perspective that both members of the marital union bring to the relationship. Admittedly, even disagreements can be too plentiful to foster a healthy marriage, as has been asserted in the previous section. It is often true that in any given marriage, a certain percentage of disagreements tend to explode into arguments. That percentage will vary depending on the temperaments of the man and wife, the extent of the external pressures around them, and so forth. With this in mind, a couple should try to keep the number of disagreements in a marriage to a minimum. And *especially* unnecessary disagreements married couples should try to keep at next to zero (Strobel and Strobel 2010; Swindoll 1998).

The reality is that an overwhelming number of disagreements are unnecessary. And because most arguments begin as disagreements, what this means is that overwhelming majority of arguments are also unnecessary. In fact, the percentage of arguments that is unnecessary is even higher than the percentage of disagreements in the same category. The reason why this is the case is that unnecessary disagreements are what they are; they are caused by factors that really made the disagreement unnecessary. But unnecessary arguments are not only caused by the same factors that cause unnecessary disagreements, they are *also* caused by necessary disagreements that somehow got out of control, i.e., the conversation should have remained at the disagreement level, but as emotions became stirred up and people were not that cautious about what they said, flared up into a argument.

Naturally, it is most crucial to reduce the number of arguments. The Bible refers to the tongue by a variety of names, but a "sword" and "knife" are among the most common (e.g., Psalm 55:21; 64:3; Proverbs 12:18). Sometimes words that individuals utter can be so cutting that they either cannot be healed over or at least easily healed over. Because of this potential damage that can result from an argument, the number and severity of marital alternations must be reduced. The best place to begin in attempting to do this is to start with a four letter word that copious people in contemporary society fear: "love" (Jeynes 2006b, 2010d). The most effective way to develop a long-term trend of little or no argumentation is to develop a long and clear history of loving your spouse and never attempting to hurt her or him (Worthington 2000). When a marriage partner truly understands that the other spouse really has motives of love and would never purposely hurt him or her, there is really no reason for that partner to allow the disagreement to become an argument. Why argue with someone who loves you so much? It does not make sense. Disagree, yes. Argue, no.

I recall really surprising my wife 1 day when I shared with her that I really felt that having arguments with each other was almost virtually unnecessary. I shared with her that we had been married over a quarter of a century and that she has seen in all those years that I have love her so much and that I never purposely hurt her. Why should she argue with me and act like my motives were any different now? Arguments generally produce some degree of pain and why would a spouse want to cause pain to a person who loves them so much? (again, assuming that this degree of love is in the heart of the other marriage partner). In fact, what couples often neglect to realize is that to start an argument with one whom loves you so much can be viewed as a insult by the other marriage partner. That loving spouse can think, "How can who speak that way to someone who loves you so much?" With the understanding in mind, a marriage partner should keep disagreements, which are sometimes necessary, at the disagreement level (Tessina 2008).

Arguments with a marriage partner who truly loves one and has never tried to hurt one are counterproductive, useless, and tend to hurt rather than help both the relationship and the partner who is showing all that love. Few patterns of activity eat away at a marriage more than a long history of argumentation. And *if* one is fortunate enough to be married to someone whose love is deep and real, they tend to be so totally unnecessary. When married to someone who truly loves you and would never purposely hurt you, one should remember: Disagreements at times, yes; arguments, no.

Affirming & Complimenting Rather than Disagreeing-Build up, Don't Tear Down-There is Enough of that in the World

It is key for any godly marriage to realize that the home is designed by God to be a place of refuge, i.e., a source of comfort, refreshment, and re-energizing. In order for this goal to be made a reality, marriages should be relationships in which complimenting and building up one another is the pattern. Disagreements should be rare and cutting one another down should never take place. From God's perspective, there is enough tearing down that transpires in the world. People are drained by a host of other people, criticized, subject to the jealousy and competition of others, and also attacked by spiritual forces. Marriage (as well as family) is God's tool to replenish one's spirit, soul, and body. In many respects, marriage works spiritually in the same way that food and rest work for the body. That is, the Lord has seen fit to use food and rest to nourish a body that each day needs to be built up again. Without that food and rest on a consistent basis, the body eventually lacks energy and begins to deteriorate to some degree. A healthy marriage and family life works in the same way. People need a happy marriage and family life. Without a healthy marital relationship, an individual loses personal energy and excitement about life. If this unsatisfactory state lasts for an extended period of time, it can begin to take a toll on one's life.

In the long term, the research is clear that marital friction and happiness can affect one's health, appetite, disposition, composure, overall sense of wellbeing, and general outlook on life (Lillard and Panis 1996; Schmeer 2011; Wilson 2005). Academic journals and books are replete with studies indicating that those who are happily married live longer and healthier lives than either those who are unhappily married or single (Lillard and Panis 1996; Schmeer 2011; Waite and Gallagher 2000; Wilson 2005). One of the primary reasons for this trend is because when there are happy marriages people become refreshed after laborious days of work and reinvigorated after being pulled down by the forces of life (Lillard and Panis 1996; Schmeer 2011; Waite and Gallagher 2000; Wilson 2005). Ultimately, then, under these circumstances the home becomes a place of refuge and a type of oasis in the mist of what can be some debilitating and even torturous paths in life. The Lord realizes that life can be difficult, painful, and even exhausting and He remembers that we, as human beings, "are but dust (Psalm 103:14, *Holy Bible*, NIV 1979)." Some people get offended by this fact, but in fact this shows the extent to which God is compassionate. He is keenly aware of what human beings can handle and what is beyond their ability to endure. With this in mind, the Lord declared that, "It is not good that man should be alone (Genesis 2:18, *Holy Bible*, NIV 1979)." Instead, he asserted that each marriage partner needed a "helper (Genesis 2:18b)."

It is important to remember that it is the Lord who uses the term "helper" and therefore this term should be defined both broadly and divinely, in the way that God would describe. Helper in God's eyes clearly means more than just someone who provides physical assistance. Such an individual in God's eyes means someone who is a helper in every sense of the word, i.e., spiritually, emotionally, and physically. One of the best ways to determine whether a husband or wife is acting like a helper is to simply ask the question as to whether the other marriage partner feels stronger or weaker at the end of the day, because of the other's presence. If the answer is yes than that other marriage partner has clearly served as a helpmate, but if not than the strength God intended to emanate from such a relationship is truly lacking.

In order for a person from a marriage to flourish, there must be an understanding in that marital relationship that it is vitally important to provide encouragement and refreshment to one another. The reality of the matter is that God has provided only one relationship in which, as a result of the relationship, the two people become one, i.e., the marriage relationship. No other family member or friend fills that role, but only one's spouse. As a result, there is no person that can provide the level of inspiration, vitality, and strength that one's spouse can in this type of holy and ideal matrimony. This level of intimacy cannot be experienced with a child, parent, brother, sister, or friend. The Lord reserves this beatific experience of unity for marriage between a man and a woman. With all that comes at a person in life, it is imperative that married couples understand that it is up to them to be a source of strength and support that is only surpassed by God Himself. Only with this cognizance of the unique source of strength and refreshment that God desires marriage to be can each partner embrace the potential benefit that marriage can yield.

The Primacy of the Husband and Wife Relationship

Over the past several decades, secularists have pounded away at most of the principle pillars of society including the church, the schools, the moral fabric, the economic institutions, and certainly the family (Jeynes 1999, 2000, 2002a, c). It is repeatedly apparent that elitists in a variety of sectors do not view the marital relationship with the degree of veneration that they once did. Regularly, the elite in Hollywood and the news media portray martial relationships as expendable and of questionable value, particularly if there are cherished secular values involved (Baehr 1998). Teachers in school who sacrifice for their students at the expense of their husbands, those engaged in civil disobedience but are flagrantly unfaithful to their wives, and those who fight for a valid cause, but lie, cheat, and steal from their spouse to accomplish their cause are elevated to the position of models of virtue and worthy of emulation (Gruwell 1999; Sawi 2000). In these cases, the feelings of the spouse are minimized and almost disregarded and on this basis the young people of today are constantly taught the limited value of loving one's spouse.

In some elements of today's society, commitment to one's husband or wife has almost become a dirty word (Waite and Gallagher 2000). Cohabitation and short-term commitments in the most intimate relationships are those promoted by Hollywood and larger society (Baehr 1998; Waite and Gallagher 2000). Many Christians dismiss the effects of Hollywood, the media, and these secular elements of society as irrelevant to their own personal marriage relationships and assert that they can pursue lives unaffected by these ponderous external forces. But the reality is that because powers are so puissant, even believers become far more influenced than they realize (Jeynes 2012c, e). Because even if they do not openly flout the institution of marriage, they do not readily acknowledge the level of intimacy and "oneness" that God desires to exist in a marriage.

The reality is the no one knows a person like his or her spouse. The husband or wife sees the opposite sex lifelong partner almost every day of every week. The spouse sees one's deepest motives and behaviors that are totally unmasked and revealed for what they are. One's husband or wife sees one "unclothed" in far more ways than in merely the physical realm. Included in this reality is also the spiritual and emotional realm. Granted, no one knows any individual like God, even including one's spouse. Among human beings, however, the relationship that a person has with his or her spouse is exceptional (Bronfenbrenner 1979; Ganong et al. 1999; Hetzendorfer 2009; Jeynes 2007a). In God's eyes, there is no other person that God declares one is truly at one with: spiritually, emotionally, and physically. Clearly, if there is sexual infidelity, there is some sense of oneness (unfortunately). It is also true that the Lord makes declarations regarding "oneness" in the church and there is a measure of "oneness" that exists in friendships (John 17:11, 21, *Holy Bible*, NIV 1979). But in Ephesians 5 and Colossians 3, as well as in other places in Scripture, it is clear that a marital relationship has an element of oneness that is apparent in no other relationship (Ephesians 5:21–33, *Holy Bible*, NIV 1979; Colossians 3:18–22, *Holy Bible*, NIV 1979). The Lord attempts to make this degree of spiritual, emotional, and physically unity more tangible and understandable to the human heart and mind by having marriage be the only human relationship that He compares to Christ's relationship with the church.

No one knows a person like one's spouse. A person's best friend or intimate relative might be second. It might be that the second person is a best friend, because best friends are likely reasonably close in age and related to each other as adult to adult for a long period of time (Bronfenbrenner 1979; Jeynes 2006a). But the extent to which this is so largely dependent on the number of years they have known each other and the depth of their relationship. It is also possible for a parent to be second. However, in order for this to take place a strong relationship between the parent and child must continue each year, so that the parent's familiarity with the child is not based on years far earlier. It is, of course, more rare for the child to know a parent very well unless a child is well into adulthood. This is largely because the perceptions of young children is limited and those of adolescents can be skewed as they struggle contending with the transition from being a child into the first exposure to some elements of adulthood. It is clear that one's spouse, who lives with a person day after day and year after year and is in a unity of relationship with him or her, generally knows one the best (Borruel 2002; Spera 2005; Wallerstein and Lewis 1998).

With all this in mind therefore, people need to do their utmost to cherish and strengthen the marital relationship (Tuch 2000). Because in a marriage "the two become one flesh," the beauty of it all is that when one seeks to encourage and strengthen one's spouse, the encourager is also strengthened, as long as the spouse behaves the same way. The result is that the spiritual dynamic of one plus one exceeding two becomes a reality (Wickman 2011; Wright and Roberts 1997). That is, the couple, as a unit, becomes stronger than what they would be collectively if they were to each continue to live as singles. People have great potential being single, of course. It's just that most of those same people in a marriage will give them even greater potential.

Important Questions to ask and Answer

To the extent that one's wife or husband knows one better than any other individual, there are some important questions to ask along these lines.

What does one's husband or wife regard as your three greatest strengths? There is a very good chance that one's spouse is right.

What does one's husband or wife regard as your greatest weakness? Here again a spouse is likely to have insight, especially if he or she is spiritual. If a spouse is less spiritual, there can be an element of projection. Nevertheless, a spouse is likely to be more accurate on this issue than any other individual.

What does one's husband or wife regard as your three greatest gifts? Often one's spouse is more perceptive about gifts than the "protagonist?"

What is one's husband's or wife's overall impression of you? Of all the people in your life, this probably is the closest to God's overall impression of you.

Does one's husband or wife really sense that you love them deeply? This is a pretty good indication of whether God knows whether we love Him deeply (Jeynes 1999, 2009a, b). Our love towards human beings, especially the closest human beings to us, is indicative of our love life with God (Cloud and Townsend 2001; DeMuth 2006; Jeynes 2010c).

What does one's husband or wife regard as your three greatest strengths? There is a very good chance that one's spouse is right.

After one has lived a certain number of years, if one has possessed a listening ear, in the truest sense of the term, it is very difficult not to have a sense of what one's greatest strengths and weaknesses are. As the years pass by, everyone has a growing list of the strengths and weaknesses that most frequently have been brought to one's attention. When an individual is 25, or in some cases up to age 28 or 30, that person can perhaps dismiss some of these comments that occur very regularly as just one person's opinion. However, when year after year, and even month after month, a copious number of individuals are mentioning the same strengths and weaknesses, it becomes difficult to ignore the overwhelming body of evidence that indicates that one possesses a particular strength or weakness (Jeynes 2009a). And indeed, by the time one is middle-aged and the same qualities or shortcomings have been brought to one's attention 30, 50, and even 100 times, it would take a stubbornness of colossal proportions to deny what is obvious to everyone else. Similarly, if a supposed weakness has only been mentioned one or twice after so many decades of living on earth, it is likely that such a viewpoint is either totally inaccurate or due to the vagaries of individual perspectives. When one's strength or weakness is consistently noted by one's spouse and close friends, in addition to a variety of other people, then an individual should stand up and take notice. They are most likely correct. As a general principle, the opinions that a person should weigh the most heavily in such circumstances are: (1) those one knows very well, i.e., those are well acquainted with one's personality traits and (2) those who are very spiritual and close to God. And certainly if a person possesses both of these attributes, the viewpoints of these people should be taken especially seriously.

Outside of the Lord, a person's spouse knows them better than anyone. This is largely because an individual's spouse is the only single human being that a person is at one with. And therefore, there is a mutual understanding and discernment of what are one another's strengths that is usually considerably greater than in any other relationship. Even one's children generally know one primarily when they are too young to fully understand what makes their parents who they are and often do not know their parents to the extent that a husband or wife does or even to the extent that a best friend might enjoy (Jeynes 2012b, d). Therefore, when a spouse states that he or she perceives certain strengths in oneself, these views need to be taken various seriously. And, in fact, a husband or wife can frequently be God's most reliable mouthpiece in conveying certain of His messages to the other marital partner. For all these reasons, if a husband or wife perceives certain strengths or weaknesses in an individual, that person should take these perceptions very seriously. This is especially true if one's spouse is in the ministry.

Human beings, almost by definition, are filled with excuses. Some of these excuses are understandable and even justifiable, but others are not (Jeynes 1999, 2003b, 2012a). Many of the great people of the Bible, who received great calls from God were initially filled with a plethora of excuses regarding why they seemingly could not respond to God's call. Abraham declared that he was too old, Jeremiah asserted that he was too young, Moses declared that he was poor of speech, Gideon averred that he was too small and insignificant, and Isaiah claimed that he was not holy enough (Holy Bible, NIV 1979; Jeynes 2006a). And yet even with God's spiritual coffer teeming with all of these various and sundry excuses, in each case God communicated that His grace was more than sufficient to address these concerns. Ultimately, each of the individuals responded in the affirmative and God used all of them in a powerful way.

God is so overwhelmingly wise and one of the ways in which this wisdom is manifested is through the godly counsel of one's spouse. From a male perspective, some have called this counsel "women's intuition," but it would probably be more accurate to say that it is "opposite sex intuition." That is, the reality of the matter is that members of the opposite gender are "wired differently" (Gray 1992; Jeynes 2011a; Lamb 1997; McLanahan and Sandefur 1994). And in spite of a myriad of attempts by seculzrists to say that basically everything is the same and of similar value, e.g., values and genders, the reality is that the full gamut of the body of research divulges a very different tapestry (Gray 1992; Jeynes 2011a; Lamb 1997; McLanahan and Sandefur 1994). The research pattern is patent that females often see truths that males do not so easily espy and males similarly identify truths that females do not perceive. In practical terms, what this means is that husbands and wives often are able to identify propensities and gifts in their opposite sex partners that the person who has these abilities does not fully (or even partially) apprehend (Gray 1992; Jeynes 2010a).

What does one's husband or wife regard as your three greatest weaknesses? There is a very good chance that one's spouse is right.

It is naturally almost always the case that a person would rather hear what the spouse views as one's three greatest strengths rather than, on the other hand, a listing of the three greatest weaknesses. The one exception is usually a case in which the spouse is insisting that one get out of the present dormant situation and use those strengths, rather than continuing in a spirit of inaction and laziness (Gray 1992; Jeynes 2010a). Nevertheless, the same truth that holds regarding a spouses' ability to perceive strengths in the marital partner is also true about the reliability of the discernment of weaknesses. No individual knows better the weaknesses that one possesses that the person who is at one with that individual (Arnold 2007; DeMuth 2006; Jeynes 2006a, 2009a). It is a person's marriage partner who sees a person at the closest range, with the highest level of transparency, and who sees the innermost parts of the heart and motives exposed (Arnold 2007; DeMuth 2006; Jeynes 2006a, 2009a). In addition, there is a sense in which if there is a fruit or potato that is rotten, it first evinces itself inside the and then works its way out. In other words, the husband or wife is generally the first to espy something and its deleterious effects as they make their way outward (Arnold 2007; DeMuth 2006). For this reason, the matrimonial partner is often the first to feel the trenchant pain of a weakness that has either failed to be controlled or has gone awry (Gray 1992; Selvaggio and Meath

2008). Even if people outside the family have not yet been influenced by the weakness' uncontrolled trajectory or its venom; it is only a matter of time before they do. Even if a person is in a prominent position such as being a pastor, if the sheep that is closest, i.e., the spouse, is hurting then a vital part of the ministry is hurting. If something is wrong with the sheep that is closest, it is hard to believe that the rest of the flock is as it should be (Selvaggio and Meath 2008).

With all of this being the case, a husband or wife should take the observations of one's spouse quite seriously. The wife and husband have an "up close" vantage point that no one else really has. One would be sagacious indeed to quickly act on the weaknesses that one's spouse points out, by coming before the Lord and asking if these shortcomings are indeed actually there. Note, that a person should not necessarily assume that one's husband or wife is correct in his or her assumptions. On the contrary, a person's humanity and set of personal experiences cause a spouses remarks to either become tainted or jaded (Arnold 2007; Gray 1992; Jeynes 2010b). Nevertheless, one should respect one's spouse and the marital institution enough so that a person at least goes before the Lord to ask that all-important question, "Lord, was that criticism from you?" If then, the answer to that question is yes, it is important that the spouse on the receiving end of that criticism respond swiftly to correct the problem.

It is also wise to look for a confirmation of one's spouse's observations by inquiring of the opinions of other close friends. If those close friends concur with the conclusions of one's husband or wife then this is a pretty good indication that the perceptions are accurate (Arnold 2007; Gray 1992).

It can also be perspicacious to consider thoughtfully the perspective of one's husband or wife for two other reasons. First, the Lord often chooses to use one's marital partner as His mouthpiece because generally there is no other person who has such unconditional love towards one as that individual. That being the case, a person's spouse can be a vessel both God's expressions of tender love, exhortation, and even rebuke in a way that will likely be received. Some truths run so intimate and are so deeply profound and meaningful that they will only be received if the conduit is a loving spouse. Second, because a spouse is the person an individual is at one with in a marital union, that person can look to the spouse to help one grow in a variety of respects and monitor one's progress as he or she attempts to develop in this way (Selvaggio and Meath 2008).

Enabling a Congregation to Strengthen their Faith as a Means to Strengthening the Marriages in a House of Worship

When one asserts that marriages need to be given more to God, this is more than just an exhortation for individuals to act in this way. The church also must assume its responsibility of preserving the marriages that exist within the church. Many times believers are oblivious to the fact that they sometimes increase the likelihood that divorce will take place. It often begins in an innocent enough form. Often what happens is that a person has a close friend who consistently complains about his or her spouse. That person believes that out of the motive of being a good friend, it is supportive to not only listen to the complaints of a friend regarding their spouse, but to comment on them. For example, imagine a situation in which a woman complains, "My husband is so lazy and unwilling to help in the home. He comes home from work, eats like a slob, and then sits on the recliner, and does nothing. He never helps out in the home and is a good-for-nothing." The friend, wanting to be supportive of the friend, declares, "You're right. He is lazy. I wouldn't put up with that." The friend may not realize it, but he or she has just contributed to the friction in that marriage. To the extent to which comments like that are allowed to continue, the chances of divorce are increased.

Ministers and Lay Leaders Can Learn to Strengthen Marriages and Reduce the Divorce Rate in the Church

People need to be aware of the extent to which they often contribute to marital friction and divorce in the marriages of their friends and acquaintances. Ministers are probably the best spiritual conduit to enable this process to take place. The reality is that families and society, as a whole, thrive when people are supportive of one another's efforts (Allen and Atkins 2012; Barclay 2010; Jeynes 2008a, b). In contrast to this more compassionate scenario are the means via which people either overtly or inadvertently tear down a marriage. The primary way that this is often done is by friends and acquaintances agreeing with and affirming a married person's complaints about his or her spouse. Ministers via counseling and pulpit ministry are often the ideal people to thwart these undermining comments and enlighten people regarding how potentially destructive such comments actually are.

In addition to pointing out the danger of perhaps well-intended, but baleful, comments, ministers, counselors, and others need to also point out what is one of the most efficacious ways that friends can support their friends' marriages. That is, in contrast, people need to be aware of the extent to which they can strengthen marriages by defending the spouses that are being criticized and pointing out their positive attributes. Although it is true that the married couple will be the primary focus of efforts to improve the quality of marital relations, the counselor is wise to acknowledge the fact that other people and factors can be major factors as well.

Concluding Thoughts

Many couples are settling for a quality of married life that is well below what is possible and those who minister to families spiritually, can incorporate faith-based principles that will help these families to flourish. The thanklessness, lack of love and commitment, and fighting do not have to have place in the marital experience. Wise spiritual guides can help couples experience marriage and family living as it was meant to be experienced.

References

Allen, E. S., & Atkins, D. C. (2012). The association of divorce and extramarital sex in a representative U.S. sample. *Journal of Family Issues, 33*(11), 1477–1493.
Arnold, L. B. (2007). *Family & communication: Theory & research*. Boston: Allyn & Bacon.
Bach, G. R., & Wyden, P. (1998). *The intimate enemy: How to fight fair in love and marriage*. New York: William & Morrow.
Baehr, T. (1998). *The media-wise family*. Colorado Springs: Victor Publishing.
Barclay, W. (2010). *Forgiveness: What the Bible tells us about forgiveness*. Edinburgh: Saint Andrew.
Block, P. (2013). *Stewardship: Choosing service over self-interest*. San Francisco: Berrett-Koehler.
Borruel, T. W. (2002). The ten p's of parent communication. A strategy for staff development. *Child Care Information Exchange, 143*(1), 54–57.
Bronfenbrenner, U. (1979). *The ecology of human development*. Cambridge: Harvard University Press.
Cahill, L. S. (1994). *Love your enemies: Discipleship, pacifism, and just war theory*. Minneapolis: Fortress Press.
Cervantes, M. (2006). *The adventures and misadventures of Don Quiote*. Charleston: Ne Plus Ulta Communications.
Clinton, T. E., & Ohischlager, G. W. (2002). *Competent Christian counseling*. Colorado Springs: Waterbrook Press.
Cloud, H., & Townsend, J. S. (2001). *How people grow: What the Bible reveals about personal growth*. Grand Rapids: Zondervan.
Coulson, R. (1983). *Fighting fair: Family mediation will work for you*. New York: Free Press.
Craker, L. (2011). *Money secrets of the Amish: Finding true abundance in simplicity, sharing, and saving*. Nashville: Thomas Nelson.
DeMuth, M. E. (2006). *Building the Christian family you never had*. Colorado Springs: Westbrook Press.
Doinick, E. (1998). *Madness on the couch: Blaming the victim in the heydey of psychoanalysis*. New York: Simon & Schuster.
Ehrensaft, D. (1997). *Spoiling childhood: How well-meaning parents are giving children too much—but not what they need*. New York: Guilford Press.
Fauteux, K. (2011). *Defusing angry people: Practical tools for handling bullying, threats, and violence*. Fair Hills: New Horizon Press.
Fine, M. A., & Harvey, J. H. (2006). *Handbook of divorce and relationship dissolution*. Mahwah: Lawrence Erlbaum.
Ganong, L. H., Coleman, M., Fine, M. A., & Martin, P. (1999). The stepparents' affinity-seeking and affinity-maintaining strategies with stepchildren. *Journal of Family Issues, 20*(3), 229–327.
Gray, J. (1992). *Men are from Mars, women are from Venus*. New York: HarperCollins.
Gruwell, E. (1999). *The freedom writers' diary*. New York: Doubleday.
Hetzendorfer, R. (2009). *The pastoral counseling handbook*. Nashville: Beacon Hill Press.
Holy Bible. (1979). Holy Bible, new international version. Nashville: Thomas Nelson.
Jeynes, W. (1999). The effects of religious commitment on the academic achievement of black and hispanic children. *Urban Education, 34*(4), 458–479.
Jeynes, W. (2000). Assessing school choice: A balanced perspective. *Cambridge Journal of Education, 30*(2), 223–241.
Jeynes, W. (2002a). A meta-analysis of the effects of attending religious schools and religiosity on black and Hispanic academic achievement. *Education & Urban Society, 35*(1), 27–49.
Jeynes, W. (2002b). *Divorce, family structure, and the academic success of children*. New York: Haworth Press/Taylor & Francis.
Jeynes, W. (2002c). The relationship between the consumption of various drugs by adolescents and their academic achievement. *The American Journal of Drug and Alcohol Abuse, 28*(1), 1–21.

Jeynes, W. (2003a). A meta-analysis: The effects of parental involvement on minority children's academic achievement. *Education & Urban Society, 35*(2), 202–218.

Jeynes, W. (2003b). The effects of black and Hispanic twelfth graders living in intact families and being religious on their academic achievement. *Urban Education, 38*(1), 35–57.

Jeynes, W. (2005). *Parental involvement and student achievement: A meta-analysis.* (Family Involvement Research Digest, Harvard Family Research Project). Cambridge: Harvard Family Research Project.

Jeynes, W. (2006a). *A hand not shortened.* Greenwich: Information Age Press.

Jeynes, W. (2006b). Standardized tests and the true meaning of kindergarten and preschool. *Teachers College Record, 108*(10), 1937–1959.

Jeynes, W. (2006c). The impact of parental remarriage on children: A meta-analysis. *Marriage and Family Review, 40*(4), 75–102.

Jeynes, W. (2007a). *American educational history: School, society, and the common good.* Thousand Oaks: Sage.

Jeynes, W. (2008a). Effects of parental involvement on experiences of discrimination and bullying. *Marriage & Family Review, 43*(3–4), 255–268.

Jeynes, W. (2008b). What we should and should not learn from the Japanese and other East Asian education systems? *Educational Policy, 22*(6), 900–927.

Jeynes, W. (2009a). *Getting closer to god.* Charlotte: Information Age Press.

Jeynes, W. (2009b). The relationship between Bible literacy and academic achievement, and school behavior. *Education & Urban Society, 41*(4), 419–436.

Jeynes, W. (2010a). *A call for character education and prayer in the schools.* Westport: Praeger.

Jeynes, W. (2010b). Religiosity, religious schools, and their relationship with the achievement gap: a research synthesis and meta-analysis. *Journal of Negro Education, 79*(3), 263–279.

Jeynes, W. (2010c). The relationship between Bible literacy and academic and behavioral outcomes in urban areas: A meta-analysis. *Education & Urban Society, 42*(5), 522–544.

Jeynes, W. (2010d). The salience of the subtle aspects of parental involvement and encouraging that involvement: Implications for school-based programs. *Teachers College Record, 112*(3), 747–774.

Jeynes, W. (2011a). Help families by fostering parental involvement. *Phi Delta Kappan, 93*(3), 38–39.

Jeynes, W. (2011b). *Parental involvement & academic success.* New York: Taylor & Francis/Routledge.

Jeynes, W. (2012a). A meta-analysis on the effects and contributions of public, public charter, and religious schools on student outcomes. *Peabody Journal of Education, 87*(3), 305–335.

Jeynes, W. (2012b). A meta-analysis of the efficacy of different types of parental involvement programs for urban students. *Urban Education, 47*(4), 706–742.

Jeynes, W. (2012c). Protestant education in Russia and the former Soviet Union and the Eastern Bloc. In W. Jeynes & D. Robinson (Eds.), *The international handbook of Protestant education* (pp. 275–294). London: Springer.

Jeynes, W. (2012d). Reaching out to make a difference. *Phi Delta Kappan, 93*(6), 80.

Jeynes, W. (2012e). The rise of home schooling as a modern educational phenomenon in protestant education. In W. Jeynes & D. Robinson (Eds.), *The international handbook of Protestant education* (pp. 77–92). London: Springer.

Jeynes, W., & Littell, S. (2000). A meta-analysis of studies examining the effect of whole language instruction on the literacy of low-SES students. *Elementary School Journal, 101*(1), 21–33.

Johnson, P. (1997). *A history of the American people.* New York: Harper Collins.

Kindlon, D. J. (2001). *Too much of a good thing: Raising children of character in an indulgent age.* New York: Hyperion.

Kostenberger, A. J., & Jones, D. W. (2004). *God, marriage & family: Rebuilding the biblical foundation.* Wheaton: Crossway Books.

Kruschwitz, R. B. (2001). *Forgiveness*. Waco: Baylor University.
Lamb, M. (1997). *The role of the father in child development*. New York: Wiley.
Lillard, L. A., & Panis, C. W. (1996). Marital status and mortality: The role of health. *Demography, 33*(3), 313–327.
McDonald, L. G., & Robinson, P. (2009). *A colossal failure of common sense*. New York: Crown.
McLanahan, S., & Sandefur, G. (1994). *Growing up with a single parent: What hurts, what helps*. Cambridge: Harvard University Press.
McLanahan, S., Tech, S., & Schneider, D. (2013). The causal effects of father absence. *Annual Review of Sociology, 39*(1), 399–427.
Meyer, J. (2002). *Making marriage work: The advice you need for a lifetime of happiness*. New York: Warner Faith.
Minith, F. B. (2004). *In pursuit of happiness: Choices that can change your life*. Grand Rapids: Fleming H. Revell.
Montague, G. T. (2011). *First Corinthians*. Grand Rapids: Baker Academic.
Murray, J. (2001). *Love, marriage, and family in the middle ages*. Peterborough: Broadview Press.
Piper, J. (2011). *Desiring god: Meditations of a Christian hedonist*. Colorado Springs: Multnomah.
Post, S. G. (2000). *More lasting unions: Christianity, the family, and society*. Grand Rapids: Eerdmans.
Sawi, B. (2000). *Coming up for air*. New York: Hyperion.
Schmeer, K. K. (2011). The child health disadvantage of parental cohabitation. *Journal of Marriage & Family, 73*(1), 181–193.
Selvaggio, A. T., & Meath, K. (2008). *A Proverbs driven life: Timeless wisdom for your work, wealth, and relationships*. Wapwallopen: Shepherd Press.
Sigman, A. (2009). *The spoilt generation: Why restoring authority will make our children and society happier*. London: Piakus.
Spera, C. (2005). A review of the relationship between parental involvement and student motivation. *Educational Psychology Review, 17*(2), 125–146.
Strobel, L., & Strobel, L. (2010). *Surviving a spiritual mismatch in marriage*. Grand Rapids: Zondervan.
Swindoll, C. R. (1998). *Joseph: A man of integrity and forgiveness: Profiles in character*. Nashville: Word Publishers.
Tessina, T. B. (2008). *Money, sex, and kids: Stop fighting about the three things that can ruin your marriage*. Avon: Adams Media.
Tuch, R. (2000). *The single woman-married man syndrome*. Northvale: Aronson.
Vangelisti, A. L. (2004). *Handbook of family communication*. Mahwah: Erlbaum.
Waite, L. J., & Gallagher, M. (2000). *The case for marriage: Why married people are happier, healthier, and better off financially*. New York: Doubleday.
Wallerstein, J. S., & Lewis, J. (1998). The long-term impact of divorce on children: A first report from a 25-year study. *Family and Conciliation Courts Review, 36*(3), 368–383.
Wickman, C. (2011). *Pastors at risk: Protecting your future, guarding your present*. Colorado Springs: WaterBrook Press.
Wilson, R. F. (2005). Evaluating marriage: Does marriage matter to the nurturing of children? *San Diego Law Review, 42*(3), 847–880.
Worthington, E., Jr. (2000). *Christian marital counseling: Eight approaches to helping couples*. Eugene: Wipf and Stock.
Wright B. N., & Roberts, W. (1997). *Before you say "I do": A marriage preparation manual for couples*. Eugene: Harvest House Publishers.

William Jeynes has served in counseling ministry for over 34 years and in academics for 23 years. He and his wife have counseled thousands of families over the years and he has three degrees in Psychology and Counseling and a fourth in a related field. He is a Professor at California State University, Long Beach and a Senior Fellow on the Family at the Witherspoon Institute in Princeton, New Jersey. He graduated first in his class at Harvard University and also graduated from the University of Chicago, where he received the Rosenberger Award for the most outstanding student in his cohort. Bill has ministered in churches in every inhabited continent and in nearly every state in the country. He has spoken a number of times at Yoido Full Gospel Church in Korea, the largest church in the world. He has spoken on family and faith issues for the White House, the U.S. Department of Justice, the U.S. Department of Education, and the U.S. Department of Health & Human Services. He has spoken for both the G. W. Bush and Obama administrations. He has spoken for foreign and UN leaders, Harvard University, Cambridge University, Oxford University, Columbia University, Duke University, Notre Dame University, and the Harvard Family Research Project. His four-point family and economic proposal given to the Acting President of Korea was passed and became the foundation for their economic and family policy to arise from the Asian Economic Crisis of 1997–1998. He has about 140 academic publications, including 12 books on family and faith issues

Dr. Jeynes has been interviewed or quoted by the Washington Post, the Los Angeles Times, The Wall Street Journal, the New York Times, the London Times, the Associated Press (AP), CBS, NBC, ABC, FOX, public radio, Al Jazeera and many other news sources. His work has been cited and quoted numerous times by the U.S. Congress, the British Parliament, the EU, and many State Supreme Courts across the United States. Dr. Jeynes has been listed in *Who's Who in the World* for each of the last 9 years and received a Distinguished Scholar Award the California State Senate, the California State Assembly, and his university. He formerly taught at USC and the University of Chicago. Bill has been married for over 28 years and has three wonderful children.

Why Families Do or Do Not Breakdown

William Jeynes and Ralph Winter

Abstract The authors present research-based evidence indicating why it is that certain families do or do not breakdown. The authors divide the factors into four distinct categories, based on the four combinations of two sets of factors, i.e., whether the factors are internal or external to the family and whether it has a positive or negative influence on the overall spiritual and psychological health of the family. The chapter is designed to strengthen families, due to an enhanced awareness of the forces at work both inside and outside the family that can serve to influence its members.

Keywords Family · Marriage · Divorce · Christianity · Prayer · Devotions · Bible · Children · Priorities · Wisdom · Example · Favoritism · Rivalry · Parenting · Counseling

It is beyond dispute that one of the most ostensible trends of the last 50 years is that the family in the United States, Europe, and much of the world has broken down to a large degree (Amato 2001; Brooks and Goldstein 2001; Chadwick and Heaton 1992; Glasser and Glasser 1996; Jacobsen et al. 2012). After declining from the 1948–1962 period, parental divorce rates surged beginning in 1963 (Becker 1981; Cherlin 1978; Fine and Harvey 2006). The research literature is inundated with the illimitable number of sobering results of the breakdown of the family, particularly on children but also on the adults involved (Allen and Atkins 2012; Bouchard and Doucet 2011; Lee and Bowen 2006). Among the children of these families, some

W. Jeynes (✉)
Witherspoon Institute, Princeton, NJ, USA
e-mail: whjharvard@post.harvard.edu

California State University, Long Beach, 6572 Red Coach Drive Huntington Beach, CA 92647, USA

R. Winter
U.S. Center for World Missions, c/o Beth Snodderly 1605 E Elizabeth St., Pasadena, CA 91104, USA

W. Jeynes, E. Martinez (eds.), *Ministering Spiritually to Families*,
DOI 10.1007/978-3-319-13302-7_2

of these effects include declining achievement in school, increased incidence of depression and other examples of psychological duress, elevated likelihood of partaking in illegal drugs, and the greater likelihood of engaging in delinquent behavior (Fine and Harvey 2006; Lamb 1997; Pong et al. 2003).

Sadly, the trend toward the break-up of the family did not end with the rising incidence of divorce, nor did it cease with the rising incidence of remarriage (Glasser and Glasser 1996; Jeynes 2006c). Rather, non-traditional family structures continued to proliferate so that never married single parent families and cohabitation surged (Guner and Knowles 2009; Palm and Fagan 2008). As time passed into the 1990s and 2000s households in which neither parent was present, although relatively small in number, increased in their incidence (Glasser and Glasser 1996; Post 2000).

There may be situations in which family breakup is unavoidable or at least understandable. Prior to the 1960s, when there was only one parent in the home often people thought that perhaps either the father or mother died (Lamb 1997; Popenoe 2000). There are also situations in which one of the marital partners commits adultery (Allen and Atkins 2012; Clayton et al. 2013). Nevertheless, there are also a plethora of cases in which the breakup of a family is viewed as unnecessary, harmful, and damaging either to couple involved, their children, and even to society at large (Nair and Murray 2005; Wallerstein 2005). There are, of course, going to be differences in the degree to which certain view particular breakups as necessary or unnecessary and the extent of the damage that is done (Glasser and Glasser 1996; Lamb 1997; Post 2000). A copious number of these differences are due to a variety of worldviews that people possess that run along the perimeter of a combination of religious beliefs, core convictions, and personal experiences (Allen and Atkins 2012; Stokes and Ellison 2010). In the midst of these dearly valued worldviews, there runs a thread of common values that are logical enough and involve common principles of decency that would lead the overwhelmingly majority of Americans and other nationalities to the conclusion that the marriage could have been saved (Weiner-Davis 2001; Popenoe 2000; Post 2000; Rein 2007). The news media daily presents stories on family dysfunction, with the understanding that the facts that they present will lead 90 % of the television audience to reach the same conclusion (Guner and Knowles 2009; McDonald and Robinson 2009).

With this background in mind, it is indubitably true that virtually all Americans concur that family break-ups should be reduced (Jeynes 1999; Post 2000). Moreover, if one were to ask virtually members of any family in the United States whether their ideal goal would be to breakup or remain together, the response would be in favor of remaining together (McLanahan et al. 2013). The issue of family harmony and togetherness impacts the vast majority of people in the world in one-way or another. This chapter could deal with few more relevant and timely topics than this one.

It is naturally easy to be critical of couples that divorce (Jeynes 2002b). At times, that criticism may be well deserved (Wallerstein 2005). Be that as it may, often individuals are quick to disparage couples who breakup in the aftermath of that divorce, but do not show as much alacrity in addressing the copious number of factors that together increase a society's proclivity toward family dissolution (McLanahan and Sandefur 1994). Only part of the solution to alleviating the high rates of divorce rests in passing laws to make divorce more difficult to initiate or complete (Stokes and Ellison 2010; Wallerstein 2005; Wallerstein and Lewis 1998). In order to have a much more efficacious impact, one must fathom some of the forces at work that increase the likelihood of family breakup. And indeed there are a host of factors, which fall under certain categories that are best conceptualized as internal and external factors. Utilizing the knowledge of these factors will not only help people adopt a strategy that will help strengthen families nationwide, but first and foremost will enable people to strengthen their own families and serve as a buttress for the marriages of those that they love. They can also be useful principles to apply in the inner city, where family dissolution is often so common (Jeynes 2003; Williams and Sanchez 2012, 2013).

Internal Factors

Positive

Marriage has many forces working on the couple to either draw the family closer or further apart. The internal factors are usually the most important ones because: (1) clearly families are almost always able to improve internal factors much more expeditiously and completely than they can the external factors; (2) external factors rarely reach levels that even approach near perfection, i.e., the environment that most families operate in is far from ideal; and (3) internal factors are more likely to have a prodigious and long-lasting impact on the family (Hayes 2011; Heaven et al. 2010; McLanahan et al. 2013; Jeynes 2005c, 2012c).

With this context in mind, it is vital that those people who are pro-family realize that much more can be accomplished they focus on the steps that families can take to increase the strength of their marriages rather than overly criticizing those who are filing for divorce (Markman et al. 2010; Post 2000; Worthington 2000). There is a place for holding responsible those who take marital agreements far too lightly than they should (Glasser and Glasser 1996; Ingram 2009; Wallerstein 2005). The research evidence is so patent on this issue that one cannot reasonably gainsay the fact that millions of Americans do not take their marital commitments seriously enough (Clinton and Ohischlager 2002; Clayton et al. 2013; Glasser and Glasser 1996; Shin et al. 2010). Nevertheless, the best times to express one's views on this subject are during the pre-marital phase, in the early days of the marriage, and well before a couple decides to break-up (Post 2000; Worthington 2000; Wright and Roberts 1997). Any efforts to preserve marriage are feeble indeed if they are only explicated when a marital breakup has occurred.

A Strong Family Begins with Right Priorities and Spending Time with The Family

For family harmony and bonding to be at its strongest, the priorities of each family member of the family should be God first, followed by the family, and everything else afterwards (Jeynes 2006a, 2010b). If these priorities are real and are seriously applied, they will be reflected in the degree to which members of the family desire to- and actually- spend time with one another (Henderson and Mapp 2002; Hoover-Dempsey and Sandler 1997). When I first became a Christian, I did not have to ask the believers that lived around me whether they loved me or not. They desired to spend an incredible amount of time with me. That was my evidence. I must confess, my priorities of God, family, friends, and then ministry represent the essence of who I am. Due to these priorities I turned down my first invitation to speak at the White House in order to ensure that we could obtain a visa for one of our children, Elisha, to join us for a ministry trip in Brazil. At the time, Brazil was one of the hardest nations to obtain a visa for minors. I had gone down to the Brazilian Consulate in Los Angeles 4 times and my wife had journeyed there once to secure our son's visa, but there had been no success. We really believed that going on trip to Brazil would change Elisha's life and it did. That is where he engaged in music ministry with other believers for the first time. I also turned down an incredible opportunity to speak in Iran, that was extended to me, largely because of an interview I did with *Aljazeera* on Christian revival in Asia that received a great deal of attention and favorable responses, including over 2800 "likes" at the *Aljazeera* website, which in an Islamic environment is rather amazing. They wanted me to come, when one of our children graduated from college. I have also taken dozens of days off from work to help my children with their homework. Family comes first.

Right priorities are salient along more than one dimension. Not only is it true that each member of the home should have the priorities of God, family, and then everything else. It is also vital that each person in the home have the right priorities in terms of the character traits that are most important in life. Biblically speaking, it is quite clear just what those traits are (Clinton and Ohischlager 2002; Montague 2011). Jesus Christ declared that the two most important qualities a person could have are love of God and love of neighbor (Holy Bible, NIV, Luke 10:27). He also declared that the greatest person in the Kingdom of God was someone who was humble (Holy Bible, NIV, Matthew 18: 3, 4). It would seem, therefore, that the three most important traits that a person can have are love of God, love of neighbor, and humility (Jeynes 2009a). In order for home-life to be spiritual, it needs to have love at its core. In addition, love and humility are never so beautifully blended as when they are inextricably harmonized in a spirit of forgiveness. That is in many ways what happened via Christ at the cross. The presence of forgiveness is necessary for any marriage to work. If a family member's foremost priorities are other qualities that are not as important this can eventually cause fundamental problems in a marriage and in family living (Clinton and Ohischlager 2002; Post 2000). For example, if a person values diligence, self-discipline, and mental toughness, these are all fine characteristics to possess. However, they should not enjoy the primacy that love and humility have. Therefore, if a person emphasizes these other traits more than love and humility, that individual may become highly successful, reach impressive heights of notoriety, and be able to handle life's stresses. However, that person may not be able to have a very serene and blissful home-life unless one has a very understanding spouse. Most marriages, especially, and families will thrive insofar as love reigns in the hearts of everyone in the household. Clearly, there are other factors that affect the quality of a marriage that go well beyond the realm of love and humility (Montague 2011; Post 2000). These forces may include financial pressures, health challenges, in-law problems, and so forth. In fact, many of these forces are external to the marriage and vary in the degree to which family members have much control over them (McDonald and McDonald 1994; Worthington 2000).

Although all of what has been shared above sounds wonderful in the ideal world, the reality is that the direction that the family goes in is often determined by the "weakest link" in the household (Post 2000; Rehm and Rehm 2002). That is, the member of the family that is least committed to a given home unit will often determine the ambience that exists in the household (Ingram 2009; Post 2000; Worthington 2000). This is why it is important for all members of the family to be oriented toward love.

Having Regular Family Devotions

It is wise to have regular family devotions. There is that old adage that states, "The family that prays together stays together." In practice, many families truly no longer know what that phrase means. Family devotions provide a wonderful opportunity to study the Bible together, pray for one another's needs, sing spiritual songs together, and encourage one another in the midst of life's blessings and trials. It is not always easy to have high quality sharing time as a family, but a family devotional time provides an opportunity to bond via sharing that few activities can rival (Jeynes 2006a; Post 2000). If at all possible, these devotionals should take place every day that the family is not going to church.

Family devotions create an atmosphere and of love and support in the family. In addition, there is the opportunity to teach the children the importance of praying specifically. They can even encourage higher rates of literacy and academic achievement among one's children (Jeynes 2010c, 2012c; Jeynes and Littell 2000). Research indicates that reading the Bible is associated with higher academic achievement (Jeynes 2010c, 2012a; Nord 2010). In fact, the difference between the average GPA of students with high Bible literacy versus those with low Bible literacy rates can be as much as the difference between an A- and C+ (Jeynes 2009b). Probably a large degree of this effect is due to the fact that if one is to understand much of American and world history, as well as literature, a working knowledge of the Bible is quite essential (Prothero 2007).

There is a fundamental strengthening that takes place in an individual, when a Bible devotional is done daily and the same principle certainly holds for the family as well (Dallman 2007; Post 2000; Worthington 2000). If they are done with discipline good thoughts become actions and actions if done consistently enough become habits. If the habits are filled with love and acceptance, what results is godly character (Dallman 2007; Montague 2011; Novak 2005).

Make Studying and Memorizing the Bible a Family Priority

The Bible serves as a moral compass to help shape family life. To the extent that godly behavior thrives in a household, family life will tend to be strengthened. The extent to which a person is committed to living out the exhortations of the Bible regarding kindness, gentleness, and upright behavior, the more likely it is that the husband, wife, and children will feel loved, valued, and appreciated (Jeynes 2009a, 2009b). As a result, it is wise to encourage a diligent and consistent study of the Bible as a means to this end. Simply attending church in order to receive one's spiritual nourishment gives one only a cursory exposure to the Scripture. Therefore, the parents should encourage the family to have morning devotionals in order to be affected by these spiritual truths every day. In addition, the members of the family should dedicate themselves to the memorization of the Bible in order to internalize many of the spiritual exhortations of the Scripture (Jeynes 2010c). Engaging in this practice will enhance the likelihood of peace, love, joy, kindness, and gentleness existing in a household.

The practice of studying the Bible and praying in the form of a personal devotional time is probably best done in the morning, because it serves as a foundation for the remainder of the day. In addition, by initiating this practice at the beginning of each day, a person is making a statement about the importance one places of personal behavior, attitudes, relationships, and particularly the family. Family devotionals are good to have at the end of the day, when everyone is home. This practice serves to draw the family closer to God and to one another (Dallman 2007).

Synchronize with What is Going on in Church and School

Communication is the lifeblood of any relationship and it is absolutely essential that parents be aware of what is going on in the church and the school and be active participants in each (Arnold 2007; Borruel 2002; Jeynes 2011b). This truism also applies to all relationships that exist within the home (Hayes 2011; Jeynes 2005a, 2005c; Williams and Sanchez 2012). Parents who have experienced raising teenagers are among the first to recognize the importance of this aspect of family living. The reality is that a myriad of the teenagers in the home are frequently uncommunicative and this fact makes synchronizing with youth activities in the church and school challenging (Kennedy 2001; Post 2000).

The synchronization via family communication, especially designed to enhance one's relationship with the children, must be ameliorative to the family's dynamics in that it needs to be supportive, free-flowing, and helpful. This is not an easy goal to accomplish, especially when parents are raising teens. If all the family members progressed through life with a plenteous amount of objectivity and compassion, accomplishing these three goals might not be as difficult as it sometimes is. However, adolescents are not usually known for their objectivity and compassion and can become defensive if adults ask them too many questions (Evertson and Emmer 2009; Williams and Sanchez 2012). It takes a certain degree of patience and creativity by the parents to create an ambience of the kind of productive communication between adults and their children that strengthen family bonds rather than weakens them. The patience that is most beneficial in these situations is one that is rooted in love (Jeynes 2002a, 2006b). In other words, the key to patience is not to declare, "Give me patience and give it now!" but rather to seek to love the individual the way that God does. Patience goes considerably farther when it is founded on love than when it is not (Jeynes 2009a).

When the parents attempt to synchronize their hearts and minds with the churches and schools, it helps their children feel more grounded in the home and the community and gives these youngsters a greater sense of belonging. Nevertheless, accomplishing this requires a good deal of communication with the children, the church, and the school (Jeynes 2005b, 2007a, 2007b). Another advantage of this synchronization is that the parents become more aware of the spiritual and academic progress of their young (Jeynes 2002c, 2003, 2011a). It is wise for parents to establish strong bonds of mutual respect and communication with the ministers, Sunday school leaders, and teachers (Jeynes 2000).

Talk About Vocations for the Children

One of the most dramatic results of being a person of faith is that one believes that God has a purpose for his or her life. The fact is naturally true not only for adult Christians, but also for young children and adolescents as well. It is very important that parents convey these truths to children (Kennedy 2001). Young people are in the midst of trying to define who they are, they are developing their self-concept, and attempting to discern God's purposes for their lives (Baehr 1998; Kennedy 2001). It is therefore vital that parents communicate with their children about God's will for their lives. This naturally includes a broad list of topics including God's will for people's lives generally, e.g., to be loving, honest, respectful, responsible, compassionate, and godly. Nevertheless, it also encompasses very specific issues such as comprehending the place of one's gifts and talents in the context of God's calling on one's life. Drawing these qualities together into a coherent whole is clearly typically more facile for an adult than it is for a youth. Therefore, it is especially important for mothers and fathers to help their children understand how all these factors interact in a way that helps them discern what type of career is best for them. This certainly does not mean that the parents should make the occupational decision for the children. To the contrary, deliberations regarding such paths as college and other occupationally-related conclusions should be largely up to the youth. These are some of the most important foundational decisions children will ever make and they should be consistent with the overall leanings of their own mind and heart. Within this context, however, it is helpful to offer parental input and wisdom.

Negative

Favoritism is a Terror

In the Bible it is clearly taught that God's essence is love. In I John 4:8 it is declared that, "God is love." Moreover, in Romans 2:11 it is declared that, "God shows no partiality." One of the most famous Bible accounts is in the Old Testament, regarding the favoritism that Jacob showed Joseph over his other sons. This proclivity for Jacob to show Joseph more loving affection than Jacob's other children almost led to Joseph's death and played a large role in Joseph's eventual selling into slavery (Jeynes 2006a).

Favoritism can cause unnecessary tension within a family. The word "unnecessary" is especially worthy of note because some challenges in life are difficult and at times even impossible to eschew. In other words, life will always have a certain degree of stress. Given that life often offers situations that are rife with stress, one would certainly not want to unnecesarily add to the list of stressors. One of the first places to do that is favoritism. This is not as easy as one might think, because one's children will *perceive* favoritism different than the parents do. Most notably, some of one's children will follow the rules of the home with greater alacrity than others. Some children will perceive that the obedient children are treated with greater trust than the others. In reality, however, in establishing the same rules for all of their children the parents are actually being very fair. Therefore, in order to parent in a way that is extricated from even the least traces of favoritism, the father and mother must know their own hearts and know them well. Perceived favoritism is quite different from actual favoritism and it is important for parents to realize that children will often be ultra sensitive to any indication of favoritism. And given that human beings, especially children, have a real propensity to feel sorry for themselves, youngsters will almost always perceive themselves as being on the lower part of the totem poll when it comes to perceived parental favoritism. Because of the capricious nature of people's perceived favoritism, it is key that people have the self-knowledge to have an accurate perception of their own heart in terms of being fair in the raising of their children (Levitt et al. 2001).

Rivalry is Serious

Virtually everyone has heard of the term "sibling rivalry." In fact, numerous people have heard of the term so many times that they can easily become anesthetized to its potentially nefarious potential (Goldenthal 1999; Levitt et al. 2001). The reality is that people are born as individuals, i.e., single human units. Whether one operates out of a secular rubric of "survival of the fittest" and "self-preservation" or one of believing that humans have a divine orientation, but concurrently also have a self-centered one, few who have lived on earth for any length of time would gainsay that human beings often behave in very self-serving ways. Young people have an unmistakable propensity to be insecure, as they attempt to define themselves in the midst of the larger world in which they live (Goldenthal 1999; Levitt et al. 2001). Given that youth, of virtually all ages, tend to be insecure in one way or another, they tend to evaluate themselves in comparison to others among their peers (Goldenthal 1999; Levitt et al. 2001). This begins in the home and the genesis of such tendencies usually begins in comparing oneself to one's siblings.

For the vast majority of young in the world, their first exposure to love comes from their parents. There are few experiences in life that are more fulfilling and generate such positive results as feeling loved (Jeynes 2006b, 2011, 2012c). Consequently, it is not unusual for children to seek to outdo their siblings in one activity or another, so that they can "earn" a greater degree of love from their parents (Kennedy 2001; Levitt et al. 2001). While such an orientation among youth is both understandable and normal, it is potentially dangerous both to oneself and at an interpersonal level. There are a plethora of disadvantages to engaging in this kind of rivalry, just some of which are listed here. They include:

1. Being defined in value based on personal perceptions entrenched in comparisons and not in reality in terms of one's worth in its own right.
2. Living a life that is focused on the acceptance of others rather than doing what is right and applying an "other orientation" that focuses on helping others become all that they can be.
3. Pursuing an existence that is concerned almost totally about one's own pursuits and successes rather than also rejoicing in the victories that others experience, especially among those that are closest.
4. Spending one's time trying to prove oneself rather than simply trying to be oneself.
5. Comparing oneself to others is generally a losing proposition because a person emphasizes his or her own inadequacies.

Parents clearly cannot always prevent such rivalries from emerging, but what they can do is recognize the potential perils of such competition and do what they can to prevent them from burgeoning.

When no One is Home After School

Communication is the lifeblood of any relationship and in no arena is this more patent than in the home (Cowan et al. 2009; Jeynes 2010d; Micklethwait and Wooldridge 2009). To whatever extent dialog does not exist whether it be through the married couple or between the parents and their children, the quality of family life will tend to suffer. In recent years, some psychologists, family scientists, and sociologists have placed an emphasis on "quality time" as opposed to the actual amount of time (Altschul 2011; Hoover-Dempsey and Sandler 1997). Granted, there is clearly some truth to this emphasis. There is no question that there is a difference between time together spent in intimate and transparent interaction as opposed to being silent at the dinner table. Having stated this, however, research does indeed support the notion that the quantity of time that family members spend together has a measurable impact on a host of outcomes, including psychological wellbeing, academic achievement, overall happiness, personal productivity, job performance and satisfaction, etc. (Dichele 2006; Frech and Kimbro 2011; Hognas and Carlson 2010; Jeynes 2010a, 2010b).

The reality of life is that getting to know one another takes time. In many respects there are really no shortcuts. Therefore, while there is clearly a sense in which there are high "quality time" activities, people would be wise to realize that sometimes children do not want or benefit the most simply from activities that involve high "quality time." These activities certainly have their place. Nevertheless, one would be wise to ascertain a salient truth: High quality time generally does not replace missed time. The presence of an individual and the time-invested by being present is generally so greatly valued by human beings, that it often cannot be replicated. For example, if my wife and have planned on 3 h of being together in an evening, I cherish every moment that I spend with my wife to such a degree that if she calls and says that she will be late and can only spend 1½ h with me, but that it will be high "quality time," I am usually quite disappointed. I enjoy just having my wife in the same room. We enjoy just holding hands. Although we enjoy the high quality times, we cherish every moment together. Therefore the word "time" is very important to us, whether it is high quality or not.

It is also true that research is quite consistent in demonstrating that on average children raised in two biological parent families accrue certain benefits to a greater degree than children raised in single parent families (Wallerstein 2005). These benefits include better academic achievement, sense of wellbeing, psychological balance, and so forth than their counterparts in single parent households (Wallerstein and Lewis 1998). There are many single parents who are able to spend quite a bit of time with their children. Nevertheless, there is no question that it easier for two parents collaborating together to make sure that children are not alone at home without parental supervision than it is for one parent to do the same. This is especially true when one considers that often single parents must go out and work in order to support the family. Consequently, research indicates that "latch key" children are far more likely to live in a home with a single parent than they are in a two biological parent home (McLanahan et al. 2013; Wallerstein 2005; Wallerstein and Lewis 1998).

When Children Don't See the Parents Praying

Academic research often confirms common sense and the idea that actions speak louder than words is one example of this fact. The Bible and various pieces of Christian literature throughout time testify to the importance of setting an example (Holy Bible, I Corinthians 11:1). Parents can discuss about the importance of praying and studying the Bible all that they want, but it is the example they set that really impacts their children the most. If mothers and fathers want their children to enhance the depth of their relationship with God, then the parents themselves need to be examples of what it means to be exemplars of dependence on God (Chapman et al. 2008; Hallett 1998; Peck 1993). Beyond this, youth need to see their parents pray as part of the initial level of strategy rather than as a last resort (Chapman et al. 2008; Jeynes 2009a). It is a humbling but true axiom that children tend to follow in some of the precise prayer habits established by their parents.

One should also note that the general trend that takes place in a family is for each generation of believers to be a bit less dependent on God and less devout than the generation that preceded them (Jeynes 2006a). In order to prevent this likely trend, the key is to encourage one's children to make an effort to have a personal experience with God. If the children's faith is simply based on being raised in a Christian home, it is going to be difficult for these youngsters to have an intimate relationship with God. If parents want their children to have a strong relationship with God, they need to have set the example of what it means to have a close relationship with God (Chapman et al. 2008; Wiseman and Rapoport 2006).

External Factors

Positive

High Ideals Can Help as Well as Hinder

It is often a good quality for a family to maintain high aspirations. However, these aspirations should be God-based and realistic. Otherwise, a family can set itself up for a long string of disappointments. If high ideals are God-inspired and yet based on realistic expectations of other people, then high ideals can be very productive and helpful. In contrast, however, if expectations cause people to depend too strictly on only the most godly behavior to proceed ahead with one's spouse and family members, then any individual with such a high degree of anticipation is likely to set themselves up for substantial disappointment. Such an attitude can result in a degree of rigidity that grace and forgiveness are both left out of the picture. It is particularly serious when this occurs because grace, love, and forgiveness are at the very core of the Christian faith (Appleby 2013; Kruschwitz 2001; Jeynes 2006a; Webster 2011). In order for a marriage to survive, these core qualities need to be active.

There are traps a family especially needs to avoid. The first is that married couples sometimes expect too much of each other. Some newlyweds enter their relationship anticipating that their spouse will meet all their needs, when in reality they are looking to their mate to fulfill many needs that only God can fulfill (Markman et al. 2010; McDonald and McDonald 1994). The second is that more than occasionally parents expect too much of their children. This often happens in the realms of academics and sports. Instead, parents need to emphasize to their children that what they want them to do is simply try their best. I recall tutoring a immigrant student for the SAT, who had above average grades and below average practice SAT scores. I have rarely seen a student as inebriated with the idea of going to Harvard as he was and the reason was because his parents insisted that he go to no university other than Harvard. His parents knew of another immigrant couple, whose daughter had been admitted to Harvard. Therefore, in their view it was quite possible for their own son, who was my student, to do so as well. However, as focused as the family was on the idea of going to Harvard, it is also true that I have rarely seen a student so overcome by stress as he. He asked me what I thought the chances were of Harvard admitting him. I told him that I felt like I needed to be honest with him and share with him that even if his SAT scores skyrocketed, his chances of admittance were near zero. This student was very diligent and he responded very well to the tutoring so that his SAT scores did indeed surge hundreds of points. Nevertheless, he persistently suffered from the stress of gaining admittance into Harvard and the intensity of the stress would rise in steady increments with each passing week. I felt badly for him because it was difficult enough to adjust to American life as an immigrant, but to see him become so encumbered by the stress of trying to gain admittance to Harvard was just too much for any human being.

In this context, however, my overburdened student came to my home one day filled with glee and laughter, as if a 500-pound weight had been lifted from his shoulders. I asked him why he has experienced such a sudden change in his countenance and disposition. He said it was because his immigrant parents, who did understand English well, had misunderstood the other family and thought that that latter had said that their daughter had gone to Harvard, when in fact they stated that their daughter had attended Haverford. Haverford is a fine school, but there is only one Harvard and Haverford is clearly not at that level. My student felt that he regained his life. Nevertheless, the stress that he had been under was venomous and this is what can happen when parents have expectations that are too high.

With this caveat in mind, however, it is indubitably true that high expectations that are realistic and subtler in nature can have a dramatically positive influence on the achievements, demeanor, and future of children. Meta-analyses, for example indicate that high expectations are probably the most salient component of parental involvement (Jeynes 2005a, 2007b, 2010d). In addition, high expectations among teachers are also extremely important (Jeynes 2010d). The explication of expectations requires careful delineation. The concept is not one of a parent foisting expectations upon their children, such as, "You must go to Harvard or Princeton" (Lancaster 2004). Rather, the type of expectations that possess the greatest impact are those that are subtle but understood by the child such as trying one's best. When these healthy balanced expectations are in place, they can yield real benefits.

The Local Church can Help

The local church can potentially be of immense help in strengthening the family, depending on its emphasis. The church has the potential to help families for a variety of reasons. First, the church can reinforce the values that already exist in a family (Kearney 2001; Weaver et al. 2002). When the church reinforces the values of the family, it serves to reassure the family that it is on the right track, the husband's and wife's trust of each other is enhanced, and the children understand that the convictions maintained by their parents are not limited to their home alone, but are widely practiced and understood to be wise (Micklethwait and Wooldridge 2009).

Second, especially based on communication with the senior pastor and youth pastor, the leaders of the church can support the parents in their attempts to raise children in a godly way. The church and its members can help youth take stands against the temptations of this life and the lascivious and corrupt ways of society that emphasize self and immediate gratification of desires that are often premature or ill-timed (Micklethwait and Wooldridge 2009).

Third, the church can via the preaching of the Word and other means cause the family, as a whole, to walk in greater righteousness. By the entire family becoming more loving, patient, kind, and compassionate, everyone in the family will be beneficiaries and they will become stronger both as a unit and individually.

Friends & Relatives can Help or Hinder

It is almost axiomatic that friends and relatives can either strengthen or weaken a marital relationship, in particular. Often this is done without the couple or the instigators being even aware of what is happening. People often unwittingly undermine the quality of a marriage because they want to be supportive of what their friend (the husband or wife) says. This becomes problematic, however, when the husband or wife, that they are seeking to support, makes pejorative statements toward the spouse. For example, the wife might say, "My husband is a no good lazy slob. All he does after work is plop down on the recliner, do nothing, and make a mess, expecting me to clean it up." The wife's friend, wanting to be supportive of her friend might say, "You're right. I wouldn't put up with that kind of nonsense." All of the sudden, the wife's friend has contributed to the undermining of that marriage. What is so sad about this scenario is that rather than even though the intentions of the friend were unlikely to be nefarious, the friend actually neglected to embrace an opportunity to strengthen the marriage. The effect on the health of the marriage would have been far more positive if the friend had stated, "Remember though, that you husband is works hard because he loves you and after a long day at work plus an grueling and debilitating commute, he is absolutely exhausted. It is only natural that after ten or twelve hours in the grind, he wants to relax and unwind." This alternative statement serves to strengthen the marriage rather than debilitate the union.

Clearly, there are situations in which the emasculating dialog above is intentional and the two friends have at least agreed in less tangible ways to disparage the thoughts, behaviors, and attitudes of the husband. Nevertheless, it is equally true that on other occasions, the friend is simply trying to demonstrate some degree of loyalty or sympathy for the complainer and is hurting the marital union unintentionally (Chapman et al. 2008; Post 2000; Worthington 2000). Whatever the motive of the friend, it is vital that churches and society as a whole more efficaciously communicate the damage that such "friendly fire" can produce (Chapman et al. 2008; Post 2000). Friends need to become more cognizant of the ameliorating actions they can take to strengthen the marriage of those they care about and how much good such strategies can do (Chapman et al. 2008; Post 2000). Moreover, ministers, counselors, and social workers would be wise to inculcate these principles to friends and family of the couple, who are willing to do what they can to help increase the likelihood of marital success for those that they love. There is indubitably an often unrealized potential for teaching people to rally around a marriage that is in trouble and to further bolster the chances of success of marriages in which greater mutual appreciation on the part of both the husband and wife is definitely needed.

It is also undeniable that in-laws can also cause the spiritual and emotional emaciation of a marriage. A considerable degree of pressure often originates from mothers- and fathers-in-law in particular (Cloud and Townsend 1999). A prodigious amount of this pressure can be eschewed or reduced if the husband and wife are able to discern the primary concerns of most parents-in-law. That is, most are concerned about how one treats their son or daughter in the marriage (Cloud and Townsend 1999). Clearly, there are all kinds of exceptions to this general principle. Nevertheless, more often than not this is their overriding concern. If the wife and husband understand this reality, they will often be able to address these concerns and actually make the role of the in-laws in a family a positive force rather than a negative one.

In order to transform the influence of the in-laws into a positive force in the marriage, the married couple needs to acknowledge and act on the following facts.

First, when one weds he or she is not merely marrying an individual, they are really marrying a family. It is naïve to think that the quality of the couples' matrimony is merely a product of the intricacies of that specific relationship. The spiritual, emotional, and physical health of the extended family can have a considerable effect on the couples experience of marital fulfillment (Chapman et al. 2008; Cloud and Townsend 1999). Second, few actions and attitudes can go farther in alleviating pressure from parents-in-law than those based on love for one's spouse. For most in-laws it is the child being loved by the spouse that they most want to see. If they see that sacrificial love emanating from almost every action and word that proceeds from their child's spouse, they will generally be quite supportive and cooperative of their child's marriage. If husbands and wives will simply remember this very important, yet basic, principle, they will go far in establishing a happy and productive marriage.

From the perspective of the parents in-law if their son- or daughter- in law is loving their spouse consistently and sacrificially, one will be amazed at the degree to which the in-laws will actually cherish their child's spouse. If the bride or groom treats their child as the most precious person on earth, one will be surprised the degree to which in-laws will usually treat one in a commensurate way (Cloud and Townsend 1999).

Negative

Superstitions About Marriage Abound

A myriad of individuals likely view superstitions as relics of the past. This may be true within certain disciplines, but one can argue that when it comes to marriage superstitions abound in greater number and to more of an expansive extent than ever before. To be sure, the superstitions held by some may not be quite as brazen as those held centuries ago. In the supposedly sophisticated era of today superstitions are best expressed via intimating and alluding to something in order to ascertain a person's reaction. Nevertheless, the superstitions are real and have risen largely due to the rampant increase in divorce, marital infidelity, and the rescinding of promised alimony payments and child support by "deadbeat dads."

The surge in horror stories pertaining to marriage has caused a precipitous decline in the level of trust that a newlywed has entering a marriage (Markman et al. 2010; McDonald and McDonald 1994). Especially since 1963 when the divorce rate abruptly started to surge after 12 years of slight decline, it was clear that a process of spiritual atrophying was taking place in most newlywed's trust in their marital partners generally and in their motives specifically (Jeynes 2002b). This fact is reflected not only in the divorce rates themselves, but also in the attenuating of the marriage rates that followed in the coming years (Carter and Glick 1976; Markman et al. 2010). And one should make no mistake about it, the ramifications of such developments could not be much more pervasive. The marriage rate is one of the most reliable predictors of future economic growth. When the United States led the world in the marriage rate during the 1945–1962 period, although the United States had only about 5–6% of the world's population it produced an astounding 56% of the world's goods (Carter and Glick 1976; Jeynes 2010a; Johnson 1997; U.S. Bureau of the Census 1975). Not surprising, Japan and Germany immediately replaced the U.S. as having the world's highest marriage rates and during the 1963–1975 period these were the two nations increasing their economic prowess at the swiftest rates (Carter and Glick 1976; Jeynes 2010a).

Superstitions often rise when fears and mistrust become elevated in any given society (Johnson 1997). Divorce, marital infidelity, and unpaid alimony checks can spawn formidable fears that can cause people to feel more uncomfortable in a marital relationship than they otherwise would. There is no question that unpleasant societal trends can cause discomfort and fear in a relationship. It is the wise couple that acknowledges this possibility and attempts to alleviate these concerns in whatever way possible.

Our School System Breaks Down Families

The effects of the public school system in breaking down the family would not be so baneful were it not for the fact that a variety of highly influential educators over the years have called for schools to supplant and some might say even usurp the place of parents in the lives of their children. This goal may be an example of "statism" at the expense of individual rights or something more pernicious (Counts 1932; Dewey 1920; Jeynes 2014). To be sure, since the Industrial Revolution the primacy of the family as the institution that raises children has declined (Dewey 1964). In the eyes of John Dewey's, it was the school's responsibility to increase the centrality of its role and execute some of the same functions previously reserved for the family (Dewey 1964). To Dewey and Counts this change was both positive and gave educators the opportunity to "reconstruct" society (Counts 1932; Dewey 1920). This shift of emphasis was slow to materialize during the 1920–1963 period, because the nation still had a core that emphasized Christian and family values (Jeynes 2007a). However, with: (1) the removal of the Bible, prayer, and character education from the public schools; (2) the sudden surge in the divorce rate that also started in 1963, this core was greatly challenged; and (3) the fact that by 1963 most teachers had by then been taught under the Dewey rubric, Dewey's ideals now largely ruled in the public schools (Egan 2002; Jeynes 2007a).

With the above trends in mind, there are an increasing number of families who are sending their children to faith-based schools or are homeschooling their children (Jeynes 2012a, 2012d). It is undeniable that some children thrive in the public schools and learn well how to share their faith. Nevertheless, it is also indubitably correct that values promoted in the schools can undermine family cohesion and the appreciation of one another. Such stresses are unnecessary and may cause many families to consider faith-based schools or homeschools for their children.

Children Aren't Supposed to Grow up in Separate Worlds

For the last 50 years or more, many Western societies in particular have engaged in a social experiment (Egan 2002). There is a sense that many believe that given the technological advances that have occurred during this period that somehow children do not need the moral input of their parents in the way they did in previous generations (Counts 1932; Dewey 1920; Egan 2002). The youth therefore can be raised by larger society in a way that is more separate and distinct than in previous generations. Consequently, within many institutions children are separated to some degree and allowed to develop in their own separate world. This is especially apparent in the public schools, but it is also evident even in churches where the interactions that children are permitted to have with the senior pastors is perfunctory at best (Jeynes 2009b). Children are often corralled into separate classes, creating age segregation that sometimes as a real as the post-reconstruction era in the South. What has emerged is a generation of youth that once they reach an adult age have almost no connectivity with the senior pastor and therefore have a sense of connectivity with their church and family.

Our Concept of the Individual Breaks Down Families—Individualization

The United States and Western Europe are clearly some of the most individualistic societies on the face of the earth (Johnson 1997). While there may be some advantages to this emphasis, a growing number of sociologists and family scientists believe that it has led to a world view that has caused people to become self-absorbed and narcissistic to the place that it undermines the health of the family. Increasingly, younger generations, in particular, have an attitude of entitlement to the place where they not only expect the government to take care of them, but they also believe that their parents and spouse owe them a certain income and certain activities around the house. In many ways it is ironic that as civilized as modern couples think that they are, this attitude of individualism and entitlement is at the very antithesis of what two of the foundational works of modern society, the *Bible* and Plato's *Republic* declare that is necessary for society to thrive (Holy Bible, NIV 1979; Plato 2000). That is, people need to come together as families and a whole society in an attitude of love, harmony, cooperation, and out of concern for the greater good in order for these institutions to work.

Our Marriage and Family Ideas can Lead to Disappointment

A myriad of individuals enter in to their weddings with unrealistic expectations about what holy matrimony will be like. Some of the ideas that are conducive to disappointment are as follows. First, is the belief that one can change his or her marriage partner. The reality is that if a person cannot accept one's husband or wife as is, the relationship already has some real potential problems. Few people change dramatically in a short period of time, unless they are committed to making certain transformations. Beyond this, the marriage will succeed or fail more on the basis of what the husband and wife are as opposed to what they should be.

Second, one can develop expectations of one's spouse based on one's experiences with a godly parent. That is, if a wife has a godly father, she may expect that her husband will act in a way that is filled with the same level of love, wisdom, and integrity. Similarly, if a husband has a godly mother, he may anticipate that the wife will be filled with the same level of compassion, sincerity, and responsibility. The reality is, however, that a spiritual mother or father has had decades to develop such a high level of character and one needs to be patient with one's spouse as he or she grows in this way (Jeynes 2010d).

The Influence of the Media

It is indubitably true that the media has contributed to the breakdown of the family, particularly Hollywood people. It is a sad commentary on Hollywood that one is generally shocked to hear of a long-time actor or actress who has not been divorced (Baehr 1998; Price and Dahl 2012). The degree of unfaithfulness in marriage is astounding and it is probably not hyperbole to call it absurd. This undermining trend has been in place so long that those who divorced frequently 40 or 50 years ago (e.g., 7–9 times) were considered unstable and abnormal, whereas those who demonstrate the same behavior today (e.g., Larry King) are viewed as just fine (Baehr 1998). It is one thing to love a person just as he or she is. That should be done. Nevertheless, to comment on the emperor's new clothes as perfectly acceptable propounds a value system that undermines the development of wise thinking among the world's youth and is an unconscionable disservice to them.

Increasingly the media almost glamorizes "doing as one pleases" rather than marital- and family- loyalty and faithfulness (Baehr 1998; Doinick 1998; Kirsh 2006; Price and Dahl 2012). Some of this tendency clearly dates back to Freud, who appeared to favor some degree of lasciviousness rather than holiness (Doinick 1998; Egan 2002). Nevertheless, Hollywood has taken this several steps farther. Hollywood disdains virginity and its leaders appear to regard illicit sex as more normal than pre-marital purity (Baehr 1998). In the view of many in the media, sleeping with prostitutes may be objectionable, but being a virgin is worthy of ponderous ridicule. It is not surprising that the Bible (Holy Bible, NIV, Isaiah 5:20, 1979) speaks of calling "evil good and good evil."

Poor Government Policies Regarding Welfare & Food Stamps

As if the factors already mentioned were not enough to substantially undermine the strength of the family, there is no question that the government contributes to the problem (Guner and Knowles 2009). There is no question that government policy influences a wide variety of family dynamics (Jeynes 2012b). The ease with which a person can qualify for welfare or food stamps from the government contributes to the weakening of the family. Two of the most prominent reasons, although certainly not the only ones, are as follows. First, nearly 50% of all the people on welfare consistently started there as unwed teens (U.S. Department of Health & Human Services 2010). It is one thing to have a safety net to support the injured, the diseased, and the suffering, but unfortunately so much more money could go to those who need it most, if the government did not provide so many loopholes so that people feel that they can easily break relationships because they know the government will support them. Second, the same phenomenon holds for those in a difficult marriage. There are many disputes in marriages that with a certain degree of love and humility can be worked out, especially for the sake of the children. However, divorce laws are often so loose and public assistance so easily procured that there is little incentive to work out marital problems. Sadly, many couples later regret that they did not do more to try to save their marriages (Wallerstein 2005).

Conclusion

A perusal of this chapter, as well as facing the everyday realities of family living, will no doubt lead many to conclude that there are many factors that work in conjunction with one another to increase the likelihood that a family will break-up. However, one can hope that this chapter will enlighten numerous families to the potency of these factors, internal ones and external ones, as well as positive and negatives ones. To the extent that the strengthening ones are utilized and the weakening ones eschewed, the family in contemporary society can hopefully look forward to a future that is brighter than one sees now. The benefits of such a development could well be irrefutable and vast.

References

Allen, E. S., & Atkins, D. C. (2012). The association of divorce and extramarital sex in a representative U.S. sample. *Journal of Family Issues, 33*(11), 1477–1493.

Altschul, I. (2011). Parental involvement and the academic achievement of Mexican American youths: What kinds of involvement in youth's education matter most. *Social Work Research, 35*(3), 159–170.

Amato, P. (2001). Children of divorce in the 1990s: An update of the Amato and Keith (1991) meta-analysis. *Journal of Family Psychology, 15*(3), 355–370.

Appleby, D. W. (2013) *Tansformative encounters: The intervention of God in counseling and pastoral care*. Downers Grove: InterVarsity Press.

Arnold, L. B. (2007). *Family & communication: Theory & research*. Boston: Allyn & Bacon.

Baehr, T. (1998). *The media-wise family*. Colorado Springs: Victor Publishing.

Becker, G. (1981). *Treatise on the family*. Cambridge: Harvard University Press.

Borruel, T. W. (2002). The ten p's of parent communication. A strategy for staff development. *Child Care Information Exchange, 143*(1), 54–57.

Bouchard, G., & Doucet, D. (2011). Parental divorce and couples' adjustment during the transition to parenthood: The role of parent-adult child relationships. *Journal of Family Issues, 32*(4), 507–527.

Brooks, R. B., & Goldstein, S. (2001). *Raising resilient children: Fostering strength, hope, and optimism in your child*. Lincolnwood: Contemporary Books.

Carter, H., & Glick, P. C. (1976). *Marriage & divorce: A social and economic study*. Cambridge: Harvard University Press.

Chadwick, B. A., & Heaton, T. B. (Eds.). (1992). *Statistical handbook of the American family*. Phoenix: Oryx Press.

Chapman, G. D., Campbell, R., & Fabry, C. (2008). *The five love languages of children*. Carol Stream: Oasis.

Cherlin, A. J. (1978). Remarriage as an incomplete institution. *American Journal of Sociology, 84*(3), 634–650.

Clayton, R. B., Nagumey, A., & Smith, J. R. (2013). Cheating, breakup, and divorce: Is facebook to blame? *CyberPsychology, Behavioral & Social Networking, 16*(10), 717–720.

Clinton, T. E., & Ohischlager, G. W. (2002). Competent christian counseling.

Cloud, H., & Townsend, J. S. (1999). *Boundaries in marriage*. Grand Rapids: Zondervan Publishing House.

Counts, G. (1932). *Dare we build a new social order?* New York: John Day.

Cowan, P. A., Cowan, C. P., Pruett, M. K., Pruett, K., & Wong, J. J. (2009). Promoting father's engagement with children: Preventative interventions for low-income families. *Journal of Marriage & Family, 71,* 663–679.
Dallman, C. A. (2007). *One-minute Bible devotions.* Lincolnwood: Publications International.
Dewey, J. (1920). *Reconstruction in philosophy.* New York: Holt.
Dewey, J. (1964). John Dewey's impressions of Soviet Russia and the revolutionary world: Mexico-China-Turkey, 1929. New York: Teachers college Press.
Dichele, A. M. (2006). Academic achievement in an age of irresponsibility. *Taboo: The Journal of Culture & Education, 10*(1), 29–33
Doinick, E. (1998). *Madness on the couch: Blaming the victim in the heydey of psychoanalysis.* New York: Simon & Schuster.
Egan, K. (2002). *Getting it wrong from the beginning.* New Haven: Yale University Press.
Evertson, C. M., & Emmer, E. T. (2009). *Classroom management for elementary teachers.* Upper Saddle River: Pearson.
Fine, M. A., & Harvey, J. H. (2006). *Handbook of divorce and relationship dissolution.* Mahwah: Lawrence Erlbaum.
Frech, A., & Kimbro, R. T. (2011). Maternal mental health, neighborhood characteristics, and time investments in children. *Journal of Marriage & the Family, 73*(3), 605–620.
Glasser, P. H., & Glasser, L. N. (1996). *Families in Crisis.* New York: Harper & Row.
Goldenthal, P. (1999). *Beyond sibling rivalry.* New York: Holt.
Guner, N., & Knowles, J. (2009). Why is the rate of single-parenthood lower in Canada than in the U.S.? A dynamic equilibrium analysis of welfare policies. *Canadian Journal of Economics, 42*(1), 56–89.
Hallett, G. (1998). *Priorities and Christian ethics.* Cambridge: Cambridge University Press.
Hayes, D. (2011). Predicting parental home and school involvement in high school African American adolescents. *The High School Journal, 94*(4), 154–166.
Heaven, P., Ciarrochi, J., & Leeson, P. (2010). Parental styles and religious values among teenagers: A 3-year prospective analysis. *Journal of Genetic Psychology, 171*(1), 93–99.
Henderson, A. T., & Mapp, K. L. (2002). *A new wave of evidence: The impact of school, family, and community connections on student achievement.* Austin: Southwest Educational Development Laboratory.
Hognas, R. S., & Carlson, M. J. (2010). Intergenerational relationships and union stability in fragile families. *Journal of Marriage & Family, 72*(5), 1220–1233.
Holy Bible (1979). *Holy Bible, new international version.* Nashville: Thomas Nelson.
Hoover-Dempsey, K., & Sandler, H. (1997). Why do parents become involved in their children's education? *Review of Educational Research, 67*(1), 3–42.
Ingram, C. (2009). *Marriage: Built to last; living intentionally and loving Biblically.* Richardson: Bluefish.
Jacobsen, L. A., Mather, M., & Dupuis, G. (2012). *Household change in the United States.* Washington, DC: Population Reference Bureau.
Jeynes, W. (1999). The effects of religious commitment on the academic achievement of black and Hispanic children. *Urban Education, 34*(4), 458–479.
Jeynes, W. (2000). Assessing school choice: A balanced perspective. *Cambridge Journal of Education, 30*(2), 223–241.
Jeynes, W. (2002a). A meta-analysis of the effects of attending religious schools and religiosity on black and Hispanic academic achievement. *Education & Urban Society, 35*(1), 27–49.
Jeynes, W. (2002b). *Divorce, family structure, and the academic success of children.* New York: Haworth Press/Taylor & Francis.
Jeynes, W. (2002c). The relationship between the consumption of 2.1 various drugs by adolescents and their academic achievement. *The American Journal of Drug and Alcohol Abuse, 28*(1), 1–21.
Jeynes, W. (2003). The effects of black and Hispanic twelfth graders living in intact families and being religious on their academic achievement. *Urban Education, 38*(1), 35–57.

Jeynes, W. (2005a). *Parental involvement and student achievement: A meta-analysis. Family involvement research digest, Harvard Family Research Project*. Cambridge: Harvard Family Research Project.
Jeynes, W. (2005b). A meta-analysis of the relation of parental involvement to urban elementary school student academic achievement. *Urban Education, 40*(3), 237–269.
Jeynes, W. (2005c). Effects of parental involvement and family structure on the academic achievement of adolescents. *Marriage and Family Review, 37*(3), 99–117.
Jeynes, W. (2006a). *A hand not shortened*. Greenwich: Information Age Press.
Jeynes, W. (2006b). Standardized tests and the true meaning of kindergarten and preschool. *Teachers College Record, 108*(10), 1937–1959.
Jeynes, W. (2006c). The impact of parental remarriage on children: A meta-analysis. *Marriage and Family Review, 40*(4), 75–102.
Jeynes, W. (2007a). *American educational history: School, society, and the common good*. Thousand Oaks: Sage.
Jeynes, W. (2007b). The relationship between parental involvement and urban secondary school academic achievement: A meta-analysis. *Urban Education, 42*(1), 82–110.
Jeynes, W. (2009a). *Getting closer to God*. Charlotte: Information Age Press.
Jeynes, W. (2009b). The relationship between Bible literacy and academic achievement, and school behavior. *Education & Urban Society, 41*(4), 419–436.
Jeynes, W. (2010a). *A call for character education and prayer in the schools*. Westport: Praeger.
Jeynes, W. (2010b). Religiosity, religious schools, and their relationship with the achievement gap: A research synthesis and meta-analysis. *Journal of Negro Education, 79*(3), 263–279.
Jeynes, W. (2010c). The relationship between Bible literacy and academic and behavioral outcomes in urban areas: A meta-analysis. *Education & Urban Society, 42*(5), 522–544.
Jeynes, W. (2010d). The salience of the subtle aspects of parental involvement and encouraging that involvement: Implications for school-based programs. *Teachers College Record, 112*(3), 747–774.
Jeynes, W. (2011). *Parental involvement & academic success*. New York: Taylor & Francis/Routledge.
Jeynes, W. (2011a). Help families by fostering parental involvement. *Phi Delta Kappan, 93*(3), 38–39.
Jeynes, W. (2011b). *Parental involvement & academic success*. New York: Taylor & Francis/Routledge.
Jeynes, W. (2012a). A meta-analysis on the effects and contributions of public, public charter, and religious schools on student outcomes. *Peabody Journal of Education, 87*(3), 305–335.
Jeynes, W. (2012b). Protestant education in Russia and the former Soviet Union and the Eastern Bloc. In W. Jeynes & D. Robinson (Eds.), *The international handbook of Protestant education* (pp. 275–294). London: Springer.
Jeynes, W. (2012c). Reaching out to make a difference. *Phi Delta Kappan, 93*(6), 80.
Jeynes, W. (2012d). The rise of home schooling as a modern educational phenomenon in protestant education. In W. Jeynes & D. Robinson (Eds.), *The international handbook of Protestant education* (pp. 77–92). London: Springer.
Jeynes, W. (2014). *School choice: A balanced approach*. Santa Barbara: Praeger.
Jeynes, W., & Littell, S. (2000). A meta-analysis of studies examining the effect of whole language instruction on the literacy of low-SES students. *Elementary School Journal, 101*(1), 21–33.
Johnson, P. (1997). *A history of the American people*. New York: Harper Collins.
Kearney, R. T. (2001). *Caring for sexually abused children: A handbook for families and churches*. Downers Grove: InterVarsity Press.
Kennedy, R. (2001). *The encouraging parent*. New York: Three Rivers Press.
Kirsh, S. J. (2006). *Children, adolescents and media violence*. Thousand Oaks: Sage.
Kruschwitz, R. B. (2001). *Forgiveness*. Waco: Baylor University.
Lamb, M. (1997). *The role of the father in child development*. New York: Wiley.
Lancaster, D. R. (2004). The psychology of parental control: How well-meaning parenting backfires. *Journal of Developmental & Behavioral Pediatrics, 25*(1), 69–70.

Lee, J., & Bowen, N. K. (2006). Parent involvement, cultural capital, and the achievement gap among elementary school children. *American Educational Research Journal, 43,* 193–218.
Levitt, J., Levitt, M., & Levitt, J. (2001). *Sibling rivalry: 8 steps to successful adult sibling relationships*. New York: Dell Publishing.
Markman, H., Stanley, S., & Blumberg, S. L. (2010). *Fighting for your marriage*. San Francisco: Jossey-Bass.
McDonald, C., & McDonald, P. M. (1994). *Creating a successful Christian marriage*. Grand Rapids: Baker Book House.
McDonald, L. G., & Robinson, P. (2009). *A colossal failure of common sense*. New York: Crown.
McLanahan, S., & Sandefur, G. (1994). *Growing up with a single parent: What hurts, what helps*. Cambridge: Harvard University Press.
McLanahan, S., Tech, S., & Schneider, D. (2013). The causal effects of father absence. *Annual Review of Sociology, 39*(1), 399–427.
Micklethwait, J., & Wooldridge, A. (2009). *God is back: How the global revival of faith is changing the world*. New York: Penguin.
Montague, G. T. (2011). *First Corinthians*. Grand Rapids: Baker Academic.
Nair, H., & Murray, A. D. (2005). Predictors of attachment security in preschool children from intact and divorced families. *The Journal of Genetic Psychology, 166*(3), 245–263
Nord, W. (2010). *Does God make a difference*. New York: Oxford University Press.
Novak, M. (2005). Sir John Templeton's three passions. In C. L. Harper Jr (Ed.), *Spiritual information: 100 perspectives on science and religion* (pp. 8–11). Philadelphia: Templeton Foundation Press.
Palm, G., & Fagan, J. (2008). Father involvement in early childhood programs: Review of the literature. *Early Child Development & Care, 178*(7/8), 745–759.
Peck, M. S. (1993). *A world waiting to be born: Civility rediscovered*. New York: Bantam Books.
Plato. (2000). *The republic*. Cambridge: Cambridge University Press.
Pong, S., Dronkers, J., & Hampden-Thompson, G. (2003). Family policies and children's school achievement in single- versus two-parent families. *Journal of Marriage & Family, 65,* 681–699.
Popenoe, D. (2000). Life without father. In C. R. Daniels (Ed.), *Lost fathers: The politics of fatherless in America* (pp. 33–49). New York: St. Martin's.
Post, S. G. (2000). *More lasting unions: Christianity, the family, and society*. Grand Rapids: Eerdmans.
Price, J., & Dahl, G. B. (2012). Using natural experiments to study the impact of media on the family. *Family Relations, 61*(3), 363–373.
Prothero, S. (2007). *Religious literacy*. New York: HarperOne.
Rehm, D., & Rehm, J. B. (2002). *Toward commitment: A dialogue about marriage*. New York: Knopf.
Rein, R. (2007). *The divorce prevention handbook: A practical guide for saving marriages*. New York: iUniverse.
Shin, S. H., Choi, H. K., Kim, M. J., & Kim, Y. H. (2010). Comparing adolescents' adjustment and family resilience in divorced families depending on the types of primary caregiver. *Journal of Clinical Nursing, 19*(11/12), 1695–1706.
Stokes, C. E., & Ellison, C. G. (2010). Religion and attitudes toward divorce among U.S. adults. *Journal of Family Issues, 31*(10), 1279–1304.
U.S. Bureau of the Census. (1975). *Historical statistics of the United States*. Washington, DC: U.S. Government Printing Office.
U.S. Department of Health & Human Services. (2010). *Statistical abstracts of the United States*. Washington, DC: U.S. Department of Health & Human Services.
Wallerstein, J. S. (2005). Growing up in a divorced family. *Clinical Social Work Journal, 33*(4), 401–418.
Wallerstein, J. S., & Lewis, J. (1998). The long-term impact of divorce on children: A first report from a 25-year study. *Family and Conciliation Courts Review, 36*(3), 368–383.

Weaver, A. J., Revilla, L. A., & Koenig, H. G. (2002). *Counseling families across the stages of life*. Nashville: Abingdon Press.
Webster, D. D. (2011). *Table grace*. Scotland: Christian Focus Publications.
Weiner-Davis, M. (2001). *The divorce remedy: The proven 7-step program for saving your marriage*. New York: Simon & Schuster.
Williams, T. T., & Sanchez, B. (2012). Parental involvement (and uninvolvement) at an inner city school. *Urban Education, 47*(3), 625–652.
Williams, T. T., & Sanchez, B. (2013). Identifying and decreasing barriers to parent involvement for inner-city parents. *Youth & Society, 45*(1), 54–74.
Wiseman, R., & Rapoport, E. (2006). *Queen bee moms & kingpin dads*. New York: Crown Publishers.
Worthington, Jr. E. (2000). *Christian marital counseling: Eight approaches to helping couples*. Eugene: Wipf and Stock.
Wright, N., & Roberts, W. (1997). *Before you say "I do": A marriage preparation manual for couples*. Eugene: Harvest House Publishers.

Prof. William Jeynes has served in counseling ministry for over 34 years and in academics for 23 years. He and his wife have counseled thousands of families over the years and he has three degrees in Psychology and Counseling and a fourth in a related field. He is a Professor at California State University, Long Beach and a Senior Fellow on the Family at the Witherspoon Institute in Princeton, New Jersey. He graduated first in his class at Harvard University and also graduated from the University of Chicago, where he received the Rosenberger Award for the most outstanding student in his cohort. Bill has ministered in churches in every inhabited continent and in nearly every state in the country. He has spoken a number of times at Yoido Full Gospel Church in Korea, the largest church in the world. He has spoken on family and faith issues for the White House, the U.S. Department of Justice, the U.S. Department of Education, and the U.S. Department of Health & Human Services. He has spoken for both the G. W. Bush and Obama administrations. He has spoken for foreign and UN leaders, Harvard University, Cambridge University, Oxford University, Columbia University, Duke University, Notre Dame University, and the Harvard Family Research Project. His 4-point family and economic proposal given to the Acting President of Korea was passed and became the foundation for their economic and family policy to arise from the Asian Economic Crisis of 1997–1998. He has about 140 academic publications, including 12 books on family and faith issues.

Dr. Jeynes has been interviewed or quoted by the Washington Post, the Los Angeles Times, The Wall Street Journal, the New York Times, the London Times, the Associated Press (AP), CBS, NBC, ABC, FOX, public radio, Al Jazeera and many other news sources. His work has been cited and quoted numerous times by the U.S. Congress, the British Parliament, the EU, and many State Supreme Courts across the United States. Dr. Jeynes has been listed in *Who's Who in the World* for each of the last 9 years and received a Distinguished Scholar Award the California State Senate, the California State Assembly, and his university. He formerly taught at USC and the University of Chicago. Bill has been married for over 28 years and has three wonderful children.

Ralph Winter was the founder of the U.S. Center for World Missions.
Time Magazine named him one of the 25 most influential Evangelicals in the United States.

Spiritual Mentoring for Healthy Family Development

Lou Selzer

Abstract This chapter presents a mentoring model that as proven effective in fostering healthy family development. It examines how dependent spirituality, one which responds to the Spirit, undergirds the effectiveness of an integrated strategy for mentoring family heads. This analysis contains a review of the interest in independent or generic spirituality, which excludes reliance upon the Spirit.

The chapter also includes a comparison of the two approaches to spirituality and a summarization of the advantages that dependent spirituality has over independent in mentoring efficacy.

The second half of the chapter contains four categories of competency for mentors and concludes with problematic mentoring or dilemmas.

The overall goal is to demonstrate that the Spirit functions as the best agent of family health and transformation. The mentor who learns to depend more upon Him gains the best results.

Keywords Family · Mentoring · Parenting · Spirituality

Today the need is great for authentic mentors who genuinely seek to establish and maintain caring relationships with those desiring spiritual moms and dads. Throughout my 35 years of ministry, I have observed how divorce and other adversities have damaged family relationships, creating in many an affective void. As a result of this condition, an escalating number of people from hurting households are craving fulfilling relationships with wise parental substitutes who will faithfully facilitate healing and not betray trust.

Even those raised in healthy, functional homes can recognize the benefits of seeking wise direction and loving support from mentors' life experiences. Most American families today live in a fast-paced culture where financial, vocational, social, moral, and various household responsibilities require informed decisions and plans, carefully implemented. Without the help of mentors, inexperienced family heads run the risk of making plans and taking actions that fail to consider harmful

L. Selzer (✉)
Christian Trinity Church, 21770 Kelly Road Eastpointe, Eastpointe, MI 48021, USA
e-mail: lselzer@wowway.com

W. Jeynes, E. Martinez (eds.), *Ministering Spiritually to Families*,
DOI 10.1007/978-3-319-13302-7_3

pitfalls. Mentors empower family leaders to navigate around these dangers by providing relevant insights, derived from life experience.

Wise mentors recognize the value of their guidance and support in assisting family heads to foster healthy family development. Michael W. Galbraith and Norman H. Cohen affirm that "mentors gradually establish a collaborative and evolving relationship with mentorees for the purpose of enabling them to take appropriate risks, deal better with stress and uncertainty, develop more self-confidence, make more informed decisions, and attain immediate and future objectives" (1995, p. 6). Lauret A. Daloz also understands that heads of households should not pursue their dreams of family health in isolation; instead, they should seek the company of caring mentors who can provide enriching resources and encouragement for their journey of developmental discovery (1986).

For Daloz, this journey of developmental discovery encompasses a progressive apprehension of the value of self-sacrificing love for family health (1986, p. 139). A growing emotional maturity that manifests as a loving concern for the common good fortifies the family, making it more resilient to destructive agents. According to the Apostle Paul, whenever people learn to remove selfishness from their love and to consider the interests of others as an essential priority, they are traveling down a path of spiritual growth and development (e.g., Phil. 2:3–4).

Being in agreement with Daloz's and Paul's perspectives on love, this chapter will show how caring mentors can guide and encourage family heads to grow in spiritual maturity by practicing a self-sacrificing love which accentuates concern for the common good of the family. However, mentors need to detect those family heads who are inclined to receive the impact of mentors for the betterment of their families.

Family heads who neglect sound advice and fail to adequately cope with real-world problems risk succumbing to cultural pressures that can overwhelm them. Galbraith believes that heads of households should establish a clear goal of one-to-one mentoring, not only to assist them in preparing for needed change but also to motivate them into a collaborative relationship where they learn to become better decision makers (1991). Cohen and Galbraith explain that mentoring functions as "a pragmatic approach that helps mentees to successfully navigate the complex and rapid social and economic transitions that characterize our century" (1995, p. 5). Therefore, family heads who seek the guidance of mentors experience many advantages over leaders who neglect or reject such assistance (cf. Murray 2001).

Spiritual Mentoring

Mentoring fundamentally consists of a relationship between someone with wisdom from life experiences and someone, usually younger, with a need for this understanding. Of course, mentoring may occur in a group, being not limited to one-to-one relationships (Parks 1992).

W. Brad Johnson and Charles Ridley explain that effective mentorships "are dynamic, reciprocal, personal relationships in which a more experienced person (mentor) acts as a guide, role model, teacher, and sponsor of a less experienced person" (Johnson and Ridley 2004, p. xv). Daloz adds that the goal of mentoring should be more than passing on a professional legacy but rather a transmission of wisdom for a transformation of the whole person (Daloz 1999, p. 18). When the wisdom that is imparted on this transformational journey bolsters the holistic development of a person, including one's emotional and spiritual need for change, one can characterize the mentoring as spiritual.

The derivation of mentoring for holistic development originates from Greek fiction where Ulysses puts his son Telemachus under the tutelage of a sage named Mentor. Keith Anderson and Randy Reese believe that "Mentor's task was to provide an education of soul and spirit as well as mind, an education in wisdom and not merely in information" (Anderson and Reese 1999, p. 35). They call this instructive relationship spiritual mentoring, since it focuses on the emotional and spiritual domains of a mentoree's total development (1999). Daloz also recognizes the value of a spiritual component to mentoring, noting that "both education and religion are centrally about growth of the spirit, and it is no accident that in less specialized societies healers, teachers, and priests are often the same person" (Daloz 1999, p. 103).

Although spiritual mentoring regards the importance of all the learning domains for transformational change, it devotes special attention to the development of the emotional and spiritual aspects of a person. The mentoring strategies chosen to achieve this goal of holistic development depend upon the perspective of the mentor regarding the meaning of spirituality. Mentors therefore need to decide whether or not to develop their understanding of spirituality from the insights of orthodox theology or somewhere else. I will examine the essence of spirituality in more detail later in the chapter.

To form a workable outlook for such a strategy or a mental model for methodology, mentors should begin by recognizing that spiritual mentoring consists of two categories: independent and dependent. Upon arriving at some understanding regarding the meaning of spirituality, mentors can then decide which category should determine and guide the strategies and goals of their mentorships.

Independent spiritual mentoring professes to be self-sufficient, professionally competent, and free from any faith-based perspective to mentoring; whereas the dependent category requires a continual sensitivity and responsiveness to the Holy Spirit's involvement in the mentoring process. Anderson and Reese describe the dependent category of spiritual mentoring as "a triadic relationship between mentor, mentoree, and the Holy Spirit," where a mentoree can discover the wisdom relevant to his or her need "through the already present action of God" (Anderson and Reese 1999, p. 12). These dependent mentorships function best within the boundaries of Christian ethics.

Although these independent and dependent categories differ in their depiction of subordination, they exhibit some similarities; for they are concerned both with solutions for heart issues which require caring relationships of authenticity and with the establishment of trust (cf., Anderson and Reese 1999, p. 3). They also make the emotional and spiritual domains of a mentoree's holistic development their priority.

This chapter explains more about these two categories later; but to illustrate better their differences now, two examples are shown here. First, as a representative of a more independent approach to spiritual mentoring, Carl Jung recognized a universal desire and need for a mentor with spiritual insight, "who appears at the appropriate time to assist a traveler on a transformational journey where insight, understanding, good advice, determination, planning, etc. are needed but cannot be mustered on one's own" (Jung 1958, p. 71). Assuming that Jung mentored others in his profession, he probably relied upon his own understanding of psychotherapy to guide his protégés rather than to seek and utilize insights from practical theology. Furthermore, his capacity to illuminate his protégés for change was limited both by his self-reliance and by his own system of ethics. As a result of this independent approach to mentoring, some of Jung's protégés could have struggles with their validation of his self-determined ability to help them legitimately. Joseph Campbell argues that mentorees can sometimes express fear and distrust within their mentorships when their mentors display a self-reliant use of their own source of power to change them (Campbell 1949).

The apostle Paul serves as an example of a dependent spiritual mentor. Gordon Fee demonstrates how the Apostle Paul utilized "God's empowering presence" in his mentoring relationship with Timothy and others (e.g., Fee 1994, pp. 758–761). Fee points out that Paul also fulfilled a group mentoring role by assisting the churches of Galatia with the Spirit's aid "to see how love, peace, gentleness, self-denial, and goodness, for example, work out in everyday life" (Fee 1994, p. 460). John Barclay summarizes that a primary goal of any service which depends upon the Spirit consists of guiding and encouraging "the bearing of one another's burdens to fulfill Christ's law of love" (Barclay 1988, p. 146, cf., Gal. 6:2).

The Apostle Paul therefore exemplifies how mentors should rely upon the Spirit and the Holy Scriptures in mentorships and how they should function within the boundaries of Christian ethics, where "God's glory is their purpose, the Spirit is their power, love is the principle, and Christ in the pattern" (Fee 1994, p. 463). This chapter demonstrates some of the advantages that this dependent approach has over other independent forms in mentoring family heads effectively for healthy family development.

A Mental Model for Spiritual Mentoring

This chapter utilizes the mental model of a bridge to make it easier for readers to understand the whole process of mentoring family heads for the betterment of their families (see Fig. 1). The bridge consists of five girders that support a five-lane road. These horizontal beams are upheld by four columns attached to piles that are

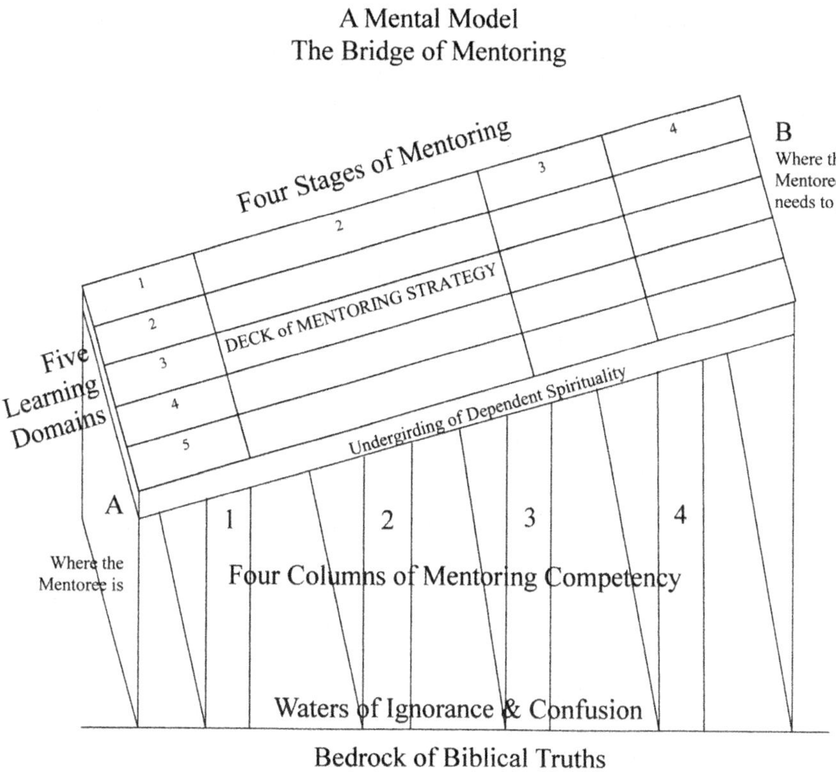

Fig. 1 The mental model of the bridge of mentoring demonstrating. How the whole process of mentoring helps families

driven into bedrock under the water of ignorance and confusion. The road is formed from four large sections that fit together in consecutive order to complete the deck of the bridge. The bridge spans from pier A to pier B.

The horizontal portion of the bridge represents the strategy of mentoring family heads from where they are (pier A) to where they need to be (pier B)—to become more effective representatives and loving leaders of their families. The five-lane road signifies the five primary learning domains—affective, cognitive, volitional, behavioral, and spiritual. A complete mentoring strategy must include all five domains to provide the range of possible solutions necessary to manage the complex and multidimensional problems that mentors often encounter today. The mentoring strategy that incorporates all learning domains for holistic wellbeing is called integrated mentoring in this chapter.

The five-lane highway of the bridge is composed of four sections that portray the four-stage strategy for the integrated mentoring of family heads—"initiation, cultivation, separation, and redefinition" (Johnson and Ridley 2004, p. 81). These four stages delineate the consecutive order of different objectives that can be achieved within the duration of mentoring.

The five girders of the bridge denote the mentor's use of dependent spirituality for each of the learning domains. This chapter will explain the meaning of dependent spirituality and disclose its many advantages over independent spirituality. The four columns that support these girders depict four categories of competency for mentors—spirituality, understanding the affects of context, mentoring and coaching skills, and the proper utilization of ten mentoring agents, which includes an accurate feedback process for continual evaluation and improvement.

The four columns of mentoring competency are anchored to four piles driven into bedrock. The bedrock represents wise principles and core values developed from a sound belief system. The pilings signify the mentor's devotion to wisdom and core values as they relate to each of the categories of competency. For instance, a mentor's spirituality must be based upon the truth derived from a reliable source. For the Christian mentor, the Bible constitutes the basis for the core values and spiritual understanding of effective mentoring. When properly understood, the Bible is the Bedrock that supports both the mentor and the whole mentoring strategy.

This chapter presents Christian mentoring as its primary means of ministering spiritually and effectively to families. The importance of Christian mentoring as a methodology for ministry requires a clear definition. Bobb Biehl describes Christian mentoring as "a lifelong relationship, in which a mentor helps a protégé reach her or his God-given potential" (1996, p. 19). Paul Stanley and Robert Clinton define mentoring as "a relational experience in which one person empowers another by sharing God-given resources" (1992, p. 38). Mentoring comprises a caring relationship where spiritual parents impart God-given wisdom from life experiences and other sources of learning to help guide and equip mentorees in their journey to fulfill their purposeful callings.

I have divided this chapter into two major portions. The strategy for integrated mentoring—the horizontal part of the bridge—will be the first portion to be examined, encompassing sections on the four-stage strategy, the five primary learning domains, and the undergirdings of dependent spirituality. The topic of dependent spirituality will include studies on the wide interest in "generic" spirituality, the meaning of independent and dependent spiritualities, and the importance of mentoring with dependent spirituality. The second portion—the vertical columns of the bridge—will scrutinize the four categories of competency for mentors and address the need for mentors who use a dependable source of bedrock wisdom and knowledge. This chapter ends with some mentoring dilemmas and conclusions.

I will attempt to show in this chapter that the Holy Spirit functions as the best agent of transformation, whether His activities are more direct, or indirect through people or giftings. As a result, the most effective spiritual mentoring requires the mentor's ability to depend upon the Spirit for the transformation of family heads and their families.

The Mentoring Strategy

The Four-Stage Strategy for the Integrated Mentoring of Family Heads

All types of mentoring follow a life cycle. Experts differ on how many stages should be identified. Most contend that mentoring requires a minimum of three stages. For example, Howard and William Hendricks recognize three: "definition, development, and departure" (1995, p. 218). This chapter's working plan selects Brad Johnson's and Charles R. Ridley's four-stage model: "initiation, cultivation, separation, and redefinition" (2004, p. 81). Awareness of mentoring stages, no matter how they are identified, enhances successful relationships, since it assists partners to anticipate and utilize the particular dynamics associated with each stage.

A mentoring design that incorporates an understanding of these stages helps family heads to achieve important learning goals. The process begins with the "initiation" stage. The proper pairing of mentors with mentorees—consisting of family heads—constitutes the first task of this stage. In a church context, mentorees are drawn to mentors who exemplify the eight components of Christian spirituality. These mentors may include pastoral staff, elders, and other church leaders who desire to share their life experiences to assist families. Family heads who persistently seek the assistance of spiritual mentors will eventually find it, if they rely upon the Lord for guidance.

In the initiation stage, mentors and mentorees set the groundwork for the learning process. Mentoring partners seek to clarify their mutual expectations, agree on the duration of the relationship, and settle the ground rules. Also during this time partners mutually delineate biblically-based purposes and establish core values to provide guidelines for the process. Guidance in volitional and affective learning likewise starts here, as mentors help family heads become more open and responsive to the motivational dynamics of the love of God. However, the primary responsibility for responsiveness and perseverance through the learning process belongs to the mentoree (cf. Stanley and Clinton 1992, p. 43).

In the second stage, "cultivation," all the essential elements of the learning process are brought into alignment by a type of systems thinking. These components include: (1) giving careful contextual consideration; (2) using core values to establish the integrity of the process; (3) utilizing biblically-based learning tasks to achieve needed learning objectives; (4) evaluating learning with an honest and valid feedback system for continual improvements; (5) defining both the primary learning goal and the learning objectives necessary to achieve various aspects of this goal; (6) selecting and implementing any of the other supportive agents of family transformation mentioned later in this chapter.

Mentors in this stage need to understand the importance of context in the learning process. Lois Zachary defines context "as the circumstances, conditions, and centralizing forces that affect how we connect, interact with, and learn from one another" (2000, p. 29). Context can hinder or enhance leadership development and spiritual formation in the Christian family. It influences motives, affects emotions, and colors perceptions and understanding. Overlooking this important factor dramatically hinders mentoring's appeal, inclusivity, duration, goals, methodology, feedback, vision formation, and Christian relevance. Effective mentors intentionally develop contextual sensitivity, which aids in discerning the types of relational operations appropriate for each situation. Sensitive mentors design their sessions by giving a careful, balanced consideration to both the context and the content of their mentoring throughout the four stages.

While mentors practice contextual sensitivity, they guide family heads to discover and use learning tasks which provide guidelines—under the direction of the Spirit—to define and achieve learning objectives. These tasks refer to the active steps required to meet a specific learning objective. For the purpose of this chapter, a learning objective describes how to achieve one aspect of the primary learning goal—holistic leadership development for family heads. Learning tasks consist of learning disciplines that assist family leaders to fulfill their responsibilities, including the need to satisfy their mentoring obligations so the appropriate learning process can occur. The Holy Spirit uses His learning objectives to lead family heads by grace toward the goal fulfillment of family transformation. For instance, His use of mentors to guide family leaders to discover and utilize certain communication skills serves to reduce misunderstandings and enhance the verbal and non-verbal expressions of love within the family. Learning how to implement these skills to achieve this learning objective illustrates the planned use of learning tasks. The Spirit directs this process and empowers mentorees to perceive, assess, believe, and act in ways that achieve necessary learning objectives, those which encompasses all the aspects of the journey toward reaching the primary learning goal.

The third stage of integrated mentoring entails "separation." Since mentors and mentorees should have already reached a termination agreement during the initiation phase, they should be able to end their relationship smoothly, concluding on a positive note. Sometimes an extension is renegotiated, but mentors should always make themselves available for any further assistance. During this phase, mentors and mentorees should plan not only to review and evaluate learning accomplishments but also celebrate any achievements.

The fourth stage encompasses a re-definitional transition. Here the mentorship changes into more of a friendship of peers—a relationship of co-mentors. The participants may go their separate ways or re-establish another mentoring relationship, on more equal terms. Mentors should strive to train mature, family heads into co-mentors, who function as facilitators for the Spirit's maturation process of other family leaders. In this way, the original mentor can perceive the mentorees of his or her mentoree as spiritual grandchildren.

Both Christian mentors and mentorees have responsibilities throughout all four stages to rely upon the Spirit and the Bible for leading and empowering the learning process. The Spirit determines ultimately how to manage the discovery process, selects the required learning tasks and objectives, and activates the grace available to transform Christian family heads and their families through Christ's resurrection power. The Spirit is the key agent of learning, regeneration, and transformation within the Christian mentoring process of discovery, trust and love.

The Five Learning Domains for Strategic Integrated Mentoring

Integrated mentoring constitutes a relational process of helping a mentoree discover pertinent truths that incorporate inputs from all the learning domains. It highlights a combination of five primary domains—spiritual, affective, cognitive, volitional, and behavioral learning—to counter the multidimensional problems that can confront contemporary families (see fig. 2).

The historian Catherine Albanese (2001) presents a four-dimensional model. She suggests that the spirituality of "knowing the divine" is required for healthy family development. Her model contains the following four dominant ways people can learn about the divine for assistance in purposeful living: "knowing through the body," which includes religious practices; "knowing through the heart," which focuses on experiential affect; "knowing through the will," which centers on social

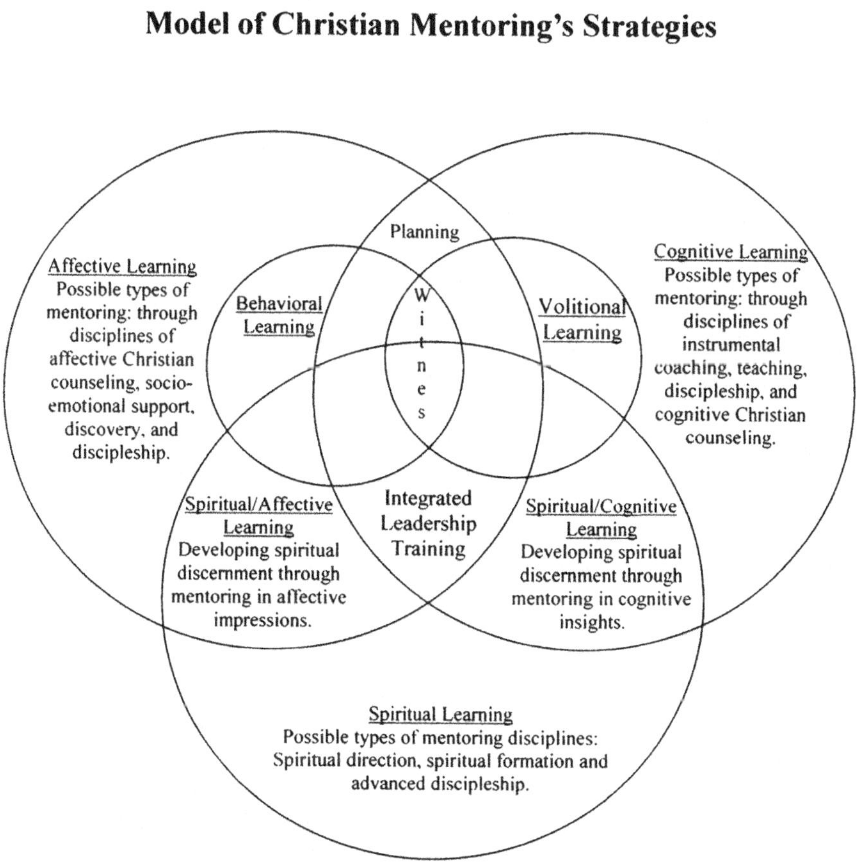

Fig. 2 Five learning domains for strategic integrated mentoring

justice; and "knowing through the mind." Since all four provide knowledge of the divine from different learning perspectives, she regards not only each domain as spiritual but also the total collection of ways to learn as spiritual. Although Albanese's model contains spiritual learning throughout her four primary domains, I prefer to include spiritual learning as a fifth domain, for the sake of simplicity.

The five-domain model of integrated mentoring presented in this section constitutes the strategic learning paradigm that enables family heads to lead their households into holistic health. It functions as a five-lane highway across the bridge of mentoring strategy, since it includes all the types of learning needed to counter the complexity of problems encountered by mentors.

The first domain to be examined is spiritual learning, which can become one of the most important domains to consider for holistic health. A person's spirit is the place of "an inner life with God that transforms the heart and builds deeply ingrained habits of virtue" (Foster 1998, p. 8). According to Mark A. Laaser, the spiritual regeneration and learning that can occur in the believer's spirit constitutes the primary means of progressively removing selfishness, which he considers the root of most family problems (2005, pp. 86–88). From many years of pastoral ministry, I have also concluded that the goal of holistic health and vitality for the Christian family cannot be reached without both spiritual learning and the activity of the Holy Spirit—His "washing of regeneration and renewing" (Titus 3:5, NASB)—taking place in the spirit of the family head who believes.

Although this input from the spiritual domain of learning serves an essential function in the family development process, holistic health also requires learning from the other four domains of integrated mentoring—affective, cognitive, volitional, and behavioral. Following are some suggestions on how a mentor can train family heads by using all five domains.

First, spiritual training at its core educates family heads on how to develop their devotional life with Jesus, which includes training in the spiritual disciplines—like prayer and meditation of Scripture. Spiritual learning also involves both the teaching of biblical principles of individual and family maturity and the exhorting of family heads to apply these principles to their lives. As they learn to cooperate with the Spirit by yielding to His inner activities and His truth, they and their families can experience more of the Spirit's transformational change. As mentors guide these leaders through this process, they establish a biblical basis upon which learning from the other domains can be built. They also assist family leaders to learn more directly from Scripture, so they can personally receive constant feedback for continual improvements.

Learning from the spiritual domain includes discovering how to recognize the wide diversity of divine communications that usually comes first to the believer's spirit; from there these divine inputs influence his or her emotions, cognitions, will, and behavior. The process of training family heads to receive divine guidance in an atmosphere of different types of prayer is often called spiritual direction. For instance, after a prayer of faith, a specific Bible reference can come into a believer's mind—after entering his or her spirit—and when it is located and read, it provides the exact insight necessary to make the best decision for the family. Mentors have been using spiritual direction for centuries, especially within certain religious orders of the Roman Catholic Church (cf. Dyckman and Carroll 1981; Edwards 2001).

God also gives spiritual gifts to the spirit of believers. Richard J. Foster points out that spiritual learning includes the receiving of charisms of wisdom, discernment, miracles, and healings (1985, pp. 9–10). He defines a charism as "a divinely inspired spiritual gift that God bestows upon individuals for the good of the community of faith and the advancement of the kingdom of God upon the earth" (1998, p. 9). From his perspective, charisms equip family heads with divinely powerful resources to help them fulfill their family responsibilities.

Second, cognitive learning pertains not only to the renewal of the mind—through faith in the transforming of the Word of God and the Spirit (cf. Rom. 12:2)—but also to the discipline of one's thoughts through wise reflection and intentional rejection of inappropriate cognitions, which are destructive to the family.

Third, volitional education encompasses biblical instruction on receiving divine guidance, surrendering to God's will, and trusting in His promises. As a result, family leaders can address selfishness and self-will, learning each day to recognize and remove some of them through faith in the Spirit's leading and empowerment (cf. Gal. 5:16–18). The Spirit frees the Christian to choose to serve one another through love, rather than deciding to act selfishly (cf. Gal. 5:13).

Fourth, affective learning encourages the building of loving and healthy relationships between spouses, parents and their children, brothers and sisters, and between men and women in the Christian community. It teaches families how to abide in peace, love and joy within these relationships. It also includes forms of training to assist family heads to receive inner healing for past wounds, which can hinder the development of healthy and vital family relationships.

Finally, behavioral learning could consist of the establishment of a mentoring policy of mutual accountability, with clear directives regarding honest and accurate personal assessments and feedback for needed improvements. Mentors and their mentorees must carefully align their actions with their core values and purposes for the family, so they can actively progress toward the fulfillment of objectives for the continual improvement of their families. For example, parents must learn to replace hurtful words spoken in haste with instructive and uplifting words spoken in love. They should also celebrate the consistent achievement of learning tasks which cooperate and correlate with the Spirit's development of the family.

Interest in Spirituality for Holistic Maturity

As interest in organized religion is declining in America, interest in spirituality is growing (Fuller 2001; Griffith 2004). Charles Taylor explains that a "culture of authenticity" inspires many today to strive to understand one's own identity and unique purpose in life. Those who seek credible answers often resist conformity to any model imposed upon them from outside by a religious authority (Taylor 2002,

p. 83). However, they recognize that their identity as humans includes a spiritual component. According to Kathleen A. Mahoney, findings from national surveys indicate that a majority of college students strongly desire to become more engaged in their own spiritual journey (2001).

The younger generations need mentors who will guide them in the process of self-discovery and personal purpose (Jacobi 1991). Some mentors believe that the ideal learning organization—"mentoring community"—is the college campus, "where faculty, professionals, and fellow students play a role in helping students find meaning in their lives" (Braskamp 2007, p. 2). Larry A. Braskamp argues that "colleges will only succeed in effectively fostering truly holistic development when faculty address the issues of meaning, purpose, religion, spiritual and moral growth along with academic learning in the classroom and in their relationships with students, when the opportunities to do so are appropriate" (2007, p. 2). Even though campuses can become important learning organizations, Christian mentors claim that the church can develop into the most trustworthy mentoring community.

Whether heads of families learn how to develop healthy family relationships from mentors in churches or on campuses, they must come to understand that holistic development requires spiritual learning (cf. Schmidt 2005; Vogel 1991). To achieve holistic maturity, family leaders must include spiritual learning with cognitive, behavioral, affective, and volitional learning.

Christian mentors often regard the spiritual domain as having central significance, since spiritual issues "lie at the core of the journey" (Daloz 1999, p. 251). Daloz argues that if educators are to properly regard the developmental needs of students as whole people, they must include spiritual learning (1996, p. 130). He explains that mentors should not separate the spirit from the intellect, but, instead, recognize that they are intimately intertwined—that "developing one depends profoundly on developing the other" (1999, p. 257). Linda Vozel (1991) also points out the importance of guiding adult seekers along a meaningful, cognitive, and spiritual journey, so they can progress more quickly and more deeply in transformational maturity. Mentors, therefore, must learn how to serve seekers of spirituality by leading them through the process of spiritual discovery.

Generic and Independent Spirituality

Does spiritual effectiveness for family health require a dependence upon the Spirit? Is there a generic form of spirituality which can be used to help the family, even though it divorces itself from a submissive relationship to the Spirit? Can generic spirituality exist—can a person be spiritual but not religious? These are the questions I will attempt to answer in this section.

Some reject the concept of generic spirituality, arguing that all forms of spirituality have some type of religious basis for interpreting spiritual experiences (Wuthnow 1998, 2003). Nevertheless, many on today's campuses claim to have discovered how to be spiritual without being religious (Bender 2004). Others assert that students' attempts to exclude various religious traditions from their spirituality merely substitute one religion with another. For instance, some experts challenge the authenticity of self-generated and non-religious spirituality. They claim that even though such spiritual seekers fail to participate within religious communities, they still can hold a religious viewpoint which can shape their perspective of spirituality (Albanese 2006; Bender 2004; Griffith 2004; Schmidt 2003).

The answer to the question regarding whether or not a person can be simultaneously spiritual and non-religious depends upon an acceptable definition of both spirituality and religion. However, the complexity of the widely diverse characteristics and historical usages of these terms makes it impossible to formulate definitions which have unanimous agreement. Courtney Bender concludes that "definitions of religion and spirituality are porous, historically variable, marked by varieties of evident and implicit theological understandings, and always remain open to the charge that they are either too general or too specific" (2004, p. 1).

The support for the existence of generic spirituality is weak, because of the difficulty of defining religion. For instance, most would agree that Christianity is a religion, and Marxism is not. Yet, the often-quoted theologian, Dietrich Bonhoeffer, describes an ideal Christianity as "religionless," where a person's call to faith constituted more than religion—i.e., it was a call of Jesus "not to a new religion, but to life" (Zerner 1984, p. 169). Bonhoeffer's understanding of a "religionless Christianity" corresponds well with the distinction between faith and religion found in the works of Karl Barth and Martin Luther. Luther even argues that faith derives from the spirit and religion from the flesh, thereby perceiving faith as spiritual but religion as carnal. Furthermore, Andrew Kerr Rule notes that some define religion with such indefiniteness that they would include Marxism as a religion—in spite of its fervent repudiation of religion (1984, p. 931). In light of this, it is unlikely for anyone to define religion in a universally acceptable way. Consequently, the existence of generic spirituality remains unresolved; for as long as more specific and definite definitions are questionable, the actuality of non-religious spirituality remains ambiguous.

Because of this difficulty with semantics, it is wise to circumvent the concept of generic or non-religious spirituality, and replace it with independent spirituality. From this perspective, the determination of whether or not a form of spirituality is religious becomes non-essential to the more relevant issue—whether people's sensitivity and responsiveness in their spirits to the spiritual realm and its dynamics involve their dependence or independence with regard to the Holy Spirit. As a result, a person who prefers independent spirituality purposefully seeks to utilize knowledge of spiritual dynamics learned from sources separate from the Spirit and from the divine revelation of the Bible.

For example, William James in his *Variation of Religious Experiences* understood spirituality as independent and pragmatic. For him, the authenticity of spiritual experiences must be tested by the pragmatic consequences of personal belief (1902). From his viewpoint, special experiences of individuals "in their solitude"—

their spirituality—can be explained and interpreted by applying psychological knowledge, rather than accepting biblical explanations without practical evidence of their validity.

Many who could be classified as independently spiritual seek to utilize the spiritual dynamics of love and compassion to better themselves and to help the personal development of others and their families. They usually attempt this altruism by utilizing their own understanding, rather than by relying upon either the Spirit or His divine revelation. Using this form of self-sufficient spirituality can benefit families temporally, but fails to adequately prepare them for eternity. By resisting both a dependence upon the Spirit and a submission to His will—as revealed in the Bible—those who manifest merely an independent spirituality forfeit all the eternal benefits that come from a "a unity of the Spirit" in the prefect bond of Christ's love and peace (cf. Eph. 4:3; Col. 3:14–15).

Examples of Independent Spirituality

Recent history contains a variety of examples of individuals from diverse backgrounds who exemplify independent spirituality—especially as it relates to unfailing love. For instance, Mitch Albom's *Tuesdays wth Morrie* contains a segment where the dying professor, Morrie Schwartz, explains life as a "tension of opposites" where "love always wins" (1997, p. 40). Albom conveys here his independent spirituality by communicating the validity of unfailing love as a spiritual dynamic for man's betterment, but he does so in a manner intentionally free from reliance upon the Holy Spirit for that perfect love.

Victor Frankl, a survivor of Auschwitz, serves as another example of a spiritual man who helped families heal and develop maturity by utilizing the dynamic of love. By using an existential process called Logo-therapy, he guided families to discover the meaning of love, work, death, suffering, and life (1969). For him, all people have a spiritual dimension which enables them to gain an appreciation of the value of love and purpose in their lives (1962). As families gained a better comprehension of revealed meaning in their lives, Frankl could guide them to use love to develop relationships and make better decisions (1978).

Even though Frankl did not utilize a Christian perspective in his therapy, much of his perception and thinking on how love weaves life's experiences into a fabric of meaning were compatible with Judeo-Christian theology (Tweedie 1961). Frankl exhibited an independence in his spirituality, for he neither appeared to acknowledge the Holy Spirit as the "Weaver of love" nor did he depend upon the Spirit for Jesus' regenerative transformation. Nevertheless, his apperception not only of the value of love and of meaning in life but also his attempts to utilize his spiritual perceptivity to guide people along a journey of purposeful development clearly constituted a valuable spirituality. As a result, the spirituality of his therapy provides important temporal benefits for families.

A final example of independent spirituality is surprisingly found in the works of Erich Fromm, an avowed Marxist and dialectic humanist. He argued that human beings show both a need for transcendence (to rise above animal behavior by being productive in love) and a need for an existential form of reference (a way of finding meaning in a world where society can pervert personality) (Mclemore 1985). It is unclear whether Fromm acknowledged these needs as spiritual in nature, but he did recognize them as necessary for holistic health, which includes spiritual well-being.

Fromm's perception and practices were spiritual, but they were independent of the Spirit and any other part of Christian theology, which he repudiated. Both his understanding of the power of unselfish love in the development of family relationships and his desire to practice it—while attempting to motivate others to follow his example—revealed a perceptivity and responsiveness to the spiritual dynamic of unselfish love (1956). This understanding and desire demonstrated his independent form of spirituality.

Fromm's rejection of Christianity limited the effectiveness of his work, for it forced him not only to arbitrarily determine the characteristics and distinctives of holistic health and goodness but also to exclude from his therapy the actual means to love unselfishly and live vibrantly—through the regenerative power of the Spirit in Christ. So, even though the spirituality of Fromm's work guided families to establish valuable spiritual goals, his refusal to rely upon the Spirit prevented him from helping them to fully obtain these goals.

The Dependence of Christian Spirituality

Christian Spirituality (CS) consists of a perceptivity and responsiveness to the spirit realm and its dynamics—as revealed by the divine revelation of the Bible, and as activated, operated, empowered, and guided by the Holy Spirit. Similar to independent spirituality, CS acknowledges that a person's spirit contains the potential for this spiritual sensitivity. Yet, unlike independent spirituality, CS remains dependent upon the Spirit; is Christ-centered rather than human-centered; relies upon the finished work of Christ's substitutional death, resurrection, and ascension; and strives by grace to find and fulfill God's callings. CS uses wisdom from above to assist the seeker to take the downward path of humility to fulfill the upward call of God, while growing "in the grace and knowledge of our Lord" (2 Pet. 3:18, NASB).

By a mystical union with Christ's Spirit through faith in Jesus' identity, a Christian potentially shines as a spiritual lamp of Jesus' love and resurrection life. As a result of this union in Christ, and this dependence upon the Spirit, CS offers countless advantages beyond what can come from its independent counterpart (cf. Nouwen 1996).

Ministering with Dependent Spiritually

To spiritually minister to family heads begins with a workable understanding of ministry. From a Christian perspective, ministering ideally means to render personal service according to the pattern of wisdom and self-giving exemplified by Jesus (Lk. 22:27). Jesus taught that ministering as servant-leaders for the good of the community constitutes the only path of authentic greatness (Mk. 9:35, 10:44). A primary Greek word used in the New Testament (NT) to convey this form of ministry is *diakoneo*, the word from which "deacon" is derived. The Early Church, therefore, expected her deacons to be servant-leaders.

A growing number of religious and secular leaders have rediscovered the value of servant-leadership. Robert K. Greenleaf, a former AT&T executive, in *The Power of Servant Leadership* provides eight essays on the value of servant-leadership in a variety of institutions or human organizations, including the family (1998). Fred Kofman and Peter M. Senge present servant-leaders as those "who lead because they chose to serve, both to serve one another and to serve a higher purpose" (1995, p. 35). For them, servant-leadership constitutes a combination not only of the idealism of strong beliefs in the dignity and self-worth of humanity but also of the pragmatism of respected leadership which inspires confidence in those led (1995).

Servant-leadership of family heads requires lifelong learning on how to serve in germane and applicable ways. Servant-leaders who attempt to develop their effectiveness continually need someone or something to empower and direct the learning process. The potency of this guidance depends upon the reliability and validity of the principle of learning.

To minister spiritually requires a sensitivity and responsiveness to both the Spirit's external and internal activity. Leaders who minister to their families by relying upon the Spirit's direction and empowerment have a great advantage over those who do not. The degree that a head of a household depends upon the Spirit determines his or her ministry proficiency to the family, thereby pragmatically demonstrating that person's level of Christian or dependent spirituality.

The Four Categories of Competency for Mentors

The Mentor's Spirituality

CS for mentors contains many fundamental components. Being able to help families more permanently and comprehensively requires a better understanding of these components, so the Christian mentor can learn how to develop into a more effective vessel of God's spiritual presence and activity. Drs. J. Robert and Richard W. Clinton (1991) divide CS into eight components: centrality, interiority, exteriority, spirit sensitivity, uniqueness of giftedness, community interaction, fruitfulness of Christ-likeness, and progressive development throughout life. These eight fundamental components of spirituality constitutes the first column of mentoring competency, which was shown in the introduction's mental model.

The first of the eight components, "centrality," focuses on a believer's connection with the person and work of Christ Jesus (1991, Ch. 4, p. 8). According to the Apostle Paul, all authentic Christians are joined to Christ, by being "baptized into His body," and by being "made to drink of one Spirit" (1 Cor. 12:3, NASB). Paul considered all Christians to be members of Christ's body—the Church—each given a divinely designated function, "for the building up of itself in love" (Eph. 4:16, NASB).

CS, therefore, starts and ends with Jesus, the one who begins and perfects transformational change in all those linked to Him by grace and through faith. James M. Houston concludes that "Christian spirituality is the outworking, then, of the grace of God in the soul of man, beginning with conversion to conclusion in death or Christ's Second Advent" (1984, p. 1047). The Christian's mystical union with Christ through faith entails a connection where the Spirit of Christ indwells each believer and provides him or her with a position "in Christ," certifiable by the Spirit himself (cf. Rm. 8:16). The Christians' position of being "in Christ" and the condition of Christ dwelling in them, divinely validates their identity as people of the Spirit—spiritual people.

The theologian Gordon D. Fee describes the spiritual person as "the person with the Spirit" (1994, p. 108). He interprets the Apostle Paul's concept of spirituality in 1 Corinthians 2:14–16 to simply mean having the indwelling of the Spirit. Since God by His grace sovereignly established this "centrality" component of spirituality as a position in His Son, He designates all true believers as spiritual. Charles K. Barrett contrasted this form of spirituality with the "natural" or "soulish" man, who has not received the Holy Spirit because of his unbelief in the gospel of Christ (1968, p. 77).

The second component of CS, "interiority," refers to the journey where believers give "attention to the life of the Spirit" in them (Nouwen 1972, p. 107). This aspect of CS "includes the capacity to develop a discerning heart among the many voices and motivations within and to determine which aspirations are seeded there by God" (Shawchuck and Heuser 1993, p. 120). It involves "one's conscious inner perception of an on-going experiential relationship with God and the activities which stimulate that relationship" (Clinton and Clinton 1991, Ch. 4, p. 11). The spiritual disciplines—such as prayer, fasting, meditation of Holy Scripture, etc.—stimulate sensitivity and cooperate with grace for growth in this relationship. Faithfulness to the spiritual disciplines not only demonstrates interior spirituality but also provides a means of expressing it (Nouwen 1981, 1989).

The third component, "exteriority," ascribes to spirituality "the outward testimony to the inner life." It consists of "a lifestyle, a spiritual tone that others sense and see which is consistent with the inner depth being experienced" (Clinton and Clinton 1991, Ch. 4, p. 13). It becomes a way of life which manifests Jesus (cf. Foster 1988). As Richard J. Foster explains, "We are to be the dwelling place of the

Holy Spirit, making the reality of God visible and manifest everywhere we go and in everything we do" (1998, p. 251).

The spiritual dimensions of interiority and exteriority correlate with each other. These two characterize a practical side of CS, as the inner life expresses itself outwardly in faithfulness and acts of love. Grace empowers believers both to discover the divine revelation of their spiritual identity in Christ and to live out this truth by a life of faith that corresponds directly with it. In light of this, Christians ascertain who they are—spiritual people—and then, by faith act in a way consistent to this vision or revelation.

Sensitivity to the Spirit constitutes another essential component of spirituality, for it includes "the believer's comprehension of Spirit activity" (Clinton and Clinton 1991, Ch. 4, p. 27). The Spirit reveals to believers "the things freely given" to them by God (cf. 1 Cor. 2:12, NASB); but to the natural man—one without the Spirit—these revelations are rejected as foolishness, because the necessary discernment comes from the Spirit (1 Cor. 2:14). Norman Shawchuck explains that "spirituality is the means by which we develop an awareness of the presence of the loving Lord in our lives, and the processes by which we keep that awareness alive and vital, to the end that we become formed in the Spirit of Christ" (1993, p. 119).

True believers, by virtue of the presence of the Spirit within them, receive a clearer discernment into the nature of both family problems and their solutions. The spiritual person utilizes the Spirit's assistance "to consider and appraise all things because he is not only inspired to understand what he sees; he is also furnished with the moral standard by which all things may be measured" (Barrett 1968, p. 77). Much of spirituality consists of discernment by the Spirit, who clearly imparts the necessary understanding as it is needed (cf. Fee 1994; Shawchuck and Heuser 1993).

Another component of spirituality refers to a certain giftedness which entails a charismatic uniqueness. In one of his letters, the Apostle Paul points out this aspect by correlating those with a prophetic giftedness with those who are spiritual (1 Cor. 14:37). Fee agrees that spiritual people and individuals manifesting the Spirit through charismatic gifts are closely linked (1994, p. 259).

The Apostle Paul uses the word "spiritual" (*pneumatikos*) to associate a person of the Spirit with a person who manifests the presence of the Spirit through some charismatic gift like prophecy (cf. 1 Cor. 12:7–10). He understands "spiritual" to describe not only one who has the Spirit (positional spirituality), but also one who can outwardly respond to Him (practical spirituality) through a spiritual gift used "for the profit of all" (1 Cor. 12:7, NKJV).

CS cannot develop in isolation nor can it exist in separation from the common good of the community. The believer's spiritual union with Christ (cf. 1 Cor. 6:17) also includes a union with all others in whom the Spirit dwells (cf. Rom. 8:9–11; 1 Cor. 12:13). In light of this, CS must embody a communal context. For instance, in Galatians (6:1–5), Paul shows that those who are spiritual should restore to fellowship those caught in trespasses, as they demonstrate authentic love to the penitent through their burden bearing (cf. vv. 1–2). They "sow to the Spirit" (Gal. 6:8, NASB) by taking advantages of opportunities to do "good to all men" (Gal. 6:10).

This horizontal accountability demonstrated in the Christian church through burden bearing constitutes another key component of spirituality—community.

As a fundamental requirement for healthy family development, communal spirituality provides a sense of connectedness with and a responsibility for others, especially those who belong to the church family (cf. Gal. 6:7–10). The educator Laurent Daloz refers to this loving concern for the common good—rather than merely for ones own benefit—a "constructive engagement with otherness" (1986, p. 139). Henri J. Nouwen describes it as the spiritual journey of "the way of the heart" (1981). Spiritual Christians, therefore, demonstrate their communal spirituality not only by family restoration and development, "but they must go beyond that by 'bearing one another's burdens,' lifting the load of the weak and needy, as it were" (Fee 1994, p. 463). The Spirit empowers and guides this love for the family in its communal context.

"Fruitfulness," another chief component of spirituality, consists of a process for growth in Christ-like characteristics, which manifest themselves in integrity and in effective service to others (Clinton and Clinton 1991). The Apostle Paul calls this creation of the likeness of Christ in character and function "the fruit of the Spirit" (Gal. 5:22, NASB). The Spirit causes this fruit to grow and mature, as Christians not only respond in faith and love to the revelations of their provisions and positions in Christ but also seek and savor the transforming presence of their Lord with joy and peace.

Obviously, only a portion of those who call themselves Christians actually act like Christ. Even the Apostle Paul recognized that he could not address some Christians as Spirit people (*pneumatikoi*), but as fleshly—those who perceive and act like others who do not have the Spirit (1 Cor. 3:1–3). Paul's choice here of the word *sarkinos* (fleshly) enabled him to distinguish these individuals from the natural man, and to do so without denying the positional spirituality that belongs even to these "carnal" Christians. Dallas Willard explains, "The babe in Christ in 1 Corinthians 3:1 has spiritual life, but in a largely incipient form. Much in his or her embodied and concretely socialized personality is not under the effective direction of the Spirit, and the reintegration of the self under God is not yet achieved" (1991, p. 67).

Even though Paul may consider these "carnal" Christians spiritual by virtue of their position "in Christ," they were still unspiritual in function—lacking fruitfulness. Fee elucidates, "Corinthians are involved in a lot of unchristian behavior, and in that sense they are 'unspiritual,' not because they lack the Spirit but because they are thinking and acting just like those who do lack the Spirit" (1994, p. 111).

Finally, spirituality includes the necessity of progressive development through constructive feedback from the Spirit. This additional component of spirituality consists of the continual process of discovery and fulfilling God's daily calling for believers—to abide in His presence, as He abides in them (Jn. 15:4–8). The Christian must not perceive this journey as an upward path of elitism, but as a downward path of servant leadership. This spiritual development leads to a deeper understanding of Jesus, who He is, and who the Spirit people are in Him. God requires believers to express outwardly their faith and love, so they can facilitate and not hinder the work of the Spirit in forming Christ "in" them—just as they were already "in" Christ through their faith in His promises.

This eight-fold model of CS should assist the reader's understanding regarding the type of comprehensive spirituality which should ideally characterize a Christian mentor's ministry to family heads.

Contextual Sensitivity

Should mentors develop their relationships with family leaders within a group or on a one-to-one basis? Should they utilize some or all the learning domains? Contextual sensitivity increases the discernment necessary not only to answer such questions but also to decide on the appropriate action to improve the influence of mentoring for the betterment of the family. By understanding contextual variables, mentors can determine whether the mentoring strategy should be formal or informal, close or long-distant, life-long or short-term, involving frequent sessions or infrequent—whatever is best for any given situation. A wise mentor, therefore, must consider contextual sensitivity an important pillar of mentoring competency.

Contextual dynamics also determine the developmental duration and extent of possible change. Some educators regard context to be so important that they believe it "should be considered with the same attention as the teaching and learning interactions occurring within it" (Merriam and Cafferella 1991, p. 306). The importance of addressing this issue is due to the many contextual factors that can influence the measure of empowerment in a mentoring relationship. Wise and effective mentors design their sessions by giving a careful, balanced consideration to both the content and the context of their mentoring throughout the four stages of the mentoring strategy.

Mentors must also address issues of cultural context. For instance, culture determines the family or clan head to be targeted as the primary agent for any needed change. As a pastor of a multi-cultural church, I have observed certain trends that have affected my choice either of mentorees or of heads of households to be trained as mentors. Among African-American families, mothers tend to function as the spiritual heads of their households, whether or not they live with the fathers of their children. However, in first generation families from Africa, the fathers usually serve as the dominant heads of their households. Among *Latino* families, the fathers are customarily recognized as heads of households; but at times some function more like figureheads, while their wives actually serve as the primary change agents. This trend can sometimes be found among *Anglo* and Philippino families, as well. With Hmong families, the clan leader and his older sons operate as heads over all the families that constitute the clan. In all of these cases, mentors should develop a contextual sensitivity to direct and support their mentoring strategy.

Mentoring Skill

Developing mentoring skills constitute the third column of mentoring competency. Throughout my thirty years of Christian mentoring, I have discovered the importance of these wise words: "let everyone be quick to hear, slow to speak, and slow to anger" (James 1:19 NASV). For me, the first and most important mentoring skill consists of learning to listen carefully with a hearing heart.

The wisdom that King Solomon asked from God means literally to have a hearing heart (2 Chron. 1:10–12). God still gives a hearing heart to those who ask Him with faith, but the recipients must develop this gift by practicing an inner listening to the Holy Spirit and to the mentorees. Only after listening with dependent spirituality can a mentor effectively guide the learning process and communicate the needed truths in love—never in anger.

Another way to listen and understand better comes from developing the skill of asking different types of relevant questions. Asking the appropriate question at the right time takes much practice, but it is worth the effort. This type of questioning takes the form of professional coaching.

Mentoring may include coaching, but it can occur successfully without coaching. Stanley and Clinton regard coaching as "a relational process in which a mentor, who knows how to do something well, impacts those skills to a mentoree who wants to learn them (1992, p. 79). When mentors guide the learning process to train someone in a skill, or when they ask questions skillfully to help a person gain needed insights, they are coaching in a mentoring context.

Mentoring skills also include learning relational ways to communicate relevant lessons from personal life experiences. Since mentors function as spiritual parents, their compassion and wealth of life experiences can attract the interest of those seeking guidance for healthy family development. When given the opportunity, mentors use their wisdom and knowledge to direct family heads away from pitfalls that can capture and hold all who fail to recognize the danger, because of their inexperience and insufficient understanding.

Ten Mentoring Agents

Integrated Christian mentoring constitutes a viable means for developing families, because it furnishes ten important supportive agents necessary for an enduring process of transformation. The Spirit uses each of these ten agents in ways that promote vitality, safeguard the holistic health of family members, and restore some of the broken and dysfunctional individuals to purposeful wholeness. These ten form one of the four columns of mentoring competency; and since they help to support the whole mentoring strategy, mentors should practice implementing this skill for greater effectiveness.

These mentoring agents of the Spirit include (1) an openness in sharing needs with assured confidentiality; (2) a development of meaningful and satisfying relationships; (3) a system of mutual honesty and accountability; (4) an accurate feedback process for continual evaluation and improvement; (5) a compassion-driven service of wise mentoring; (6) a discovery process which guides the training of family leaders by utilizing all the learning domains; (7) a procedure for teaching wise parenthood; (8) a use of spiritual direction and spiritual gifts for needed understanding and healing of emotional and spiritual trauma, (9) a modeling of moral integrity in family leadership and spirituality; (10) a Spirit-led process that supplies grace to enable mentors and mentorees to actualize their potential development within a facilitating environment or structure.

These ten agents of integrated Christian mentoring ideally work together to counteract, remove, and replace most of the factors which contribute to family failures and relational weaknesses. The more spiritual mentors utilize these supportive agents—while giving careful consideration to the full range of learning required for holistic development—the better they are able to encourage family heads to take proactive measures to cooperate with the Spirit for needed assistance.

The Need of Trustworthy Mentors Who Use a Dependable Source

When heads of households seek mentors, they prefer ones who demonstrate consistent trustworthiness. Erik Erikson asserts that people mature through eight stages of development, enabling them to resolve "life-crises" by developing basic trust, identity, intimacy, and productivity (1950). He believes everyone must develop a basic trust, which begins to be learned in a parent's arms, before children can progress further in development. For him, trust fosters the security that enables a person to utilize tensions in life to progressively mature. Daloz also claims that "growth is fundamentally seated in a sense of basic trust" (1999, p. 128). Reliable mentors can facilitate relationships of trust, resulting in the security necessary for progressive maturity.

Mentors, in turn, must seek out a dependable source of wisdom and knowledge—one which can enable them to appropriately interpret their own life experiences and to gain useful insights to assist the more inexperienced in their developmental journey of self-sacrificing love. For the Christian mentor, the Bible serves as an inerrant source.

Since all mentors' trustworthiness depends upon what they have proven reliable, they must be careful of the accuracy and authenticity of their source for mentoring. Family heads are more inclined to receive input from mentors who have a dependable source of knowledge to help them along their journey of spiritual growth and development for the benefit of themselves and their families. Therefore, I am fully convinced that the most reliable source of knowledge and wisdom is the Bible. It constitutes the bedrock that anchors the columns of a mentor's competency, enabling him or her to be "equipped for every good work" (2 Tim. 3:17, NASB).

Mentoring Dilemmas and Conclusions

Mentors today encounter many mentoring dilemmas (cf., Murrel et al. 1999; Murray 2001). Due to limited space, this section will address only two major dilemmas of the Christian mentoring which uses dependent spirituality properly.

First, many who utilize independent spirituality, and who are content with its results, do not perceive a need for Christian mentoring. Misconceptions regarding the value of dependent spirituality abound among those satisfied with the wisdom of man. The Apostle Paul wrote that the Spirit enlivens or awakens the spirit of genuine Christians, so they can appraise the worth of "the things of the Spirit of God" (1 Cor. 2:14, NASB). Further, he pointed out that these things and the ways of the Spirit appear foolish and incomprehensible to those who seek independence from Him (1 Cor. 2:14). As a result, without attempting to examine the evidence for the Spirit's transformation of families, many still reject Christian integrated mentoring as foolish and unworkable for helping families. Some even view it as religious nonsense.

Second, when Christian mentorees seek to control the change process from a carnal perspective, they often experience incomplete results. For example, a limited effectiveness occurs whenever family heads seek superficial change that appears to fulfill merely immediate demands, as they reject or neglect the efforts necessary to meet the need for deeper and more permanent, character formation. Yet, since these demands frustrate or interfere with the learning process—i.e., by making it client-controlled rather than Spirit dependent—the final results are partial and disappointing. This absence of complete achievement appears to tarnish the glory of the Spirit's stellar record of successes, which occur when mentoring partners depend fully upon Him. Therefore, in the initiation stage, a wise mentor should decline assistance to carnal family heads who refuse to trust his or her key conditions for spiritual mentoring.

Integrated Christian mentoring that adequately utilizes dependent spirituality provides holistic benefits for committed households and their constituents—especially the family heads—because it relies upon the Spirit for His divine intervention and revelatory insights. Mentoring that functions with independent spirituality fails to supply the same results, for it divorces itself from the only authentic source of resurrection life and light.

When mentors depend upon man's wisdom and exclude the wisdom from above—the way of the Spirit—they tend to accept at least partial credit for any major accomplishments. When mentors rely upon God's wisdom found in Jesus, they value faithfulness to their call, no matter what happens; for they do not take responsibility for a mentoree's unwillingness to finish the journey of development in only God's terms. As Parker J. Palmer insightfully asserts, a person expresses spiritual life through life-giving actions; and he or she should judge personal performance "not by the results it gets, but by its fidelity to his [or her] own calling and identity" (1990, p. 76). Christian mentors who are dependently spiritual, therefore, recognize their calling and spiritual position in Christ's body—the Church—and remember to give Him all the glory for every one of His gracious accomplishments for the betterment of families, by His Spirit and Word, working together through their love.

References

Albanese, C. L. (2001). *American spiritualities: A reader*. Bloomington: Indiana University Press.

Albanese, C. L. (2006). *A republic of mind and spirit: A cultural history of American metaphysical religion*. New Haven: Yale University Press.

Anderson, K. R., & Reese, R. D. (1999). *Spiritual mentoring: A guide for seeking and giving direction*. With a foreword by James M. Houston. Downers Grove: InterVarsity Press.

Barclay, J. M. G. (1988). *Obeying the truth: A study of Paul's ethics in galatians*. Edinburgh: T and T Clark.

Barrett, C. K. (1968), *The first epistle to the Corinthians*. In H. Chadwick (Ed.), *Harper's new testament commentaries*. New York: Harper and Row.

Bender, C. (2007). Religion and spirituality: History, discourse, measurement. *The Religious Engagements of the American Undergraduate*. http://religion.ssrc.org/reforum/Bender.pdf. Accessed 11 May 2007.

Biehl, B. (1996). *Mentoring: Confidence in finding a mentor and becoming one*. Nashville: Broadman and Holman.

Braskamp, L. A. Fostering religions and spiritual development of students during college. *The Religious Engagements of the American Undergraduate*. http://religion.ssrc.org/reforum/Braskamp.pdf. Accessed 14 May 2007.

Campbell, J. (1949). *The hero with a thousand faces*. Princeton: Princeton University Press.

Clinton, J. R., & Clinton, R. W. (1991). *The mentor handbook: Detailed guidelines and help for Christian mentors and mentorees*. Altadena: Barnabas.

Cohen, N. H., & Galbraith, M. W. (1995). Mentoring in the learning society. In M. W. Galbraith & N. H. Cohen (Eds.), *Mentoring: New strategies and challenges* (pp. 5–14, Vol. 66). San Francisco: Jossey-Bass.

Daloz, L. A. (1986, 1999). *Mentor: Guiding the journey of adult learners* (2nd ed., *Effective Teaching and Mentoring*. San Francisco: Jossey-Bass.

Dyckman, K. M., & Carroll, L. P. (1981). *Inviting the mystic, supporting the prophet*. Mahwah: Paulist Press.

Edwards, T. (2001). *Spiritual director, spiritual companion: Guide to tending the soul*. Mahwah: Paulist Press, Inc.

Erickson, E. H. (1950). *Childhood and society*. New York: Norton Publishers.

Fee, G. D. (1994). *God's empowering presence: The holy spirit in the letters of Paul*. Peabody: Hendrickson Publishing, Inc.

Foster, R. J. (1988). *Celebration of discipline: The path to spiritual growth*, rev. and exp. San Francisco: Harper and Row.

Foster, R. J. (1998). *Streams of living water: Celebrating the great traditions of Christian faith*. With a foreword by Martin Marty. San Francisco: Harper San Francisco.

Frankl, V. E. (1962). *Man's search for meaning*. Boston: Beacon Press.

Frankl, V. E. (1969). *The will to meaning*. New York: World Publishing.

Frankl, V. E. (1978). *The unheard cry for meaning*. New York: Simon and Schuster.

Fromm, E. (1956). *The art of loving*. New York: Harper and Row, Inc.

Fuller, R. (2001). *Spiritual, but not religious: Understanding inchurched America*. Oxford: Oxford University Press.

Galbraith, M. W. (1991). *Facilitating adult learning: A transactional process*. Malabar: Krieger.

Galbraith, M., & Cohen N. H. (1995). Issues and challenges confronting mentoring. In M. W. Galbraith & N. H. Cohen (Eds.), *Mentoring: New strategies and challenges* (pp. 89–93, Vol. 66). San Francisco: Jossey-Bass.

Greenleaf, R. (1998). Servant: retrospect and prospect. In L. C. Spears (Ed.), *The power of servant leadership*. With a foreword by Peter B. Vaill, 17–59. San Francisco: Berrett-Koehler Publishers, Inc.

Griffith, M. R. (2004). *Born again bodies: Flesh and spirit in American Christianity*. Berkeley: University of California Press.

Hendricks, H., & Hendricks, W. (1995). *As iron sharpens iron: Building character in a mentoring relationship*. Chicago.: Moody Press.

Houston, J. M. (1984). Spirituality. In W. A. Elwell (Ed.), *Evangelical dictionary of theology* (pp. 1046–1051). Grand Rapids: Baker Book House.

Jacobi, M. (1991). Mentoring and undergraduate academic success: A literature review. *Review of Educational Research*, 61(4), 501–32.

Johnson, W. B., & Ridley, C. R. (2004). *The elements of mentoring*. New York: Palgrave MacMillan.

Kofman, Fred, & Senge, P. M. (1995). Communities of commitment: The heart of learning organizations. In S. Chawla & J. Renesch (Eds.), *Learning organizations: Developing cultures for tommorow's workplace* (pp. 14–43). Portland: Productivity Press.

Jung, C. J. (1958). *Psyche and Ssymbol*. New York: Doubleday.

Laaser, M. R. (2005). Sexual wholeness: A biblical understanding of healthy sexuality. *Enrichment, 10*, 84–89.

Mahoney, K. A., Schmalzbauer, J., & Youniss, J. (2001). Religion: A comeback on campus. *Liberal Education, 87*, 36–41.

Mclemore, C. W. (1985). Erich fromm. In D. G. Benner (Ed.), *Baker encyclopedia of psychology* (pp. 432–433). Grand Rapids: Baker Book House.

Merriam, S. B., & Caffarrella, R. S. (1991). *Learning in adulthood*. San Francisco: Jossey-Bass. Quoted in Zachary, L. J. (2000). *The mentor's guide: Facilitating effective learning relationships*. San Francisco: Jossey-Bass.

Murray, M. (2001). *Beyond the myths and magic of mentoring: How to facilitate an effective mentoring process*. New and rev. ed. San Francisco: Jossey-Bass.

Murrell, A. J., Crosby, F. J., & Ely, R. J. (Eds.). (1999). *Mentoring dilemmas: Developmental relationships within multicultural organizations*. Mahwah: Lawrence Erlbaum Associates.

Nouwen, H. J. M. (1981). *The way of the heart*. Minneapolis: The Seabury Press.

Nouwen, H. J. M. *The living reminder*. New York: The Seabury Press, Inc., 1977. Quoted in Job, R. P., & N. Shawchuck. (1983). *A guide to prayer for ministers and other servants*. Nashville: The Upper Room.

Nouwen, H. J. M. (1989). *In the name of Jesus: Reflections on Christian leadership*. New York: The Crossroad Publishing Co.

Nouwen, H. J. M. (1996). *Ministry and spirituality*. New York: Continuum.

Palmer, P. J. (1990). *The active life: Spirituality of work, creativity, and caring*. San Francisco: Jossey-Bass.

Parks, S. (1992). *The university as a mentoring environment*. Indianapolis: Indiana Office for Campus Ministries.

Rule, A. K. (1984).Religion. In W. A. Elwell (Ed.), *Evangelical dictionary of theology*(pp. 168–169). Grand Rapids: Baker Book House.

Schmidt, L. E. (2003). The making of modern mysticism. *Journal of the American Academy of Religion, 71*, 273–02.

Shawchuck, N., & Heuser, R. (1993). *Leading the congregation: Caring for yourself while serving the people*. Nashville: Abingdon Press.

Stanley, P. D., & Clinton, J. R. (1992). *Connecting: The mentoring relationships you need to succeed in life*. Colorado Springs: NavPress.

Taylor, C. (2002). *Variation of religion today: William James revisited*. Cambridge: Harvard University.

Tweedie, D. F. (1961). *Logotherapy: An evaluation of Frankl's existential approach to psychotherapy*. Grand Rapids: Baker Book House.

Vogel, L. (1991). *Teaching and learning in communities of faith: Empowering adults through religious education*. San Francisco: Jossey-Bass.

Willard, D. (1988). *The spirit of the disciplines: Understanding how god changes lives*. New York: Harper Collins Publishers, Inc.; Harper San Francisco, 1991.

Wuthnow, R. (1988). *After heaven: Spirituality in American since the 1950's*. Berkeley: University Press.

Wuthnow, R. (2003). *All in sync: How music and art are revitalizing American religion*. Berkeley: University of California Press.

Zachary, L. J. (2000). *The mentor's guide: Facilitating effective learning relationships*. With a forward by Laurent A. Daloz. San Francisco: Jossey-Bass.

Zerner, R. (1984). Dietrich bonhoeffer. In W. A. Elwell (Ed.), *Evangelical dictionary of theology*. (pp. 168–169). Grand Rapids: Baker Book House.

Lou Selzer PhD has pastored and engaged in family counseling for several decades. He is currently pastoring Christian Trinity Assembly of God in Eastpointe (Metro Detroit), Michigan. He also has served as an adjunct Bible college professor for many years.

The Power of a Husband's Delight in his Wife

Gary Rieben

Abstract It is the premise of this chapter that the rise of the self-focused American male has birthed a plague of fractured marriages, frustrated wives, insecure children and a confused community. It further identifies the husband's chief failure as his refusal to pursue his delight in the delight of his wife. When a husband makes his wife's joy the passion of all that he does, his marriage will be solidified, his children's lives will be edified and his purpose for living will be satisfied.

The assumption of the author is that God the Creator designed marriage and provided the Bible as the unique and authoritative manual for how to build marriages and families that flourish. Jesus Christ is the supreme model. Christ came and died to present to Himself a radiant bride, the Church. He lived and died for His bride not out of duty but out of His delight. When a husband follows Christ's example, when he is willing to die for his wife, when he makes her welfare more important than his career, his bank account, his buddies or his toys, his wife will find deep joy and his children will find health and happiness.

The dissertation of fathers from the home has had a disastrous effect upon our children. Over 30 % of our children now live with one parent, and of that number, 83 % live with their mother. Recent studies have shown that children without a father experience "poor performance in school, early sexual experimentation, drug use and involvement with law enforcement."

Real men are not remembered for their tattoos, their bank accounts or their fast cars. Real men will protect, provide and persevere for their families. If our husbands would redirect their devotion toward their wives and children, we would see a profound and positive effect that would transform the character of our nation. When children see their dads loving their mothers with the same kind of love they have, when they know that his love for her is even more important than his love for them; when they know that he will never leave or desert his family, they are given a precious and safe environment in which to grow into confident and mature adults.

Keywords Marriage · Family · Spirituality · Husband · Counseling · Bible

G. Rieben (✉)
Give Me That Book, Box 1045, La Quinta, CA 92247, USA
e-mail: grieben@aol.com

W. Jeynes, E. Martinez (eds.), *Ministering Spiritually to Families*,
DOI 10.1007/978-3-319-13302-7_4

The 2006 hit film, *The Pursuit of Happiness*, portrays a man by the name of Christopher Gardner, [Will Smith] whose great ambition and drive is blocked at every turn by disappointments and frustration (Mancino 2006). Set in the early-1980s San Francisco, the film charts how Gardner had invested all of his money in a bone scanner that wouldn't sell. In the financial disaster that followed, his wife left him, he lost his home, his bank account and his credit cards. Forced to live on the streets, the film displays this man's incredible determination to find success while facing a series of setbacks that would drive a normal man into despair or drunkenness.

What distinguishes this "rags to riches" story from other "success chronicles," is Gardner's total devotion to his son. In the midst of his failed marriage, failed occupation and failed dreams, he refuses to fail as a father. He prevents his wife from taking his son [Hayden Smith] with her when she leaves the marriage. We get a hint as to the cause of this commitment when he confesses, "I met my father for the first time when I was 28 years old. I made up my mind that when I had children, my children were going to know who their father was." In a day when so many fathers are deserting their families for shallow and selfish pursuits, this film does an awesome job of depicting both the responsibilities and the rewards of being a faithful father.

However, in spite of this film's excellent quality and redemptive plot, I left the theater feeling somewhat ambivalent. I know that the film was based on a real life story so its parameters were fixed by a real life storyline. But, I felt that the film and indeed our whole society had overlooked a crucial, life enhancing principle: The positive trickle-down effect of a husband's love and devotion for his wife upon the welfare of his children. This film showed only the aftermath of the fights and feuds of a failed marriage. Some would say that was an accurate portrayal of the world we live in. But, *must* we live that way? I resist that fatalistic and dismal conclusion. The future welfare of our nation, our marriages, and our children are riding upon the back of an opposite affirmation. I insist that it is not too late, that our marriages and families can be restored to health and happiness by applying divine and time-tested principles to our marriages.

It is the premise of this chapter that there is no more positive influence upon the welfare of the children than for their father to find his joy in the joy of their mother (Bledsole 2012; Cornwell 2014). I base that conclusion upon my own personal experience of being raised by a busy, successful father who was also totally devoted to his wife of 55 years. That conviction has been reinforced by observations spanning over 40 years as a clergyman, counselor, teacher, and grateful husband. I have found that this principle, when applied, "works." Whether it is in the ghettos of Manila, the compounds of Lusaka, the villages of Kenya or the plains of the Patagonia, when a husband loves his wife, joy floods the family producing an environment that fosters healthy and happy children (Piper 1996).

I affirm that it is the man, the husband, who has the primary responsibility for establishing a healthy environment for the family and the most important thing he does in that regard is to love and serve his wife with joy (Piper 2009). That may seem naïve, politically incorrect and offensive to some, but I am convinced it is the foundation necessary for building strong and healthy families. Seeing my father cherish the most important woman in my life, my mother, had an incredible, positive effect upon me and my family. We knew our father would never desert our mom. We knew our family would never be divided. Loud laughter rather than loud arguments filled our house. Our favorite place was the evening table where my father presided over a daily celebration of life. Life was satisfying, my family was special and I was secure.

Please understand, I am not merely advocating a return to the "traditional" family. What I am promoting is far more important and profound than sociological constructs. The relationship I will describe and defend has its origins not in historical, sociological or evolutionary processes, but in divine and sacred purposes (Piper 2009; Piper and Gruden 2006). God, the creator of all things, established the institutions of marriage and the family and uniquely designed them for the good of his people and the glory of his name (*Holy* Bible, NIV, Ephesians 5:22–33). By studying and applying God's directions for our marriages, we can experience the liberation and celebration he intended for our most cherished relationships (Mack 1998).

I am fully aware that my affirmations fly in the face of the strong winds of a culture that is pluralistic and postmodern, which dismisses and disdains any claims to objective and ultimate truths (Carson 2000). Complexity wins over simplicity. Theories trump truth. Feelings are favored over facts (Jeremiah 2009). But, I ask you to look around. What has such thinking brought upon us? In all of our sophistication, what has happened to the celebration? Look at the broken marriages, the shattered families and the confused children that lie scattered across the landscape of our culture (Marriage and Family Fact Sheet 2012). Is our new found dependency upon medications the result of solving the brain's complexity or because we have lost our sense of human dignity? Are we not observing a society that is out of control, without purpose, without meaning, and without a center (Breggin 1991; Lockerbie 1986; Wells 1993)?

It is my conviction that there is a God at the center of all things whose purpose is to create cosmos out of chaos (Sproul 2009). He is the still point in a swirling universe. He has created all things and directs them toward his own ultimate purposes. He is a God who speaks and communicates his will and his ways in a book we call the Bible (Packer 1979; Packer 1996). That Book is as eloquent and relevant today as it was when it was first inspired thousands of years ago (*Holy* Bible, NIV, Psalm 119:89). From its pages we will discover that the relationship between the husband and his wife is a critical component in God's comprehensive plan to reveal his wisdom and beauty to his creation. If we are to find the purposes and principles that can create marriages that sing, we must go to the Source. The Bible is *the* manual on how to have a holy and happy marriage and a healthy and happy family (Mack 1998).

Before we take up our study in God's Word, let me further clarify my purpose for writing this chapter and the assumptions I will be operating upon.

My Reason for Writing It is my intention to show that a husband's calling to love his wife should not be a duty but a delight (Piper 2009). He does not have to serve her. He gets to. I will attempt to show how a husband's devotion to his wife will not only give her great joy, but will bring him great satisfaction. Drawing from contemporary evidence, personal experience and Biblical principles, I will show why the husband's delight in his wife is a crucial ingredient for the establishment of strong, successful marriages and healthy, happy children. When Biblical principles are taught, understood and applied to marriages and families of any culture, they produce fulfilled, satisfied and productive people (Broger 1994).

My Unique Perspective I write as a son who had the great privilege of watching my father devote himself to loving my mother for over 55 years of marriage. I write as a husband who has personally experienced the joy and delight of loving and being loved by one woman for over 40 years. I write as a pastor-counselor who has witnessed marriages healed and thrive on the principles taught in the Scriptures. I write as a teacher who has applied these same principles in diverse cultures and found them as powerful there as in America. I write as a Christian thinker who is convinced that the principles of Scripture, when understood and applied rightly, not only make sense, they work. I write as a follower of Jesus Christ, who has a passion that all men and women would experience the delight and fulfillment he gives to all who love him and obey his teachings.

My Foundational Assumptions

- When a husband devotes himself to bringing delight to his wife, his marriage will be solidified, his children's lives will be edified, and the husband's primary desire will be satisfied (Piper 1996).
- The self-focused and unfulfilled American male has birthed a plague of fractured marriages, frustrated wives, insecure children and a confused community (Popenoe 2011).
- God designed marriage and he has written the Bible to be the unique and authoritative manual for building satisfying marriages, healthy children and dynamic communities.
- The Bible's picture of the delight that Jesus Christ displayed in dying to present to himself a radiant Bride, the Church, is the model and motivation of how a husband can and should do the same kind of thing for his wife (*Holy* Bible, NIV, Genesis 2:22–24; Ephesians 5:28–30).
- The wife will know how precious she is to her husband when he demonstrates his delight in her by making her welfare more important to him than his career, his bank account, his male friendships, his toys and any other rival to this precious relationship.
- If husbands will build their lives upon the unchanging, foundational truths of the Bible, God will send a new wave of joy and satisfaction to our marriages that will result in healthy kids and hope to a hurting society.
- Finally, it is the over-arching purpose of God to reveal his awesome beauty in all things (Piper 2000). Marriage is one of the ways he has chosen to reveal how good and great he is. When a husband and a wife learn to trust God and obey his commands, they will discover a deep satisfaction that can only be found through the wisdom and grace that he supplies. In the end, we are satisfied and he is glorified.

Getting Back to the Beginning The Genesis account displays the purposes for which God created the universe, man and woman, and marriage. First, Genesis reveals that man and woman together are created in the image of God:

> Then God said, "Let us make man in our image, in our likeness, and let them rule over the fish of the sea and the birds of the air, over the livestock, over all the earth, and over all the creatures that move along the ground." So God created man in his own image,
> in the image of God he created him; male and female he created them. (*Holy* Bible, NIV, Gen 1:26–27)

Man and woman are the unique and crowning act of God's creative work (Gruden 1994). Both have a dignity that sets them above and over all of creation. We are like God not only in our ability to rule but also in our ability to relate. God exists in a community of persons who commune and communicate in an environment of love and unity. We were designed with a capacity to participate in that intimate and infinite oneness that exists in the Eternal God. We will see that the institution of marriage is intended to be a sacred bond where the love between a man and his wife reflects something of the intimacy and unity that exists within the Godhead. (John *Holy* Bible, NIV, 17:20–23; Rieben 2012).

Marriage Is Given for Deep and Satisfying Oneness In Genesis 1, it is recorded that seven times God declared that the results of his creative acts were "good." In Genesis 2:18 (*Holy* Bible, NIV), we see the first instance where God recognizes something as being "not good." "The LORD God said, 'It is not good for the man to be alone. I will make a helper suitable for him.'" Solo man was incomplete. In himself he was not able to live up to God's glorious purposes for him. He was created with a need of someone to complement him and to fill him up (Keller 2012).

The author of Genesis illustrates this in a very unique way. In Genesis 2:19–20 (*Holy* Bible, NIV), we are told that God assembles all of the other creatures that he has made and marches them past the man, Adam. Revealing his unique authority over other creatures, Adam is given the privilege of naming the animals. But this episode is intended to show more than Adam's uniqueness. It also reveals his incompleteness. Genesis 2:20, sums up: "But for Adam no suitable helper was found." It is obvious that man needs someone to communicate with him on a level that corresponds with his dignity. It is great to have a dog for a pet, but it will never be able to see, appreciate and share a beautiful sunset on the shores of the Pacific; or hear, enjoy and share the melodious strains of Mozart's *Symphony Number 41;* or hold, love and share the baby created out of an act of intimate union. Adam needed someone like him and unlike him to fill him up (Keller 2012). The story continues to unfold.

> So the LORD God caused the man to fall into a deep sleep; and while he was sleeping, he took one of the man's ribs and closed up the place with flesh. Then the LORD God made a woman from the rib he had taken out of the man, and he brought her to the man.
> The man said,
> "This is now bone of my bones
> and flesh of my flesh;
> she shall be called 'woman,'
> for she was taken out of man."
> For this reason a man will leave his father and mother and be united to his wife, and they will become one flesh. The man and his wife were both naked, and they felt no shame. [Gen 2:20–25, *Holy* Bible, NIV]

The woman was created out of the side of the man, not from his head to rule him nor from his foot to be ruled, but from his side to be his friend and partner in life. This passage pictures God bringing the woman to the man as a special gift and that is just the way Adam receives her. His response is hard to translate into our English, but it has the sense of great excitement and pleasure. “God you did it! Just what I wanted! Wow!” [I confess I felt the same kind of excitement the first time I laid my eyes upon my wife Barbara. I still feel the same way after 44 years of marriage.]

I believe that God still presents our wives to us as a gift to be loved and treasured, not as trash to be used and discarded. The woman we have been given is more like God than any other creature on the earth. She is to be handled and cared for as if she was the most valuable and fragile vessel we possess. Just one slip of the hand or one careless act could destroy our priceless present. Of course, our wives are not easily broken but we should treat them as if they could be. And, yes, we will have moments when our selfish focus will cause a lapse in this commitment, but it is always handled with regret and with apologies. We have been entrusted with treasure and I believe we will answer to the Giver for our stewardship of her heart.

This text also shows that the marriage relationship supersedes all others in importance (Piper 2009). Even the father and mother of the family of birth are now relegated to an advisory role instead of the previous supervisory role. Two individuals are transformed into a new and seamless unit. Literally, the text says that the two are now “glued together.” There is a mysterious oneness that is created that cannot be explained by science or psychology. It is a miracle of divine origin. In the early days of marriage it is experienced in the delight of discovery. The intimacy afforded by the exclusive commitment of marriage cracks open the door to the awesome secrets that have been deposited in the personality of the one we love. Every day and every experience becomes an opportunity to know and celebrate the pleasure of finding new treasure that has been hidden in our partner’s heart. Because of the promise of growth and maturity, it is a process that need never end. After 44 years of marriage, I am still being surprised and blessed by the precious jewels I uncover as I mine the depths of my wife.

Within the sacredness of marriage, sexual intimacy can flourish without shame or regret. God is not against sex. He designed it and gave it to his creatures as a gift (Piper and Taylor 2005). But, he did set down parameters for its practice. When we fail to follow those guidelines we stand guilty before the One who made us. We have tried to purge the idea of guilt from our culture but it remains whether we like it or not (Schaeffer 1971). We live in a moral universe because we were created by a holy and moral God. All men and women are created responsible for their decisions. We suffer the consequences of our wrong actions both inwardly in a deterioration of integrity; or outwardly, in broken trust with meaningful others. This principle is especially true in the area of sexual fidelity in marriage (Piper and Taylor 2005).

As I write this chapter, one of the most popular and venerated sports figure of all time has confessed to a series of marital “transgressions.” He admitted to violating a sacred trust to his wife *and* his family. The infidelity apparently went on for several months. We are not privy to the way it affected the unity of that marriage, but we can be assured that it did. Something was gone. A barrier was erected. Communion was stilted. Communication was shallow. Intimacy was awkward and unfulfilling. Adultery breaks the bond of marriage even if it does not rise to a conscious awareness. Something is profoundly wrong and it is felt within the family.

We have also seen a strong movement in our culture that seeks to reduce sexuality to be something akin to animal behavior (Watts 2008). If we are nothing more than the result of evolutionary forces and chance chemical reactions, then there is no ultimate purpose or absolute wrongs. We just are. So, like the animals, we are free to seek pleasure whenever the opportunity presents itself, as long as it does not hurt others. But, simple reflection and honest observation would reveal the fallacy of such thinking.

No wife or husband responds to a spouse's marital infidelity by saying, "Oh, well, they are just expressing their animal freedom. No big deal." Trust is broken, feelings are hurt and the relationship is shaken at its most meaningful level. My wife has informed me that if I ever did such a thing to her and if I survived the shotgun blast I would be singing soprano the rest of my days. Although that may seem a little extreme, she has captured the seriousness of betrayal to this sacred commitment. Fidelity to this core commitment is absolutely essential to creating and maintaining the unseen but felt atmosphere of peace needed to raise healthy families (Keller 2012).

That is why the pornography industry is such a threat to our marriages. Fifty years ago, if one wanted to experience pornography, he had to sneak down to the seedy part of town (Easton 1994). Now, it comes right into our living room in the form of videos and internet. Sex is presented as a recreational sport and anonymous women are "things" who come to satisfy our most sordid fantasies. How can *that* not impact our relationships with our wives? How can they compete with *that*? Sexual joy was meant to be experienced as a celebration that arises out of the deep love that comes from a life-time commitment. Our culture tends to idolize the man who makes many conquests. But, true manhood is just the opposite. A real man is one who finds the woman of his dreams and devotes the rest of his life to being faithful to her alone. Dogs run around. Men remain faithful.

How Things Went Wrong Our Designer knows what is best for us. He is holy and has determined that holiness, living according to his commands, would be the criteria needed for humans to experience the satisfaction and fulfillment for which He created them. So, when Adam and Eve disobeyed and ate of the fruit of the prohibited tree [*Holy* Bible, NIV, Genesis 3:1–6], their lives immediately disintegrated. We see this when God sought out the two in the garden [*Holy* Bible, NIV, Genesis 3:8].

Their first reaction was to hide. Where once they looked forward to communing with God, they now hide in fear. They were not fully aware of all the ramifications of their disobedience, but they knew something was radically different and it was not good. They no longer felt comfortable in God's presence. So, they sought to distance themselves from him.

Not only did their relationship with God radically change, so did their relationship with each other (Gruden 1994). In the first report of a marital tiff, Adam defends himself by blaming his wife for his failure to obey God's command. Adam's refusal to take responsibility for himself established a pattern of behavior often duplicated by weak and "whimpy" husbands throughout history. Rather than "manning up," taking responsibility for their failures and making necessary corrections, they blame their wives and bale out.

Because this couple failed to follow the one restriction God placed upon them, their marriage became a drag instead of a delight. To the woman, God pronounced this curse: "Your desire will be for your husband, and he will rule over you" (*Holy* Bible, NIV, Genesis 3:16). Instead of the wife joyfully coming along side of her husband to help him become the accomplished leader God intended, she seeks to manipulate him into meeting *her* demands and *her* expectations. Instead of the husband, focusing upon humbly serving his wife and seeking to make her life radiant with joy and satisfaction, he rules her and uses her for his own selfish and short sighted ends.

That is why today we see so many marriages begin with hilarity and hope and end in despair and disappointment. The facts are that feelings fade and fantasies fail when confronted by life's painful realities. Once cultural mores held couples together for no other reason than for the sake of the children. Now, the emphasis on self-fulfillment and personal happiness has made it almost a sin to fight for a marriage when it fails to meet not only our needs but also all of our wild fantasies.

The tragic results of such loose thinking is seen in the statistics of failure. One study determined that only one third of all first time marriages will likely stay together until widowhood. (Bumpass et al. 1990) Within three decades after the implementation of the no-fault divorce in 1969, the rate of divorce for American couples doubled. By 1990, the marriage rate had fallen to 41 %, from 148 marriages per 1000 women to 87 per 1000 in 1990 (Webster et al. 1995).

The innocent victims of divorce are the children. Since 1970, at least a million children a year have witnessed the divorce of their parents (Wallerstein 2000). Forty percent of children today do not live with their fathers and the rates are climbing (Popenoe 2011). And the results of divorce have had a disastrous effect upon the well being of the children. Studies have shown them to be more aggressive toward parents and teachers; more likely to be depressed; 2–3 times more likely to need psychological counseling; to experience earlier sexual activity and more likely to have children born outside of marriage (Wallerstein 2000). Perhaps the most disturbing result is that many children blame themselves for their parents divorce (Schramm 2009).

Instead of having the security of a close and loving family, the children's lives are torn apart. They are faced with the pressure of choosing sides. The two most significant people in their lives are fighting with each other. In trying to determine what caused the break, too often they blame themselves. Inwardly, the child inherently believes that love is forever and their family will remain unbroken. But the tragic break-up of marriage and family instills within the child a deep sense of insecurity that is often missed by the parents who are caught up in a self-centered split. The negative side effects of divorce affect the personality development of the children and may create attitudes and fears that they will struggle with the rest of their lives. Not only will they miss out on the warmth and security a forever-loving family provides, they will be denied the blessing of seeing how love and commitment can conquer any problem that life can throw at it.

How the Curse Was Overcome The God of the Bible is both great and good. He created us so that may know Him and enjoy his glory forever. So, we should not be surprised when we discover that He removes the curse he has placed on marriage at a very great cost to himself. In the New Testament, Paul records how God sent his Son, Jesus Christ, to redeem a people who he would forgive and restore to fellowship. Paul, inspired by the Holy Spirit identified the redeemed family as the bride of Christ. In giving instructions to the husbands on how they should treat their wives in the new order, Paul penned,

> Husbands, love your wives, just as Christ loved the church and gave himself up for her to make her holy, cleansing her by the washing with water through the word, and to present her to himself as a radiant church, without stain or wrinkle or any other blemish, but holy and blameless. In this same way, husbands ought to love their wives as their own bodies. He who loves his wife loves himself. After all, no one ever hated his own body, but he feeds and cares for it, just as Christ does the church—for we are members of his body. "For this reason a man will leave his father and mother and be united to his wife, and the two will become one flesh." This is a profound mystery—but I am talking about Christ and the church. However, each one of you also must love his wife as he loves himself, and the wife must respect her husband. (*Holy* Bible, NIV, Eph 5:25–33)

Paul is in the process of identifying the different roles the wife and the husband play within God's design of marriage. Although both are equal in dignity and worth, they each have unique roles that are complimentary (Piper 2006). Both roles are essential for couples to find soul satisfying-marriages. Both seek the welfare of each other [called "mutual submission" in Ephesians 5:21], but do it in different ways. The wife willingly seeks to come alongside her husband to help him become the godly leader he was meant to be. She is to follow the example of the Church. Just as the Church, the Bride of Christ seeks to honor her husband, Jesus Christ, by serving and respecting Him, she is to live that same kind of life before her husband. [*Holy* Bible, NIV, Ephesians 5:21]

Although this appears to be a daunting task for the wife, the husband's part is just as challenging. He is to love his wife in the same way that Jesus Christ loved his bride. In other words, he is to give up his life for his wife. He is to sacrifice his own comfort and position for the sake of seeing his wife become radiant in every aspect of her being. In the same way that Jesus died to produce a holy Church without spot or wrinkle, radiant in splendor, so the husband puts the welfare of his wife above all of his personal interests.

What is completely overlooked by most men is the implicit reward he receives for putting his wife first: what the husband does for his wife, he does for himself (Piper 2009). Paul puts it like this: "No one ever hated his own body, but he feeds and cares for it, just as Christ does the church." The wife and the husband are united in the same way that Christ and the Church are. What Christ does for the Church he does for himself and what the husband does for his wife he does for his own body, for they are one. No one hates his own body. Every man and woman feeds and cares for their body. They naturally think about themselves, their welfare, the comfort, their needs and their desires, first. From birth we seek our own welfare and need no one to teach us that.

What we do need to be taught is how to put others first (Keller 2012). When husbands enter into marriage, they are faced with the crucial challenge of loving their wives in the same way they *already* love themselves. It is here that faith enters in. God promises that although it is costly up front, it is always more rewarding in the long run. Faith trusts in a God who never lies and has the power to always deliver what he promises. In one unbelievable demonstration of humility and love, God gave his Son for us [*Holy* Bible, NIV, John 3:16]. In that one act of unmatched sacrifice, he showed us what it means to put others first. He proved that he is a God worthy of love and complete devotion. He showed us that "love never fails," both in its actions and its rewards.

Jesus Christ came and died to "to present her [the Bride] to himself as a radiant church." In other words, Jesus died to present to himself the gift of a redeemed Church, His Body. It cost him up front unimaginable suffering and pain. But, the joy of receiving us as his Bride, pure and radiant, was worth the cost to him. In like manner, living for our wives may be painful at times. We may act and look weird to our peers and the culture in which we live. But, we know a secret. We are finding more joy and satisfaction than any man can imagine by finding our joy in the joy of our wives.

How to Develop Delight There is an old saying that expresses just the opposite of what we are advocating. It goes like this: "Once I was looking for an ideal. It became an ordeal. Now I want a new deal." (Carmody 2014, p. 1) That unfortunate pattern seems to becoming more and more prevalent in our world today. We think love just happens and when we lose "that loving feeling" then there is nothing to do but to pack the bags. But, love does not "just happen" and neither does it "just grow." It takes work and perseverance and battle. The pressures and choices of our ever changing world can sap our energy and distract us from what really matters.

Too often our media is plastered with the stories of Hollywood romances gone sour. Lately, there has also been too many headlines of politicians who have proclaimed a pro-family, pro-marriage message in public but were caught messing around in private. There is a temptation to think that great marriages are rare and only happen by accident. But, that is not true. When a man and a woman follow certain laws, their marriage will sing. And, if we will look, we can find busy and influential persons, who have lived successful and powerful lives and still managed to experience a marriage that was the joy of their lives. One example we can point to is the marriage of Prime Minister Winston Churchill and his wife Clementine. One writer, Laura Wood (2009, p. 1), describes what she found when she studied their relationship.

> I discovered a tender and unwavering partnership that spanned 57 years and the major world crises of the 20th Century. Their marriage included great sorrows, the death of a young child, the suicide of an adult daughter, petty annoyances, disagreements, mutual loneliness and incompatibilities. But, if there is a pantheon for married couples, Clementine and Winston deserve to be admitted. It is a story that leaves at least one valuable lesson for those seeking marital harmony and is a reminder that all great marriages are worthy of study. Why do we spend so much time looking at the bad ones?

It has been reported that near the end of his life, Churchill was attending a dinner in his honor. A time came for questions and answers and he was asked by one guest this provocative question: "Sir Winston, if you could live your life all over again and come back as any other man in history, who would it be?" There was a moment of silence and many wondered who he would choose. Would it be some military leader like Julius Cesar or Napoleon; or, a great philosopher like Plato or Socrates; or, maybe, another distinguished statesman like William Wilberforce or Benjamin Disraeli? When the time came for his answer, Churchill got up from his chair and moved behind his wife. Putting his hands on Clementine's shoulders he said, "If I could come back as any man in history I would choose to come back as Lady Churchill's second husband."

That is what I am talking about! No regrets! Pure satisfaction! Now, anyone who was acquainted with Winston knew that he was not easy to live with. Not only did he have a lot on his table but he could be rather cantankerous and stubborn. But, with all that working against him, he loved his wife and worked hard at making his wife know how much he loved and appreciated her. A lot is written about what made Churchill such a strong and confident leader at a time when men of similar position were shaking in fear. One commentator gave this perspective: "Her advice on personal matters was usually followed by Churchill and her political judgments were often wiser and steadier than her husband's." I suspect that his wife's love, support and counsel had as much to do with his success as any quality within him (Wood 2009, p. 1).

If you are searching for one principle to guide you in your search for a marriage that sings, you need to go no further than the Author of marriage. In Matthew 6:19 (*Holy* Bible, NIV), Jesus was teaching his disciples the absolute necessity of getting our priorities straight. Addressing our proclivity to store and horde things he admonished, "Do not store up for yourselves treasures on earth, where moth and rust destroy, and where thieves break in and steal. But store up for yourselves treasures in heaven, where moth and rust do not destroy, and where thieves do not break in and steal." [Matt 6:19–20, *Holy* Bible, NIV] The things in this life will disappear. Only what we invest in the future life will survive our death and the world's rust. Then Jesus gave us our principle: "For where your treasure is, there your heart will be also." [Matt 6:21, *Holy* Bible, NIV] Where you place your treasure, your heart will follow. What you work at, what you devote to, what you invest in, that will have your heart, devotion and love.

You can see how that is applied to our wives. When the wellbeing of our wives takes precedent over occupation, sports, friends and all other desires of manhood, she *will* be treasured. Our heart will follow our investment. Seeing a smile on her face and knowing that you did it is a reward in itself. Where many see marriage as dire duty, the loving husband sees it as pure delight (Piper 2009).

A few years ago I was traveling between the Philippines and Argentina and had a layover in Los Angeles. I had been away from my wife Barbara for a couple of weeks and it was our anniversary. I was missing her big time! On another trip I had found a clock that she had seen years before but we could not afford it. It was half-price so I purchased it. Knowing that I would be absent on our anniversary, I hid it in my closet. So, the night of our anniversary I called her from Los Angeles. In our conversation I told her to go to the closet where I had put a surprise for her. When she came back she was all excited and said, "Oh Babe, It is great! Thank you!" She was thrilled, not just because she got her clock, but also because I thought of her and took the time to plan ahead for her joy.

Now, what if upon receiving that clock she said to me, "Why did you do this? How could you give me such a great surprise?" and I answered, "I was just doing my duty," that would not have worked. She does not want to know that I took the time and effort to surprise her just because I had to be a good husband. She wanted to know that I did that because I wanted to please her because I treasured her and wanted to make her happy. Her joy was my joy.

Out of that one principle flow many corollaries. Here are some of them.

Your Wife Wants to Know that She is Number One My profession has called for me to be away from home in foreign lands for extended times. It is what I have been called to do. But, the thing I *want* to do more than any other is to be with my wife, sharing her presence and friendship. Knowing that, she has never complained about me being away from her or even my golf time with the guys or my love of sports. I naturally have other interests, but if I had to choose, she knows I would choose her every time. Why wouldn't I? She is my best friend.

My Wife Wants to Know that I Want to Understand Her Notice I said she wants to know that I "*want*" to understand her. In other words, I have made it a life's project to study her. I will not always "figure her out" for in many ways she remains a mystery. Men, can I hear an "Amen?" But I try.

The apostle Peter gave men this instruction: "Husbands, in the same way be considerate as you live with your wives, and treat them with respect as the weaker partner and as heirs with you of the gracious gift of life, so that nothing will hinder your prayers." [1 Peter 3:7] In God's economy, the way we treat our wives affects the way he relates with us. If we treat our wives badly, he will not listen to our prayers. It is as simple as that. We may lead a great and famous ministry, which attracts large numbers and great acclaim, but if we are failing to love our wives, we are fooling ourselves if we think God is blessing us (*Holy* Bible, NIV, Psalm 1:1–3; Psalm 119:1–3).

We are to live with our wives in knowledge ["considerate"]. We are to treat them, not as one who has no strength but as one who is precious. She is to be treated like a priceless vase where one mishandling might cause it to fall and be forever destroyed. Most wives are not that fragile, but we are to treat them as if they are. They are precious to God and they should be precious to us.

The first year of our marriage was a time of intensive learning on my part. I came from a family who showed their love for one another by teasing. If you were not teased, you needed to worry. My wife came from a southern home where there was no teasing. So, when I teased her she took it personal. She thought I was serious. I took note that she would spend extended times in the bathroom and when she came out her eyes were red. At first I thought she had an unknown allergy. Then I would get in bed and I would see that way on the other side of the bed was a back. Now, I do not claim to be real smart but I was smart enough to know something was wrong.

So, I would crawl over to her, turn her face to me and say, "Babe, I know you are upset with me and I don't know why. So, I am not going to let you go to sleep until you tell me what I have done." It is not without reason that the Bible says, "In your anger, do not sin. Do not let the sun go down upon your anger" [*Holy* Bible, NIV Ephesians 4:26]. Time does not heal differences. More often than not it causes a festering rather than a healing (Adams 2009). By dealing with the problem quickly, I not only became aware of the problem, I showed her that I really cared about her. She also learned that teasing was a sign of love and she has adjusted quite well, becoming a "master kidder" in the family gatherings.

My Wife Wants to be Included in all Important Decisions I believe that God has made me responsible for the spiritual direction of our family. But, I would be a fool to not seek the counsel of my wife in the making of important decisions. She has gifts and perspectives that I do not have. I look long term and see in generalities and she looks short term and sees details. I have come to greatly appreciate her wisdom and council and been saved from many costly mistakes by listening to her. God gave me her for a reason.

My Wife Wants to be Able to Help Me Grow Without My Reacting in Anger I entered marriage like any other man, with plenty of need for growth. And, my wife was given to me to help bring about that growth. My wife has graciously fulfilled that calling by pointing out areas in my life where I need to grow, not because she was seeking to manipulate or control me, but because she loves me. She is my friend and wants my best. Part of being in a loving relationship is receiving counsel that at the time is not comfortable for it challenges our way of living. But, my wife has a tender way of approaching me. She will say something like, "Honey, you are my man. I am so proud of who you are and how you love me." It is only after reinforcing her love and care for me, that she shares her concern. Someone once commented to me, "Your wife is the best part of your ministry." She was absolutely right.

I heard of the supposed true story of the mayor of Philadelphia traveling through his town with his wife when he suddenly realized he needed gas. So, he stopped at a corner gas station to fill up. While he was in the station, he noticed that his wife was having an animated conversation with the service attendant. He was a little upset by what he saw so after traveling a few blocks he asked his wife who that man was that she was talking to. "Oh," the wife said, "that was my old boyfriend I had before I met you." The mayor was quiet for a moment and then observed, "I guess you are glad you married me and not that gas attendant." The wife shot back, "You don't understand. If I married him, *he* would be the mayor." True or not, it is a great illustration of my life.

My Wife Wants to Hear How Much I Love Her It is so easy to take our love for granted. We are like the husband whose wife asked him why he never told her he loved her anymore. He responded, "I told you when I married you didn't I? If anything changes I will tell you." Not smart or good. Expressed words have power to hurt and heal. Our wives need to hear how much we love them in words sincerely felt and carefully thought out on a regular basis. Doubts can slip in and bring unnecessary pain when love is not regularly expressed.

Early in their marriage and after the birth of their first child, Clementine wrote a letter to Winston expressing a tinge of jealously and concern for his love for her. We are not sure of the reason for her nervousness, but we have a record of Winston's response. He wrote,

> We do not live in a world of small intrigues, but of serious and important affairs. I could not conceive myself forming any other attachment than that to which I have fastened the happiness of my life here below. And it offends my best nature that you should—against your true instinct—indulge small emotions and wounding doubts. You ought to trust me for I do not love and will never love any woman in the world but you, and my chief desire is to link myself to you week by week by bonds which shall ever become more intimate and profound. (Wood 2009)

He then closed his letter with these words: "Beloved I kiss your memory—Your sweetness and beauty have cast a glory upon my life. You will find me always, Your loving and devoted husband. W." If there was any doubt or jealousy in the mind of Clementine, that lter should have dismissed it. Our wives need the same kind of expressions regularly (Wood 2009).

"My Wife Needs to Know that She Can Depend Upon Me to Protect Her from All Enemies" When we hear a noise in our basement, I am the one who goes down to see if a burglar has penetrated the defenses of our home. There is a reason for that. I am the man. Even if the woman is physically stronger, the husband inherently knows that he should take the initiative in protecting his bride. We are given the charge to protect our wives even if it means laying down our lives.

That not only applies to their physical wellbeing but also their emotional wellbeing. To my knowledge, I have never publicly said anything that cast a shadow over the beauty and value that is in my wife by her being. She is not my "old lady." She is my dearest friend. I am proud of her and I want everybody to know it. If we are working through some issues like every couple will, I do not need to gather supporters to my position at the expense of my dear friend. And, if you want to see a lady turn into a tiger, attack me. We protect each other. Lovers do that.

"My Wife Needs to Know that I Will Never Ever Leave Her or Forsake Her" One of the dearest and clearest love letters that has ever been written was delivered in a speech by the President of Columbia Bible College, and sent in letter form to the students, faculty and alumni of that school. In the communication, Dr. Robert McQuilkin explains why he is resigning his position as President of the school to stay at home with his wife who suffered from Alzheimer's disease. Although he loved to serve the students in that capacity, he loved serving his wife more. Here is the text of the letter. It is so moving I have included the address in its entirety.

> I haven't in my life experienced easy decision making on major decisions, but one of the simplest and clearest decisions I have had to make was this one because circumstances dictated it. Muriel, now in the last couple of months, seems to be almost happy when with me and almost never happy when not with me. In fact, she seems to feel trapped, becomes very fearful, almost terror, and when she can't find me she can't get to me there can be anger… she's in distress. But when I am with her she is happy and contented, and so I must be with her at all times …and you see, It's not only that I promised in sickness and health, till death do us part, and I am a man of my word. But as I have said [I don't know if with this group but I have said publically] it's the only fair thing. She sacrificed for me forty years of her life to make my life possible…so if I cared for her forty years I would still be in debt. However, there's much more…It's not that I have to, I get to. I love her very dearly, and you can tell it's not easy to talk about. She is a delight. And it is a great honor for me to care for such a wonderful person. (McQuilkin1981)

That letter captures the deep love and joy that is possible for all husbands who will learn to love their wives as Christ loved his Bride. We don't have to love or live or die for our wives. We get to. It is the highest calling a man can enter into. It reaps benefits, not only for us but also for our family.

Can We Transfer this Gift to Our Sons? Late night show host David Letterman once asked an actor: "Tell me. You're a sex symbol who plays all sorts of exciting roles with gorgeous women. How does that compare to your life, off-screen?" The actor reminded Letterman that he had been married for 20 years. Then he said, "Here's the difference in a nutshell. In the movies, life is mostly about sex and occasionally about children. Married life is mostly about children and occasionally about sex." Isn't that the truth? Is not life less about sex and more about family? Is it not the responsibility of men to discover the highest values of life and transfer those blessings to their children?

My father was a minister for 55 years. He was a man among boys. He was like a tree, not a weeping willow but a northern red oak. He had integrity. He was the same in the pulpit as he was in the parsonage. But for all the lessons of character I learned from my dad, I will never be more grateful than the one I learned when I saw the way he loved my mother. I can remember him grabbing my mother and bringing close to his body, and my mother screaming out, "Oh, Bob, not in front of the kids." Although I did not appreciate it at the time, I am glad he did it in front of us. It was not phony or fake. My dad had a passion for my mom. He declared it publicly so none of us would miss the point. She was the joy of his life and we were second. We did not mind.

When my father lay on a hospital bed, suffering from a heart attack, I visited him. Being a pastor myself I thought I would do my duty and pray for him. He would have none of it. He grabbed my hand and prayed for me. He prayed that I would be a man of God and a servant of men. He prayed that God would bless me and my family. When he was finished, I asked him if he was worried or concerned about anything. He said, "No. I am only concerned that if something happens to me, your mother will be taken care of." I assured him that her kids would take care of her.

It was the last moment I had with my dad. It was precious not only because of his fearlessness in the face of death, or his prayer for me, but because he still had one passion, the welfare of my mom. I will always be thankful for that. It shaped my life.

I have prayed one prayer throughout my married life: That I would love my wife and be faithful to her until death. It has been my hope that my boys would see the same kind of devotion and care of their mom that I saw in my father's love for his bride. A few years ago, my son came home from Paris for the holidays. He had met a young lady from Ecuador and they were dating regularly. We had the opportunity to communicate with her and met her briefly on our visit to Paris. While sitting at the table 1 day, I asked my son what her impression was of me. He responded, "She really respects you." I responded, "How is that? She hardly knows me." He responded, "She respects you because I treat her like you treat mom." My boy could not have given me a higher compliment.

We were created to know God and to enjoy Him forever (*Holy* Bible, NIV, I Corinthians 10:31; Lawson 2007). He has planted within his creation clues that point to the unbelievable treasures that are found only within His person. One of the means he has given us to discover and experience his joy is marriage. As a husband loves his wife as Christ loved his Bride, he experiences deep within his soul something of the joy God has for us. As he pledges a life-long commitment to his wife and by the strength God provides keeps that covenant, he displays to his children and the world that there is a God who is there and who is good. No other relationship on earth testifies to the greatness of God more than a sacred marriage lived out in obedience to his laws. Our children need to see this great lesson lived out before their eyes. I believe that one of the greatest gifts I could give my boys is to be devoted to loving their Mom with the same kind of passion that their Lord is devoted to loving them.

References

Adams, J. E. (2009). *Competent to counsel*. Grand Rapids: Zondervan.

Bledsole, J. G. (2012). The single greatest thing a dad can do for his children. http://jackiebledsoe.com/the-single-greatest-thing-a-dad-can-do-for-his-children/. Accessed 1 Aug 2014.

Breggin, P. R. (1991). *Toxic psychiatry*. New York: St. Martin's Press.

Broger, J. (1994). *Self-confrontation: A manual for in-depth discipleship*. Nashville: Thomas Nelson.

Bumpass, L., Sweet, J., & Castro-Martin, T. (1990). Changing patterns of remarriage. *Journal of Marriage and Family, 52*(3), 747–756.

Carmody, C. (2014). Malachi 2:10–16: God hates divorce. http://www.challengenews.org/show-clf.php?s=sermon&sermon=Carl_Carmody/Malachi_2_10-16_God_hates_divorce. Accessed 14 Aug 2014.

Carson, D. A. (2000). *Telling the truth: Evangelizing postmoderns*. Grand Rapids: Zondervan.

Cornwell, S. W. (2014). Five guidelines for no-regret fatherhood. http://www.millersvillebiblechurch.org/_files/live/noregretfatherhoodpdf.pdf. Accessed 9 Aug 2014.

Easton, S. (1994). *The problem of pornography: Regulation and the right to free Speech*. London: Routledge.

Gruden, W. (1994). *Systematic theology: An introduction to Biblical theology*. Grand Rapids: Zondervan.

Jeremiah, D. (2009). *Living with confidence in a chaotic world: What on earth should we know*. Nashville: Thomas Nelson.

Keller, T. (2012). *The meaning of marriage: Facing the complexities of commitment with the wisdom of god*. New York: Riverhead Books.

Lawson, R. (2007). *The shorter catechism*. Ross-shire: Christian Focus.

Lockerbie, B. D. (1986). *The cosmic center: The supremacy of Christ in a secular wasteland*. Sisters: Multnomah Press.

Mack, W. A. (1998). *Marriage and family counseling*. Glenside: Christian Counseling and Education Foundation.

Mancino, G. (2006). *The pursuit of happiness*. United States: Sony Pictures.

Marriage and Family Fact Sheet. (2012). http://firstthings.org/marriage-family-fact-sheet. Accessed 9 Aug 2014

McQuilkin, R. (1981). Robert McQuilkin's resignation speech. http://reforming.wordpress.com/2006/10/20/robertson-mcquilkins-resignation-speech/. Accessed 9 Aug 2014.

Packer, J. I. (1979). *God has spoken*. Grand Rapids: Baker Books.

Packer, J. I. (1996). *Truth & power: The place of scripture in the Christian life*. Chicago: Harold Shaw Publishers.

Piper, J. (1996). *Desiring god* (2nd ed.). Sisters: Multnomah Press.

Piper, J. (2000). *The pleasures of god: Meditation on god's delight in being god*. Sisters: Multnomah Press.

Piper, J. (2009). *This momentary marriage: A parable of permanence*. Wheaton: Crossway.

Piper, J., & Gruden, W. (Eds.). (2006). *Recovering Biblical manhood and womanhood: A response evangelical feminism*. Wheaton: Crossway.

Piper, J., & Taylor, J. (Eds.). (2005). *Sex and the supremacy of Christ*. Wheaton: Crossway.

Popenoe, D. (2011). *Families without fathers: Fathers, marriage and children in American society*. New Brunswick: Transaction Publishers.

Rieben, G. (2012). *Give me that book: A treasury of truth for troubled times*. Enumclaw: Winepress.

Schaeffer, F. (1971). *True spirituality*. Wheaton: Tyndale House.

Schramm, D. G. (2009). http://familyinamerica.org/journals/fall-2009/counting-cost-divorce-what-those-who-know-better-rarely-acknowledge/#.U-eBYFYyH1o. Accessed 10 Aug 2014.

Sproul, R. C. (2009). *The consequence of ideas: Understanding the concepts that shaped our world*. Wheaton: Crossway.

Wallerstein, J. S. (2000). *The unexpected legacy of divorce: A landmark study*. New York: Hyperion.

Watts, S. (2008). *Mr playboy: Hugh Hefner and the American Dream*. Hoboken: Wiley.

Webster, P. S., Orbuch, T. L., & House, J. S. (1995). Effects of childhood family background on adult marital quality and perceived stability. *American Journal of Sociology, 101*(2), 404–431.

Wells, D. (1993). *No place for truth*. Grand Rapids: Wm. B. Eerdmans.

Wood, L. (2009). Clementine and Winston. http://www.thinkinghousewife.com/wp/2009/08/famous-couples-clemetine-and-wonston/. Accessed Aug 2012.

Gary Rieben is president of the international counseling ministry, Give Me That Book. He has a D. Min. from Fuller Theological Seminary. He also served as a pastor in Southern California and the Mid-West for many years. He is presently based in Malawi, AFRICA.

Preparing for Your Future Spouse

William Jeynes

Abstract The chapter provides guidance for those contemplating the very important decision of anticipating- and pursuing- the decision of preparing for one's future spouse. The author provides principles that young adults can apply to each stage of the preparation process, including building the right personal foundation for making this event possible, how to believe for the right person, and what actions to take once one thinks he or she might have met that person.

Keywords Marriage · Pre-marital counseling · Counseling · Family · Wedding · Spirituality · Faith · Christianity · Religion

The Journey Toward Marriage

Most people either do not fully acknowledge or do not practice the principle that probably the most important time for securing the success of a relationship with a future spouse is actually before the relationship commences (Wright and Roberts 1997). The foundation that one permits God to create when one is single will also serve as the genesis of the foundation that emerges when one is first married (Jeynes 2006a). Although, at first glance, this fact may seem burdensome, in reality if one examines this fact from the right perspective it is truly exciting (Wright and Roberts 1997). That is, the time is now to begin the journey toward a fulfilled family life. Why wait until one's wedding to prepare for marriage, when this is the time to initiate this journey?

There are several principles, that when fathomed and applied, will enlighten one with the realization that the trek toward holy matrimony begins when one is single.

First, the foundation for one's happiness commences when one is single. Myriad individuals view marriage as a path via which one can transcend the quagmire of

W. Jeynes (✉)
Witherspoon Institute, Princeton, NJ, USA
e-mail: whjharvard@post.harvard.edu

California State University, Long Beach, 6572 Red Coach Drive Huntington Beach, CA 92647, USA

W. Jeynes, E. Martinez (eds.), *Ministering Spiritually to Families*,
DOI 10.1007/978-3-319-13302-7_5

dissatisfaction and unfulfilled dreams to enter a life of ethereal bliss (Meyer 2002; Piper 2011; Post 2000; Worthington 2000). In reality, however, the degree to which one is happy before marriage is a good predictor of how happy one will be after the wedding has taken place (Meyer 2002; Piper 2011). Marriage, unlike the regeneration that a person undergoes when he or she is born-again in Christ, is not a radical transformation, but the uniting of two lives (Jeynes 2009a; Meyer 2002). It is, if you will, the continuation of two lives that have chosen to live together in spiritual, emotional, and physical unity (Post 2000; Worthington 2000).

One can certainly think of copious individuals both in the Bible and historically, as well as in every day life, that are fine examples of this. In the Bible, Jacob is a very good example of this principle. Before Jacob was married he was a disgruntled individual and after he was married he was as well (Barber 2010; Wallace 2001). This principle, however, is not merely limited to biblical experience, but is also supported in academic research (Barber 2010; Jeynes 2010e; Wallace 2001). That is, the research literature indicates that there is a strong relationship between premarital satisfaction with life and the satisfaction that one experiences after marriage (Jeynes 2010b; Minith 2004; Murray 2001).

Second, the spiritual level that a person is at prior to marriage will have a dramatic impact on the maturity of the person that one will ultimately marry. The reality is that people of similar stages of spiritual inclination tend to attract one another (DeMuth 2006; Jeynes 2006b; Meyer 2002; Strobel and Strobel 2010). This is a tangible and practical truth that one can apply to one's prayer life. Because there are many ministers who will encourage young singles to pray for roughly ten or twelve traits that they desire their future spouse to possess (Strobel and Strobel 2010). This is certainly a worthy undertaking. Nevertheless, it is rare indeed to hear a minister or any other individual to exhort young people to pray for ten or twelve traits they desire God to produce in themselves. And yet the truth of the matter is that even if one meets a potential future spouse who possesses all of these traits, unless one exhibits a roughly equivalent degree of character it is unlikely that this person of one's dreams will be interested in the relationship that one desires. If one realizes this truism, he or she will eschew a great deal of pain. Commonly, young people endure a prodigious amount of unnecessary pain because they fail to be cognizant of this fact. Almost without exception, adolescents and young adults spend more time praying for godly traits to be manifest in their potential spouse than they do for these same traits to be exhibited in themselves. Consequently, they sometimes encounter the dilemma of meeting and desiring someone who possesses these traits, but is not the least bit interested in pursuing an intimate relationship with oneself.

Third, where one works and operates are likely to be the places where one meets one's spouse and one needs to be realistic about this fact. If one spends a lot of time in bars, in questionable establishments, in neighborhoods where licentiousness reigns, that is likely where one will meet his or her future spouse. If one spends a lot of time at work or on the internet, that is also likely to be the place where one meets his or her future spouse. If, on the other hand, an individual is deeply involved in a church and volunteers to help others in faith- or community-based outreaches meeting one's future spouse is most likely to take place there (Dobson 2007; Jeynes

2009b, 2009c; Strobel and Strobel 2010). I recall ministering to a lady who had a history of alcohol destroying her life. She was miserable over this fact, had been arrested for driving under the influence of alcohol, and worked as a bartender. By God's grace, she was touched by what I shared with her over time. At my advice, she decided to change her job and left her job as a bartender. One of the reasons she was so willing to make the change is because she realized that she was "better off meeting her future husband at a church or community center than in a bar."."

This is a particularly salient principle for some of the most devout individuals to apply. That is, if one wants to meet someone with an equivalent degree of spiritual intensity, then he or she would be wise to go about the ministering of love, compassion, faith, caring, and commitment that is consistent with who one is as an individual and the kind of person that one anticipates uniting with in holy matrimony (Strobel and Strobel 2010). It is important that individuals seeking a calling in life in one capacity or another realize that because one is setting high standards that it is particularly vital that one be deliberate in thinking through the ramifications for the potential of future relationships of engaging in particular tasks and in frequenting specific locales (Baehr 1998; Dobson 2007; Strobel and Strobel 2010). Granted, that the tasks in which a person applies oneself and the places where one goes potentially influences the kind of relationships that all people develop, this principle is especially weighty for people who believe that their purpose in life is quite unique and potentially demanding.

Many times people can greatly bolster their chances of having a rewarding marital relationship if they first humbly realize that being married to someone with their call in life is not an easy task and likely requires that the spouse be an understanding, flexible, dedicated, and unique individual. What makes this issue especially complex is that some of the occupations that might fit under the category of challenging call are not immediately obvious. For example, people who own a restaurant or a store may not view their occupational choice as a particularly challenging call, but when marriage enters the picture it can be so. Unless an owner finds a magnificent assistant to consistently act in relief, the store can quickly become one's life. The hours can become excessive and late, as well as early. Moreover, vacation times can be hard to come by. It takes a special spouse to be married to someone with this career. Being a physician or a minister can also be a demanding call, because the essence of one's purpose becomes helping other people. Consequently, that individual's schedule is highly influenced by the people that he or she is seeking to help. Once again, although the salary of physicians tends to be high, the emergencies that occur with almost no warning can be stressful even for the most patient individuals. The challenges of being a minister are often considerably greater, on average, than that of a doctor, largely become the compensation is so much lower (Dobson 2007; Wickman 2011). It therefore takes a special person to be married to a minister.

With the above facts in mind, it is therefore wise to realize that one is far more likely to meet one's future spouse in some environments and locales than in others. Additionally, it is far more preferable and forward thinking to understand that it is far better to meet one's future spouse in some locales rather than others.

Fourth, the time during which one is single is an excellent opportunity to prepare the qualities needed to be a good spouse and parent. There are a number of traits that, scripturally speaking, are some of the most salient that one can possess (Jeynes 2006b, 2010a, 2010d). From the Bible, it is apparent that the Lord values three traits above all the rest and it is important that people develop these traits in order to have successful marriages. First, Jesus teaches that the commandments of God are based on two overriding principles: that one should love God and his or her neighbor (Holy Bible, NIV 1979, Luke 10:27, 28; Jeynes 2007, 2012a). The third of these prevailing traits is based on Christ's assertion that it is the person who humbles himself like a child who is greatest in the kingdom of heaven (Holy Bible, NIV, Matthew 18:3, 4).

These three traits can probably go farther in securing a strong marriage than just about any other similarly sized set. Any intimate relationship should be saturated in love (Jeynes 1999, 2003, 2005). Christ asserted that this love must radiate from God's love, which the Bible declares is the only pure form of love. In fact, the Bible declares that love is so completely central to Christian faith that the Bible declares that, "God is love" (Holy Bible, NIV 1979, I John 4:8). The Bible declares that as one relies on God's love and becomes filled with that love, He is then capable of loving others with a God-based love. By having a marriage relationship that is based on God's love, the intimacy is therefore founded on absolute truths that can enable the relationship to be well-founded on principles that are eternal and do not change. By founding their relationship on eternal truths, the idea is that it will be more likely that there marital relationship will also last eternally. And naturally any long-lasting relationship that entails this degree of intimacy must be founded in love (Jeynes 2002b, 2011a, 2013).

Humility is also a key ingredient that one needs to develop ideally before one marries. Few traits will have such a baleful effect on a marriage as pride. Moreover, it takes humility to both ask for forgiveness and to forgive (Barclay 2010; Cloud and Townsend 2001; Jeynes 2002a; Kruschwitz 2001; Swindoll 1998). Engaging willingly in each practice is indispensable if a marriage is to thrive (Barclay 2010; Swindoll 1998). The cross, the central symbol of Christianity, conveys a message of forgiveness (Barclay 2010; Cloud and Townsend 2001; Swindoll 1998). This primary message differentiates Christianity from every other religion in the world (Barclay 2010; Jeynes 2012b, 2012c; Swindoll 1998).

There are a variety of other traits that one should use his single years to develop in preparation for marriage (Kostenberger and Jones 2004). Some of these traits are inextricably connected to the three qualities just mentioned. For example, loyalty and its sister trait commitment are absolutely essential to develop before one marries, rather than after the fact. One of the reasons why it is so vital to develop loyalty before one marries and to value this trait in others is because the presence and practice of loyalty before marriage is predictive of loyalty after marriage (Selvaggio and Meath 2008; Strom 2002). One of the key questions that counselors would be wise to ask after one marriage partner has committed adultery is whether that person had engaged in pre-marital intercourse before marriage (Allen et al. 2005; Anderson 2004; Selvaggio and Meath 2008; Tuch 2000). In the overwhelming percentage of cases if one committed adultery after marriage, that same person engaged in pre-marital intercourse before marriage (Hetzendorfer 2009; Selvaggio and Meath 2008). The reason that this close relationship exists is because pre-marital behavior is very predictive of after-marital behavior (Allen et al. 2005; Anderson 2004; Selvaggio and Meath 2008; Tuch 2000). If one was not disciplined and loyal enough to refrain from coitus before marriage takes place, it is unlikely that this behavior will change after a wedding. Naturally, if one was an unbeliever before marriage and a Christian afterward, this is an important exception. Nevertheless, pre-marital behavior is highly predictive of what is likely to occur afterward (Allen et al. 2005; Anderson 2004; Tuch 2000). Along these lines, the way a person treats his opposite sex parent is often indicative of how he or she will treat one's spouse after marriage. This is an important trend to note not only in choosing a marriage partner, but also to eye in oneself.

Steps to Believing God for One's Best Partner

Faith in God's Plan

It is a very spiritual declaration to proclaim that one believes that God's plan for his or her life is better than one's own. Moreover, there is no better time to believe this than when a person is trusting God to provide a future spouse. Thinking realistically, however, to what extent is this generally speaking actually the case? And to the extent to which this is true generally, how much more is this so when one encounters the specific experience of trusting God to provide one's spouse. Most people, even Christians and other people of faith, proceed with the pursuit of the dream of a future spouse operating under the assumption that no one knows who is best as a potential marriage partner than oneself. Nevertheless, if he or she truly believes that God's plan is best, this conviction should apply to all things, including meeting and developing a very special relationship with one's future spouse.

There a number of reasons why it is both wise and practical to view God's plan as superior to one's own when it comes to believing for one's future spouse. First, a primary principle of the Bible is that God's plan is better than one's own (Holy Bible, NIV 1979, Isaiah 55:8, 9). Second, God as Creator knows people more than anyone else. He knows their hearts better than does any other individual. He also knows the types of individuals into which people will develop. Third, God knows the future circumstances that will unfold and how people will develop and behave in the future better than any human being. If one is a person of faith, it makes perfect sense to reach a logical conclusion that God's wisdom is better than human insight on these matters.

The Input of Godly People Who Know One Well

One truth that many couples experience is that when one enters into a serious relationship with a member of the opposite sex, there is usually no shortage of the number of people that are willing to offer advice. Almost always these people mean well, but the question is whether these individuals are offering advice that is reliable. There is certainly a propensity that is almost innate in human beings that cause them to look toward those who could offer some insightful advice (Dobson 2007). Most young singles are cognizant of the fact that they lack the experience necessary to consistently act in the best interests of God, their beloved, and themselves. Insightful advice from the right people can therefore be of immense help (Dobson 2007). The quandary that so many couples encounter is that it is not always clear just who the right person is. The key is to find a person who *both* has a close relationship with God and knows one well. There are many people who meet one of these criteria or the other, but there are seldom individuals who meet both. Naturally, some are going to know at least one member of the couple quite well and will be able to offer some insight from this perspective. Nevertheless, most of these people will not be particularly close to God and therefore may not be able to offer the deep spiritual understanding that people close to God might possess. On the other hand, there are other individuals who will have a special relationship with God that will indubitably mean well, but they really do not know about your personality traits, preferences, tastes, and convictions. Therefore, the most they can really offer is general principles on which to act rather than real insight that can address one's own particular relationship. For these reasons it is best to procure advice for a person who is both spiritual and knows one well.

Thoughts to Consider When Meeting Someone Who Potentially Might Be One's Future Spouse

In the vast majority of circumstances, one first meets someone with potential as a future spouse before he or she knows with certainty that this person is that special someone with which one will experience holy matrimony. One of the most important questions a person can ask along these lines is, "What are the indications that the person I am interested in would make a good husband or wife?" Here a few ideas to consider. First, it is wise how to observe how this person treats his or her mother and father. These are the closest personal relationships that he has and probably the best indicator of how one can expect to be treated in the future. An individual might feel that one's potential future spouse might be a nice person now, but that is while both members of the potential couple are young and good looking and there is great incentive to put one's best foot forward. How a person treats their parents, however, is a very good indicator of how one will likely be treated in the future. It is especially insightful to observe carefully how one's potential spouse treats the parent of the same gender that one is. Patterns that a person's potential future spouse show are trends that usually continue into marriage and it is vital that people be aware of this fact. In decades of counseling families, my wife and I can tell you that people who have been verbally abusive to their parents are almost always very abusive to their spouse, unless they have experienced a dramatic spiritual change (DeMuth 2006).

Second, one demonstrates perspicacity when one observes how the individual of interest treats other people as well. There is an old adage that states, "If a person does not treat waitresses well, he or she is not a nice person." There is a lot of truth to that statement. While it is quite possible that the person will treat one well *now*, personality traits tend to reside quite deeply in a person and will likely surface over time. Whatever negative attitudes and behavior are directed at coworkers, strangers, and acquaintances now will probably be aimed at a spouse at various times along one's lifespan. Anger, disloyalty, condescension, disrespect, maliciousness, and nastiness will tend to manifest themselves toward different people at various times. This is because one's personality tends to be quite consistent over time (Cervone and Shoda 1999; Hetzendorfer 2009; Zuckerman 1991).

Third, consider that the person one marries will not only be one's spouse, but will also in all likelihood function as the parent of one's children. With this in mind, it is therefore wise to ask, "Would this person make a good parent of my future children?" Admittedly, there is and should be a considerable overlap between those people who will make good spouses and those who will make good- fathers and mothers (Jeynes 2011b; Lamb 1997; Wilson 2005). Nevertheless, it is frequently the case that a potential future spouse may make a fine husband or wife, but a very poor mother or father (Hetzendorfer 2009; Wilson 2005). For example, some of the most important qualities if one is to be a good husband or wife include being loving, loyal, faithful, a good provider, a reliable communicator, romantic, a strong team-player, and someone who can build bonds with in-laws. Some of the most salient qualities for a parent to possess include being loving, a great example, someone who balances kindness and giving children a sense of structure to their life, someone who is willing to take time to both care for and interact with the children, a person who can relate to people much younger than he or she is, and someone who realizes that children are people too (Vangelisti 2004; Wright and Oliver 1999). While it is patent that there are certain similarities between the qualities necessary for effective motherhood and fatherhood on the one hand and married life on the other, it is clear that there are also differences (Jeynes 2010c; Waite and Gallagher 2000). With these ideas in mind, it is therefore wise for one to ponder and pray about whether the person one is considering marrying would not only make a good spouse, but also whether this person would make a virtuous parent.

Fourth, one should consider how one's future spouse treats God. The Scripture is clear that how one treats God and other human beings are closely related (Holy Bible, NIV 1979, I John 4:20, 21). One of the most powerful traits that people associate with God is that He keeps his word. In fact, the entire Christian faith is built on the notion that God keeps His word. With this in mind, one can make an argument that one of the most vital traits that a person can have is that he or she keeps his word, because this is truly godly. A valuable question to ask, therefore, regarding one's future spouse, is does he or she keep his word (McDonald and Robinson 2009). Does the person one is interested in keep his or her word with God? with others (McDonald and Robinson 2009)?

Actions to Take Once a Person Finds Their Future Spouse

What is very important after a person thinks that he or she has found one's future spouse and the couple is engaged, is that a strong spiritual foundation for the relationship be established (Cloud and Townsend 2001). It is vital that the couple be cognizant of the fact that the formation of this foundation begins before the marriage is consummated (Cloud and Townsend 2001). Naturally, a spiritual foundation must begin with God and that means that prayer and the study of the Bible are important. Therefore, it is wise for the couple to begin every meeting with prayer. It can be brief, but this simple act produces a number of advantages. First, the couple's relationship is dedicated to glorifying God. Second, the man and woman are acknowledging their dependence on God. Third, acts of anger, spite, jealousy, and others that potentially can undermine a relationship are minimized because the couple is attempting to walk in the grace and love of God. Similarly, it is wise to conclude each time together with some prayer.

In addition to these actions, it is important to try to have joint devotional times as much as possible. These can involve times of studying the Bible together praying, and spending some time worshipping God as a couple. The latter is especially beneficial if either the man or the woman is musically inclined. They can sing around a piano together and play the guitar and sing. These times are essential and the couple must not take the engagement period lightly, even though the marriage has not yet taken place. There is a sense in which there is a foundation that is clearly built once a wedding takes place. That is, the early days of a marriage are very important. Nevertheless, the salience of the pre-marital period must not be underestimated. In many respects, the true foundation for the relationship commences during this period (Arnold 2007). Given that when a man and a woman get married they become one, it is important that the couple become spiritually united in the most positive way possible. This process can be realized the extent to which the couple studies the Bible-, prays-, worships-, and fellowships- together. To become united in these ways eventually creates a married couple that is single minded and single hearted (Cloud and Townsend 2001). Marriages in which the husband and wife view the Bible in a similar way tend to thrive more than when this unity is not extant. Naturally, this does not mean that the husband and wife will have total unanimity in their view of Scripture. Disagreements do, and to some extent, should happen in the sense that iron sharpens iron (Holy Bible, NIV 1979, Proverbs 27:17).

A second act of wisdom the prenuptial couple should take is to try to iron out whatever concerns they have and interactive irritants that might exist. Specifically, it makes a lot of sense to ask the question, "If there was one way in which I would like my future spouse to improve in, this would be the way." It is sagacious to focus on one primary quality, for the following reasons. First, often if the couple is able to see victory in their main area of concern, they are usually able to prevent major harm coming to the relationship. Often what causes relationships to either crumble or become debilitated is a direct result of one area that has not been adequately addressed. Second, human beings by nature are quite stubborn. Change can be difficult and time consuming. Generally speaking, if a person has rather obvious faults that need to be worked on, most people can only effectively work on one fault at a time. That is particularly true in a marriage or other intimate relationship.

Third, the engagement period must be used efficiently in another respect. It is an excellent time for the man and woman to get to know their in-laws. Virtually no one would gainsay the fact that the quality of a couple's relationship with their in-laws can have a major impact on their marital relationship. Tensions between in-laws can sometime emerge because of problems that are predictable and, at times, unavoidable (Arnold 2007; Chapman et al. 2008; Cloud and Townsend 2001). However, there are other in-law problems that arise due to miscommunication. Miscommunications can be reduced if there is enhanced communication before the marriage takes place. This often is not as facile as it might seem, because most young couples are not especially jubilant about the idea of meeting their future in-laws. Nevertheless, engagement couples must jettison any predispositions toward avoiding meeting their future in-laws and think about what is best for the future of the marriage and family. Showing a willingness to meet one's in-laws produces a number of immediate benefits. For example, it indicates to the family the way you are likely to treat them in the future (Barber 2010; Swindoll 1998). Many times the family draws conclusions about how their future son-in-law or daughter-in-law is likely to treat them after the marriage takes place (Hetzendorfer 2009). If one thinks about it, such a perspective is quite reasonable and logical (Hetzendorfer 2009). In fact, how sons-in-law and daughters-in-law treat their future parents-in-law before marriage actually is a good indication of how they treat them after the wedding takes place (Barber 2010; Hetzendorfer 2009).

Fourth, reaching out to the in-laws in this way can also enhance a person's relationship with his or her future spouse. A person generally loves it when an individual, especially someone close such as a future spouse, demonstrates love and show interest in his or her family. It is difficult for most individuals who are about to become a husband or wife to feel totally accepted unless one also loves their family (Jeynes 2011b; Swindoll 1998).

Fifth, it is wise for a couple to talk about any potential problems they foresee once the wedding takes place. It is vital to discuss this issue before the wonderful day of matrimony takes place. To whatever extent pre-nuptial discussions can reduce marital surprises later can be a real boon for a marriage. Often what happens in a marriage, especially among newlyweds, is that the sudden unexpected nature of an event causes them to overreact more than the event itself does (Barber 2010; Hetzendorfer 2009). Therefore, couples would be prudent to try to anticipate any potential problem that might arise following marriage including problems related to finances, in-law problems, mutual expectations, future direction, occupational hazards, employment demands, college and graduate school training, anticipated timelines, and so forth. The more that these subjects are discussed prior to the wedding, the more likely the newlyweds will find building bonds between them as being facile rather than a source of an act producing difficulty.

Concluding Thoughts

It is humbling but true that most people make a majority of the most important decisions of their lives between the ages of sixteen and thirty. Moreover, it is also true that for the person of the faith, the decision to marry is second in importance only to one's decision to follow the Lord. To the extent to which this is true, preparing for one's future spouse is one of the greatest acts of wisdom that one can make. To the extent that counselors, spiritual leaders, and moral examples can help young adults in this process of preparation, they will be participating in a work of eternal worth.

References

Allen, E. S., Atkins, D. C., Baucom, D. H., Snyder, D. K., Gordon, K. C., & Glass, S. P. (2005). Intrapersonal, interpersonal, and contextual factors in engaging in and responding to extramarital involvement. *Clinical Psychology: Science & Practice, 12*(2), 101–130.

Anderson, N. C. (2004). *Avoiding the greener grass syndrome: How to grow affair-proof hedges around your marriage*. Grand Rapids: Kregal.

Arnold, L. B. (2007). *Family & communication: Theory & research*. Boston: Allyn & Bacon.

Baehr, T. (1998). *The media-wise family*. Colorado Springs: Victor Publishing.

Barber, C. J. (2010). *Profiles of the patriarchs: Jacob*. Eugene: Wipf & Stock Publishers.

Barclay, W. (2010). *Forgiveness: What the Bible tells us about forgiveness*. Edinburgh: Saint Andrew.

Cervone, D., & Shoda, Y. (1999). *The coherence of personality: Social-cognitive bases of consistency, variability, and organization*. New York: Guilford.

Chapman, G. D., Campbell, R., & Fabry, C. (2008). *The five love languages of children*. Carol Stream: Oasis.

Clinton, T. E., & Ohischlager, G. W. (2002). *Competent Christian counseling*. Colorado Springs: Waterbrook.

Cloud, H., & Townsend, J. S. (2001). *How people grow: What the Bible reveals about personal growth*. Grand Rapids: Zondervan.

DeMuth, M. E. (2006). *Building the christian family you never had*. Colorado Springs: Westbrook.

Dobson, J. C. (2007). *Life on the edge: The next generation's guide to a meaningful future*. Carol Stream: Tyndale House.

Hetzendorfer, R. (2009). *The pastoral counseling handbook*. Nashville: Beacon Hill.

Holy Bible (1979). *Holy Bible, new international version*. Nashville: Thomas Nelson.

Jeynes, W. (1999). The effects of religious commitment on the academic achievement of black and hispanic children. *Urban Education, 34*(4), 458–479.

Jeynes, W. (2002a). A meta-analysis of the effects of attending religious schools and religiosity on Black and Hispanic academic achievement. *Education & Urban Society, 35*(1), 27–49.

Jeynes, W. (2002b). *Divorce, family structure, and the academic success of children*. New York: Haworth/Taylor & Francis.

Jeynes, W. (2003). The effects of Black and Hispanic twelfth graders living in intact families and being religious on their academic achievement. *Urban Education, 38*(1), 35–57.

Jeynes, W. (2005). Parental involvement and student achievement: A meta-analysis. *Family involvement research digest, Harvard family research project*. Cambridge: Harvard Family Research Project.

Jeynes, W. (2006a). *A hand not shortened*. Greenwich: Information Age.

Jeynes, W. (2006b). Standardized tests and the true meaning of kindergarten and preschool. *Teachers College Record, 108*(10), 1937–1959.

Jeynes, W. (2007). *American educational history: School, society, and the common good*. Thousand Oaks: Sage.

Jeynes, W. (2009a). *Getting closer to god*. Charlotte: Information Age.

Jeynes, W. (2009b). The relationship between Bible literacy and academic achievement, and school behavior. *Education & Urban Society, 41*(4), 419–436.

Jeynes, W. (2009c). The relationship between Bible literacy and academic achievement, and school behavior among Christian- and public school-students. *Journal of Research on Christian Education, 18*(1), 36–55.

Jeynes, W. (2010a). *A call for character education and prayer in the schools*. Westport: Praeger.

Jeynes, W. (Ed.). (2010b). *Family factors & the educational success of children*. New York: Routledge.

Jeynes, W. (2010c). Religiosity, religious schools, and their relationship with the achievement gap: A research synthesis and meta-analysis. *Journal of Negro Education, 79*(3), 263–279.

Jeynes, W. (2010d). The relationship between Bible literacy and academic and behavioral outcomes in urban areas: A meta-analysis. *Education & Urban Society, 42*(5), 522–544.

Jeynes, W. (2010e). The salience of the subtle aspects of parental involvement and encouraging that involvement: Implications for school-based programs. *Teachers College Record, 112*(3), 747–774.

Jeynes, W. (2011a). Help families by fostering parental involvement. *Phi Delta Kappan, 93*(3), 38–39.

Jeynes, W. (2011b). *Parental involvement & academic success*. New York: Taylor & Francis/Routledge.

Jeynes, W. (2012a). A meta-analysis on the effects and contributions of public, public charter, and religious schools on student outcomes. *Peabody Journal of Education, 87*(3), 305–335.

Jeynes, W. (2012b). Character instruction in protestant education throughout history. In Jeynes, W. & Robinson, D. (Ed.), The *international handbook of protestant education* (pp. 3–24). London: Springer.

Jeynes, W. (2012c). The removal of character education from the public schools and America's moral decline since 1963. In Jeynes, W. & Robinson, D. (Ed.), *The international handbook of protestant education* (pp. 25–49). London: Springer.

Jeynes, W. (2013). Father involvement, African Americans, and reducing the achievement gap. In Pattnaik, J. (Ed.), *Father involvement across the globe* (pp. 71–87). Amsterdam: Springer.

Kostenberger, A. J., & Jones, D. W. (2004). *God, marriage & family: Rebuilding the biblical foundation*. Wheaton: Crossway Books.

Kruschwitz, R. B. (2001). *Forgiveness*. Waco: Baylor University.

Lamb, M. (1997). *The role of the father in child development*. New York: Wiley.

McDonald, L. G., & Robinson, P. (2009). *A colossal failure of common sense*. New York: Crown.

Meyer, J. (2002). *Making marriage work: The advice you need for a lifetime of Happiness*. New York: Warner Faith.

Minith, F. B. (2004). *In pursuit of happiness: Choices that can change your life*. Grand Rapids: Fleming H. Revell.

Murray, J. (2001). *Love, marriage, and family in the middle ages*. Peterborough: Broadview.

Piper, J. (2011). *Desiring god: Meditations of a Christian hedonist*. Colorado Springs: Multnomah.

Post, S. G. (2000). *More lasting unions: Christianity, the family, and society*. Grand Rapids: Eerdmans.

Selvaggio, A. T., & Meath, K. (2008). *A proverbs driven life: Timeless wisdom for your work, wealth, and relationships*. Wapwallopen: Shepherd.
Strobel, L., & Strobel, L. (2010). *Surviving a spiritual mismatch in marriage*. Grand Rapids: Zondervan.
Strom, B. (2002). Communicator virtue and vice: Neglected constructs of relational communication. *Atlantic Journal of Communication, 10*(1), 84–103.
Swindoll, C. R. (1998). *Joseph: A man of integrity and forgiveness: Profiles in character*. Nashville: Word Publishers.
Tuch, R. (2000). *The single woman-married man syndrome*. Northvale: Aronson.
Vangelisti, A. L. (2004). *Handbook of family communication*. Mahwah: Erlbaum.
Waite, L. J., & Gallagher, M. (2000). *The case for marriage: Why married people are happier, healthier, and better off financially*. New York: Doubleday.
Wallace, R. S. (2001). *The story of Joseph and the family of Jacob*. Grand Rapids: W.B. Eerdmans.
Wickman, C. (2011). *Pastors at risk: Protecting your future, guarding your present*. Colorado Springs: WaterBrook.
Wilson, R. F. (2005). Evaluating marriage: Does marriage matter to the nurturing of children? *San Diego Law Review, 42*(3), 847–880.
Worthington, E., Jr. (2000). *Christian marital counseling: Eight approaches to helping couples*. Eugene: Wipf and Stock.
Wright, H. N., & Oliver, G. J. (1999). *Raising kids to love Jesus*. Ventura: Regal.
Wright B. N., & Roberts, W. (1997). *Before you say "I do": A marriage preparation manual for couples*. Eugene: Harvest House Publishers.
Zuckerman, M. (1991). *Psychobiology of personality*. Cambridge: Cambridge University Press.

Prof. William Jeynes has served in counseling ministry for over 34 years and in academics for 23 years. He and his wife have counseled thousands of families over the years and he has three degrees in Psychology and Counseling and a fourth in a related field. He is a Professor at California State University, Long Beach and a Senior Fellow on the Family at the Witherspoon Institute in Princeton, New Jersey. He graduated first in his class at Harvard University and also graduated from the University of Chicago, where he received the Rosenberger Award for the most outstanding student in his cohort. Bill has ministered in churches in every inhabited continent and in nearly every state in the country. He has spoken a number of times at Yoido Full Gospel Church in Korea, the largest church in the world. He has spoken on family and faith issues for the White House, the U.S. Department of Justice, the U.S. Department of Education, and the U.S. Department of Health & Human Services. He has spoken for both the G. W. Bush and Obama administrations. He has spoken for foreign and UN leaders, Harvard University, Cambridge University, Oxford University, Columbia University, Duke University, Notre Dame University, and the Harvard Family Research Project. His 4-point family and economic proposal given to the Acting President of Korea was passed and became the foundation for their economic and family policy to arise from the Asian Economic Crisis of 1997–1998. He has about 140 academic publications, including 12 books on family and faith issues.

Dr. Jeynes has been interviewed or quoted by the Washington Post, the Los Angeles Times, The Wall Street Journal, the New York Times, the London Times, the Associated Press (AP), CBS, NBC, ABC, FOX, public radio, Al Jazeera and many other news sources. His work has been cited and quoted numerous times by the U.S. Congress, the British Parliament, the EU, and many State Supreme Courts across the United States. Dr. Jeynes has been listed in *Who's Who in the World* for each of the last nine years and received a Distinguished Scholar Award the California State Senate, the California State Assembly, and his university. He formerly taught at USC and the University of Chicago. Bill has been married for over 28 years and has three wonderful children.

Marriage Preparation: A Ministry with Lasting Benefits

Joe D. Wilmoth

Abstract With the vast majority of marriage preparation provided in a religious setting, churches are uniquely positioned to help couples improve marital quality and stability by providing research-based and biblically sound premarital counseling. This chapter discusses the importance of church-based premarital counseling and gives tools for developing an effective ministry. The chapter includes background information about clergy involvement in premarital counseling; best practices for marriage preparation; and the attitudes and behaviors of U.S. clergy related to this ministry that we have discovered in our research. We offer specific suggestions to help the minister develop appropriate skills, recommend tools to address the unique needs of each couple, and suggest strategies for utilizing additional resources. An appendix lists websites that provide specific resources.

Keywords Marriage preparation · Premarital education · Premarital counseling · Divorce prevention

Marriage Preparation: A Ministry with Lasting Benefits

Marriage preparation (also called premarital counseling or premarital education) is an effective ministry of the church that usually leads to marriages that are happier and more likely to stay together (Stanley et al. 2006). An increasing number of therapists and secular agencies provide various kinds of premarital education or counseling, but the vast majority of marriage preparation in the United States takes place within a religious setting (Glenn 2005).

The benefit of marriage preparation goes far beyond the welfare of the couple getting married. In light of the significant social costs of divorce and marital discord (Wilcox et al. 2005), religious leaders are uniquely positioned to impact the economic, social, and emotional well-being of individuals and families by providing this service. However, there is reason to believe that this vital ministry could

J. D. Wilmoth (✉)
Mississippi State University, Mail Stop 9745, Mississippi, MS 39762, USA
e-mail: jwilmoth@humansci.msstate.edu

W. Jeynes, E. Martinez (eds.), *Ministering Spiritually to Families*,
DOI 10.1007/978-3-319-13302-7_6

be much more effective when pastors use proven methods and resources. Although adequate discussion of marriage preparation would require at least book-length treatment, in this chapter I want to introduce several important aspects of effective marriage preparation: (1) background information related to clergy involvement in marriage preparation; (2) best practices for marriage preparation, based on the research; and (3) the attitudes and behaviors of U.S. clergy related to marriage preparation, as discovered in our own research.

Background Information Related to Clergy Involvement in Marriage Preparation

Marriage Preparation in the United States

In the United States, the risk for divorce is higher than in other Western countries, with approximately half of marriages expected to end in divorce (Schoen and Canudas-Romo 2006). The Centers for Disease Control (2009) reported that the marriage rate is 7.1 per 1000 people and the divorce rate is 3.5 per 1000 people. The financial cost of marital dissolution for the state, local, and federal governments has been estimated to range from $ 33.3 to $ 112 billion per year (Scafidi 2008; Schramm 2006). In addition to financial costs, the individuals involved in a divorce often experience negative outcomes: depression and reduced commitment to marriage (Amato and DeBoer 2001; Simon 2002), maternal stress and quality of parenting (Osborne and McLanahan 2007), and unhealthy relationship dynamics (Booth and Amato 2001). Increased risks for negative emotional, behavioral, and health outcomes for children also have been associated with family fragmentation (Amato 2007). In contrast, Wilcox et al. noted the opposite to be true for healthy marriages:

> Communities where good-enough marriages are common have better outcomes for children, women, and men than do communities suffering from high rates of divorce, unmarried childbearing, and high-conflict or violent marriages. Moreover, as we have seen, the benefits of a strong marriage culture extend across lines of race, ethnicity, and class. (2005, p. 32).

Multiple studies have demonstrated the potential for adverse impacts from marital conflict or divorce not only for couples but particularly for children. Many of the effects are especially apparent in the months immediately following parental divorce (Hetherington and Stanley-Hagan 1999). For example, immediately following parental divorce children are more likely to participate in early sexual activity (Ellis et al. 2003; Jeynes 2001c) and to consume alcohol (Jeynes 2001a; Tomcikova et al. 2009) and other drugs (Jeynes 2001b). Furthermore, effects often linger into adulthood (Amato and Cheadle 2005; Cherlin et al. 1998). Some of the long-term effects identified in the literature include reduced educational attainment (Amato and Cheadle 2005; Biblarz and Gottainer 2000; Jeynes 2000), reduced levels of marital commitment and confidence (Whitton et al. 2008), marital problems, and tension between parents and children (Amato and Cheadle 2005; Yu et al. 2010). Of particular interest to clergy is the finding that individuals whose parents divorce are less likely to maintain their connection to religious congregations as adults (Myers 1996).

On average, children whose parents divorce are more likely to have adjustment problems socially, emotionally, and academically compared to children in nondivorced families. The greatest effects for the adjustment of children are most likely to be externalizing disorders such as aggressive, antisocial, and noncompliant behavior as well as low social responsibility, absence of self-regulation, and diminished cognitive achievement and agency. Internalizing disorders associated with divorce include anxiety and depression, and children are more likely to have difficulties in relationships with siblings, parents, teachers, and peers (Hetherington and Stanley-Hagan 1999).

Premarital education has been shown to be one of the most effective interventions available to prevent marital dissolution and improve marital satisfaction (Stahmann and Hiebert 1997; Stanley 2001). For example, Stanley et al. (2006) found marriage preparation to be associated with a 31 % lower rate of divorce in a large multi-state random survey.

Clergy Involvement in Marriage Preparation

Although barely one third of couples currently receive premarital counseling, more than 90 % of couples that receive marriage preparation do so from a church or religious institution (Glenn 2005). Among the respondents to our national survey, a clergyperson performs an average of 4.91 weddings annually ($SD = 6.19$), although nearly half conduct two or fewer a year. Even though clergy already provide most premarital education, scholars and marriage advocates have called for an increased emphasis on effective premarital education by churches and clergy (e.g., Institute for American Values 2000; Stanley 2001; Stanley et al. 2001). Clergy often have been singled out as having several advantages for providing marriage preparation: access to and influence with couples, since as many as 80 % of first marriages occur in religious organizations (Stanley et al. 2001); a belief in the value of marriage; a strong educational tradition; and an institutional base of operations (Stanley et al. 1995).

In addition to having unparalleled opportunities for providing marriage preparation, clergy also have the ability to provide the service effectively. For example, Stanley et al. (2001) discovered that clergy and lay religious leaders were as effective in the short run as university staff in presenting PREP (Prevention and Relationship Enhancement Program; Markman et al. 1988), a program created to prevent marital distress and divorce.

Well-constructed premarital programs show evidence of having a significant short-term effect on behaviors related to marital satisfaction (Carroll and Doherty 2003; Fagan et al. 2002). However, long-term effects have not been established as definitively (Halford et al. 2008). Also, since many studies showing efficacy of premarital education have been conducted with mainly white, highly-educated couples (see Halford et al. 2008; Hawkins et al. 2008), it is possible that these programs might not have the same effect among groups with social disadvantages that are highly correlated with the risk of divorce (Ooms and Wilson 2004).

Schumm et al. (2010) found that the quality of premarital counseling, specifically within a religious setting, predicts both the short- and long-term helpfulness of premarital counseling in a couple's relationship. Although clergy have the opportunity and capability to provide quality marriage preparation, questions remain about the current effectiveness of clergy-provided programs (Wilmoth and Smyser 2007). Because little was known about the content and requirements of marriage preparation provided by clergy (Wilmoth and Fournier 2009), we conducted a national study to see what marriage preparation looks like in the United States. This study is the first to use national random sampling to determine the behaviors and attitudes of clergy related to marriage preparation. More details about the study are discussed later in the chapter.

Best Practices in Premarital Education Based on Research

After pastors have made the decision to prepare couples for marriage, they have several important questions to answer:

- *What kind of structure will I use?* This broad question includes aspects such as the number of sessions to have with a couple; how long the sessions will be; how long before the wedding they will start; whether to use an assessment inventory; whether to include the couple alone or in group classes; whether to conduct all the sessions personally or to ask someone else to help, such as a mentor couple, a financial counselor, a therapist, or a relationship educator; and whether the process will be information-based or skills-based.
- *What content will I cover?* Marriages are complex relationships, and their success includes many dimensions. Which are the most important areas of content for the pastor to cover during marriage preparation?
- *What resources will I incorporate?* Pastors can use homework, readings, videos, and other sources. In addition, a number of formal programs and curricula designed specifically for marriage preparation are available. Many pastors have joined healthy marriage initiatives and have signed Community Marriage Policies®, agreeing to a common set of standards for marriage preparation: Is this something the pastor wants to participate in?

Structural Components of Marriage Preparation

One of the important decisions pastors must make is how to structure marriage preparation. Murray (2005) observed that dosage, format, and approach are three important process-related aspects of effective marriage preparation. In addition, Hawkins et al. (2004a) identified intensity and methodology as crucial components of decision-making for marriage educators.

Timing and dosage For long-term behavioral change to occur, the length and intensity of marriage preparation are key factors. One study revealed that couples that had attended four or more education sessions rated their marriage preparation significantly higher than those that attended no sessions or one session of premarital education. Additionally, the study's findings suggested that 10 or more education sessions did not increase the perceived value of the marriage preparation and may even be counterproductive (Williams et al. 1999). Hawkins et al. (2008) meta-analysis revealed that programs with a moderate dosage of instructional time produce significantly stronger effects.

Stahmann and Hiebert (1997) recommended that, for counseling to be more beneficial, clergy should provide at least five to seven, 2-h sessions beginning several months before the wedding. Barlow (1999) also noted that premarital education should be 6–8 months before the wedding and consist of six to eight 1-h sessions. Sullivan's small study ($n=62$; 2001) found that clergy most frequently provided four to six education sessions with a range of 30–90 min per session. Our national study looked at the structural components that pastors require for marriage preparation. When a preparation or waiting period before the wedding was required, the average length of time was 3.21 months ($Mdn=4.00$, $SD=1.01$). When meetings or sessions with the pastor were required, the average number of sessions required was 3.98 sessions ($Mdn=4.00$, $SD=2.12$). The average time per session required was 68.5 min ($Mdn=60.0$, $SD=27.16$).

Another component of marriage preparation that has been recommended by scholars is follow-up sessions after the wedding (Stahmann and Hiebert 1997). Murray (2005) noted that some providers have expressed an interest in providing booster sessions to refresh the couple's skills. My Oklahoma study (2005) found that very few Oklahoma clergy provide such post-wedding services. Among pastors who include sessions after the wedding, our national study found the average was 1.65 sessions ($Mdn=1.00$, $SD=1.00$). These meetings or sessions took place an average of 5.47 months after the wedding ($Mdn=6.00$, $SD=3.35$).

Format Murray (2005) noted that marriage preparation employs diverse formats such as one-on-one sessions, classrooms, and support groups. Williams (1992) found that engaged couples prefer the following formats: counseling sessions with a minister, weekend retreats, meeting with a married couple, and small group discussions. Private sessions with a sponsor or mentor couple also were highly regarded (Williams et al. 1999). My 2005 study of Oklahoma clergy found that mentor or sponsor couples and group premarital classes were among the least required components of marriage preparation. Our national study found that 68.9 % never required group classes and 73.5 % never required meetings with mentor couples.

Skills The format of marriage preparation also is distinguished by whether the approach is information-based or skills-based. Information-based premarital education promotes understanding of a concept (i.e., knowledge or attitudes about marriage) through lectures, demonstrations, and/or audio-visual presentations. Skills-based marriage preparation not only promotes understanding and knowledge but also provides opportunities to practice relationship skills and receive feedback on these skills (Halford et al. 2003; Hawkins et al. 2004a; Trathen 1995). Skills most often addressed are communication, conflict resolution, and problem solving. As noted by Halford (2004), examples of skills-based relationship education are PREP, Relationship Enhancement program (RE; Guerney 1977), and Couple Commitment and Relationship Enhancement program (Couple Care; Halford et al. 2004).

An example of teaching communication skills is PREP's use of the Speaker-Listener technique. The process is based on the idea of letting one person at a time have the "floor," while the other person in the dyad focuses on listening. Rules for the speaker are (1) Speak for yourself, don't mind read! (2) Keep statements brief. Don't go on and on. (3) Stop to let the listener paraphrase. The listener has two rules: (1) Paraphrase what you hear. (2) Focus on the speaker's message; don't rebut. During a PREP seminar, each couple has multiple opportunities to practice the technique as they discuss low-conflict topics, and the instructor or an assistant will observe the discussion to provide feedback on using the technique effectively (Stanley et al. 1999). Another example is the Couple Communication model (Miller et al. 1992), which guides couples through the use of the Awareness Wheel and the Listening Cycle, providing hands-on practice and feedback from the instructor.

Similarly, skills-based curricula often teach methods of conflict resolution and problem solving. For example, PREPARE-ENRICH (Olson et al. 1986) provides a couple feedback form that includes exercises for practicing assertive communication, active listening, managing conflict, and solving problems. The pastor typically will ask the couple to work through the exercises during the marriage preparation sessions, and the pastor can provide feedback on ways to improve the skills.

Research has shown that this type of premarital education is effective because crucial relationship skills can be learned (Halford et al. 2004) and because the training is based on variables that influence relationship outcomes (Halford 2004). Hahlweg et al. (1998) found that skills-based premarital education is associated with higher levels of relationship satisfaction and functioning even after 5 years of marriage. Additionally, skills-based education improves couple communication (Hahlweg et al. 1998) and reduces the risk of future relationship problems (Halford et al. 2003).

Although research has found skills-based premarital education to be useful in influencing marital outcomes for most couples (see Halford 2004; Halford et al. 2003), only 26.5 % of clergy in our national sample reported using a skills-based strategy, "which not only promotes understanding but also provides the opportunity to practice learned skills" (Wilmoth 2005). Given that the skills-based approach is the only method of marriage preparation that has reliably demonstrated its effectiveness (see Hahlweg et al. 1998; Halford et al. 2003; Hawkins et al. 2004a), this finding suggests that the majority of clergy are still using programs that have not been proven effective.

Using a skills-based approach to marriage preparation requires an investment by the pastor on multiple levels, but the difference in outcomes is worth the extra effort. Buikema (2001) determined that pastors generally are uncomfortable with communication, conflict resolution, and problem solving so teaching premarital couples those skills can be intimidating. Using skills-based curricula such as those mentioned above usually requires 2 or 3 days of training, but I believe most pastors who take advantage of these programs will feel much more confident about their ability to work with premarital (and married) couples.

Premarital Assessment Questionnaires Premarital assessment questionnaires (PAQs) are considered a meaningful component of many premarital counseling and educational programs (Larson et al. 2002), including programs provided by clergy. For example, the United States Conference of Catholic Bishops (2008) asks couples to take a marriage preparation inventory, such as Facilitating Open Couple Communication, Understanding, and Study (FOCCUS; Markey and Micheletto 1997), the PreMarital Inventory (PMI; Burnett 2004), or the PREmarital Personal and Relationship Evaluation (PREPARE; Olson et al. 1986). One partial explanation for the widespread use of premarital inventories is the structured training and implementation available for individuals who utilize these instruments (Halford 2004).

Stahmann and Hiebert (1997) suggested six advantages for using PAQs, including the promotion of couple involvement, the investment of couples in the process, and the opportunity to elicit information more efficiently than through an interview. Halford (2004) also reported that some PAQs, such as FOCCUS, PREPARE, and RELATionship Evaluation (RELATE), assess factors relevant to relationship satisfaction, as evidenced by their ability to predict satisfaction in the early years of marriage (e.g., Holman et al. 1994; Larsen and Olson 1989; Williams and Jurich 1995), and provides couples the opportunity to use this information to assess their personal risk and resilience profiles. Busby et al. (2007) also noted that inventories provide information to facilitators and couples that make it possible to focus on specific issues that are particularly relevant for the couple.

Halford (2004) suggested two weaknesses of inventory-based premarital education. First, there is no empirical evidence of long-term benefits, and some would suggest that revealing partner differences or relationship weaknesses might actually create problems for the couple unless they have necessary skills to deal with the revelations (Silliman et al. 2002, cited in Halford 2004). Second, some self-report assessments may not identify dynamics, such as certain communication deficits, that can be detected only with observational assessments (Larson et al. 1995; Sanders et al. 1999). Therefore, Halford (2004) recommended using an inventory in conjunction with development of cognition and skills, an approach that Busby et al. (2007) suggested would alleviate some of these concerns.

Clergy report using a variety of assessment instruments in marriage preparation, some of which may not be optimal for use with premarital couples (Sullivan 2001; Wilmoth 2005). Larson et al. (1995) suggested that for premarital inventories to be adequate they must (1) be designed primarily for assessing the premarital relationship, (2) collect comprehensive data that are relevant to marriage preparation, (3) be easy to administer and interpret, (4) have a wide application, and (5) be reliable and valid. After analyzing various premarital assessments, Larson et al. (1995) concluded that the following instruments were the most psychometrically sound: PREPARE, the PREP-M (PREParation for Marriage), and FOCCUS. They specifically excluded the Taylor-Johnson Temperament Analysis (T-JTA; Taylor and Morrison 1984) and the Myers-Briggs Type Indicator Relationship Report (MBTI; Hammer 1987) "because they assess only personality and couple personality matches and do not focus on the broader dimensions of premarital relationships" (Larson et al. 1995, p. 247). Subsequent analysis determined that PREPARE, FOCCUS, and RELATE (previously known as the PREP-M) "may be confidently used in premarital assessment and counseling" (Larson et al. 2002, p. 238). Although the MBTI and T-JTA possibly can provide helpful supplemental information, I do not recommend that pastors use them as their primary assessment tools for premarital couples. Some pastors also find it helpful to develop their own questionnaires to cover topics not covered in the PAQs, especially items related to distinctive doctrinal issues.

The PREPARE inventory, oldest of the "big three" PAQs, originally was developed through research at the University of Minnesota. It consists of 30 background questions and 165 additional items, measuring 20 relationship areas dealing with personality, family-of-origin, and other significant issues for couples (Olson et al. 1986). The latest version of FOCCUS, which was developed at Creighton University, a Catholic institution, consists of 156 items and 33 additional, optional items that were designed to give couples a relationship profile, detailing both the weaknesses and strengths in the relationship. RELATE, developed by scholars at Brigham Young University, consists of 271 items that measure how variables such as family background, personality, values, and social relationships will affect future marital quality and stability (RELATE Institute 2009).

As Halford (2004) noted, a fundamental weakness of using inventories in premarital education is the lack of published systematic evaluation of the long-term effects on relationship outcomes. Although evaluation of inventories has been limited to short-term outcomes, some studies have shown at least moderate effectiveness. Knutson and Olson (2003) evaluated the effectiveness of the PREPARE Program by comparing couples ($n=59$) who received an average of four feedback sessions after completing the inventory with a control group ($n=48$) and with couples ($n=27$) who took the inventory but had no feedback. Both PREPARE groups significantly increased scores on the Couple Satisfaction Scale, while there was no change in the control group. Additionally, both PREPARE groups also made gains in several relationship skills and other relationship areas. Of the highest risk couples, 83 % moved to a more positive couple type (Knutson and Olson 2003).

Busby et al. (2007) compared the effectiveness of three models of premarital education: self-directed, using a 20-page workbook that all couples receive when they apply for a marriage license in the State of Texas; therapist-directed, assigning participants to meet for six 1-h sessions with professionally trained therapists; and assessment-based. Couples in the assessment-based group received the RELATE inventory and accompanying report, and each couple met with a facilitator trained to use the report in a six-session program. At the sixth month follow-up, the assessment-based treatment resulted in significantly better scores on the problem area scales than either of the other treatments and had significantly better scores in satisfaction and communication compared to the therapist-directed treatment (Busby et al. 2007). Larson et al. (2007) found that RELATE is a positive intervention tool, improving couple communication skills, preventing future relationship or marital problems, increasing preparedness for marriage, and improving relationship satisfaction (Larson et al. 2007).

Although PAQs show evidence of being an important component of premarital education, few clergy use one of the three instruments identified by Larson et al. (1995, 2002) as being appropriate for premarital couples. Of those clergy who used an inventory (51 %), Sullivan (2001) found that 18 % used PREPARE, and none reported using either RELATE or FOCCUS. Sullivan (2001) also found that 11 % of clergy used MBTI and 28 % used T-JTA.

Similarly, our Oklahoma study (2005) found that 47.1 % of clergy used some kind of inventory. Of these, 28.3 % used the MBTI at least some of the time, 19.3 % used PREPARE, 17.9 % used T-JTA, 4.5 % used FOCCUS, and 2.1 % used RELATE. In addition, 12.7 % indicated they used another inventory, including informal questionnaires the clergy constructed. In our national study, when clergy required a premarital inventory, the most frequently required instrument was PREPARE ($n = 111$, 13.6 %) followed by FOCCUS ($n = 57$, 7.0 %).

Besides the traditional pencil and paper format, RELATE and PREPARE also are now available for couples to take online. Generally pastors that use PREPARE must attend a 1-day training workshop, which usually costs about $ 175. Those who have a master's degree or doctorate in the field of counseling also have the option of completing a self-training program at a cost of $ 225. Facilitators who use FOCCUS also must attend a 1-day training workshop, at a cost of about $ 100. The widely used Marriage Savers program also provides training for FOCCUS facilitators as a foundation for their mentoring program. Pastors who desire to use RELATE must provide proof of their ministerial card.

Almost two-thirds of the clergy in our national study say they require a couple inventory at least part of the time, and 40 % say they always require an inventory. However, many of the instruments either were not designed specifically for marriage preparation or have not been proved to be reliable or valid. I believe that using one of these three PAQs designed for premarital assessment is one of the most versatile and effective tools at a pastor's disposal, particularly when combined with alert observation of relationship patterns that might not show up in a pencil-and-paper inventory. In addition, the 1-day training workshops will be a profitable experience, providing much valuable information in addition to securing the privilege of using the premarital inventory.

Marriage Mentors

Sandstrom defined marriage mentoring as "the actions of a more experienced married couple (mentor) who empower and support a premarital couple (mentee) and who act as a guide and role model, sharing resources and relational experiences" (2004, p. 7). Although the effectiveness of using marriage mentors in premarital education has not been evaluated thoroughly (Doherty and Anderson 2004), anecdotal evidence and limited empirical data suggest that marriage mentors can provide support, skills, and inspiration that clergy and other professionals cannot (Institute for American Values 2000; McManus 1995; Wages 2003).

Barlow (1999) noted that mentor couples "allow for the benefit of experience to enter into the premarital preparation process" (1999, p. 7–8). Similarly, McManus (2001) observed that engaged couples relate better to a married couple than to a pastor or counselor, develop more honesty and rapport with another married couple, and use the mentor couple as a positive marriage role model. Wages (2003) found that mentor couples provide a more realistic view of marriage and help resolve relationship issues for engaged couples. In addition, Sandstrom's (2004) findings showed that marriage mentoring potentially has both short- and long-term effects on premarital couples. One short-term effect was that mentor couples were beneficial in providing support for the engaged couple, giving them confidence in starting their marriage. Long-term effects included dealing with in-law relationships and family-of-origin issues. Sandstrom (2004) also suggested that these benefits derived from including mentor couples in premarital education could help decrease the divorce rate, especially during the first year of marriage.

Although there has been little research to demonstrate the effectiveness of including marriage mentoring, experience suggests that it has potential to be an effective approach to preparing couples for marriage. More important, it is an example of incorporating biblical principles for discipleship into the marriage preparation process (2 Timothy 2:2, Titus 2:1–5). Internet sites describing several mentoring programs are listed in Appendix 1.

Prohibition of Premarital Sex and Cohabitation

Our national study found that 42.7% of clergy say they require couples to remain sexually abstinent. However well-intentioned they may be, policies such as these can be problematic considering the high percentage of couples that have been sexually active before marriage and considering that 49% of cohabitating couples marry within 5 years of cohabitation (Kennedy and Bumpass 2008). As far back as 1993, Markman et al. found that 80% of the couples participating in their study were sexually active and 39% of the couples were living together before marriage. Hawkins et al. (2004b) suggest that premarital education may be particularly beneficial for cohabiting couples and that churches may need to be proactive in reaching this audience:

> … marriage educators have an important role to play with couples who choose to cohabit before marriage. Religious organizations that require couples—cohabiting or not—to participate in premarital education before marrying will help, especially if they are designed to emphasize needed skills and knowledge, and not dwell as much on issues, such as sexuality, with which cohabiting couples are already familiar. It is important for these religious institutions to involve rather than shun cohabiting couples who may need their services more than couples who do not cohabit before marriage. (2004b, p. 44)

While Hawkins et al. (2004b) make a compelling case that churches can—and should—help cohabiting couples prepare for marriage, not all clergy would agree with the recommendation that it is best to avoid dwelling on sexuality. Research indicates that cohabitors, compared to non-cohabitors, are more likely to have had more sexual partners, and cohabiting women are more likely to be unfaithful after marriage (Forste and Tanfer 1996). Thus, increased sexual experience could be a disadvantage in forming healthy sexual attitudes and behaviors. Similarly, suggest that the experience of cohabitation may affect commitment levels in marriage.

Topics Covered in Marriage Preparation

Research and theory have identified content appropriate for effective marriage preparation. Hawkins et al. (2004a) suggest that the following three subdivisions of content should be included in premarital education: (1) relationship skills; (2) awareness, knowledge, and attitudes; and (3) motivation and virtues. In addition, Bradbury et al. (2000) determined that the following topics should be included in marriage preparation since research has associated them with marital satisfaction: communication, conflict resolution, social support, careers, children, life stressors and transitions, and family background. Larson and Holman (1994) included additional factors that are significant for marital quality and stability: family-of-origin effects; socioeconomic factors such as age, education, income, and occupation; personality traits; similarity of attitudes, values, and beliefs; interactional history such as length and nature of acquaintance, cohabitation, premarital sex, and premarital pregnancy; and interactional processes such as communication, conflict, and consensus building.

Participants often list communication as one of the most helpful topics in marriage preparation programs (Williams et al. 1999). Research has found that communication processes are able to predict future relationship quality and stability (Clements et al. 2004; Markman et al. 1993), and research-based relationship education programs (e.g., PREP and PREPARE) typically focus on teaching communication skills as a core part of the curriculum (Olson and Olson 1999; Stanley et al. 1999). In addition, Russell and Lyster (1992) found family of origin, finances, conflict resolution, and sexuality among the most helpful content topics. Family-of-origin issues are particularly important to address in premarital education since families of origin influence an individual's expectations and cognitions about and behavior in extrafamilial relations including future romantic relationships (Larson et al. 2001;

Roisman et al. 2001). Phillips et al. (2009) found that individuals who perceive their families of origin as healthy tend to be more satisfied in their romantic relationships. Negative experiences in one's family of origin create poorer attitudes and esteem about adult relationships (Busby et al. 2005) as well as increase dating anxiety and decrease relationship satisfaction and commitment (Larson et al. 2001). The family-of-origin effect is particularly evident in the relationship between parental divorce and children's subsequent marital stability and interactional processes (Amato and DeBoer 2001).

Our national survey tried to get an indication of the topics that pastors include in marriage preparation. Overall, clergy believe they adequately address most of the topics associated with premarital education. For 14 of the 18 topics measured, the mean was at least 3 on a scale of 1 (*Not at All Effectively*) to 5 (*Very Effectively*). The content area that clergy believed they had covered most effectively was the wedding ceremony ($M=4.34$, $Mdn=5.00$, $SD=1.10$), and the topic covered least effectively was legal issues ($M=1.91$, $Mdn=2.00$, $SD=1.59$). Legal issues also was the content area that was least likely to be addressed at all ($n=247$, 30.3 %). Clergy believe the three content areas they cover most effectively are the wedding ceremony, communication, and relationship to God, whereas family planning, career, and legal issues are the areas that clergy believe are least effectively covered in the premarital services they provide.

Resources Pastors Use in Marriage Preparation

Homework Many pastors utilize homework assignments in their work with premarital couples (Wilmoth 2005). Given their own experience of being assigned homework throughout their school years, it is not unexpected that they would intuitively use a similar tool for marriage preparation. Homework also is a component of programs such as PREP, which encourages couples to practice communication skills between workshop sessions (Stanley et al. 1999). L'Abate (1999), a clinical psychologist, has made homework an essential element of his therapeutic, structured environment and distant writing programs, in which assignments are tailored for the specific needs of each couple. Our Oklahoma study (2005) found that more than 80 % of Oklahoma clergy indicated they assigned some homework to engaged couples. Among respondents to our national survey, 36.5 % say they always require homework, and 25 % said they never require it. Among those who gave homework, the average number of assignments required was 3.29 ($Mdn=3.00$, $SD=2.44$).

Some pastors devise their own homework assignments, and others use materials provided with marriage preparation programs such as PREPARE (Olson et al. 1986), *Before You Say "I Do"* (Roberts and Wright 1978), or *Saving Your Marriage Before It Starts* (Parrott and Parrott 1995). As L'Abate (1999) suggests, homework can be tailored to the specific needs of each couple. Assignments can be particularly useful in helping couples work through issues such as setting goals, budgeting, and family of origin.

Premarital Education Programs Dozens of premarital education curricula are available for use in marriage preparation (Stanley 1997; National Healthy Marriage Resource Center 2010). These programs differ according to theoretical orientations, format, length, and content (Carroll and Doherty 2003).

Williams (2003) identified six of the best-known programs in the marriage and family field that are used in premarital counseling. These programs are Relationship Enhancement (Guerney 1977), Couple Communication (Miller et al. 1992), PREP (Stanley et al. 1999), Practical Application of Intimate Relationship Skills (PAIRS; Gordon 1996), PREPARE (Olson et al. 1986), and Association for Couples in Marriage Enrichment-style (ACME; Mace and Mace 1974). These marriage preparation programs also have been distinguished as skills-based education programs, meaning these programs not only promote understanding and knowledge about marriage but also provide opportunities to practice relationship skills and receive feedback on these skills (Halford et al. 2003; Hawkins et al. 2004a; Trathen 1995).

Markman et al. (2004) noted the following as essential components for prevention programs to be empirically based: (1) content is based on basic relationship research, (2) ongoing research examines the program's effectiveness, and (3) content is updated to reflect new research findings. Unfortunately, many popular premarital programs have not reported their effectiveness in peer-reviewed research journals (e.g., Engaged Encounter, Pre-Cana, and Saving Your Marriage Before It Starts; Silliman and Schumm 2000). Of the curricula identified by Williams (2003), only PREP and PREPARE have been evaluated significantly by research. The lack of standardization in curriculum (Callaway 1993), which makes program evaluation difficult, is one explanation for limited research. In addition, religious curricula are less likely to be developed in an academic setting, where there is a greater emphasis on research and publication. Another shortcoming of research is that empirical evaluation of premarital programs generally has focused only on short-term outcomes instead of the more important long-term outcomes such as marital stability (Carroll and Doherty 2003; Stanley 1997).

PREPARE-ENRICH, PREP, and Engaged Encounter were the programs clergy in our national study said they were most likely to use. We are going to describe these at greater length, not only because of their frequency of use but also because they illustrate three different approaches to marriage preparation.

PREP PREP is a marriage preparation program that uses a skills-based approach that focuses on thoughts and behaviors that research has found to be associated with marital success (Renick et al. 1992; Stanley et al. 1999). Specifically, the program focuses on attitudes, expectations, communication, conflict resolution, and commitment (Stanley et al. 1999). The four main goals of PREP regarding couple outcomes are as follows: (1) to teach more efficient communication and conflict resolution skills, (2) to help clarify and evaluate relationship expectations, (3) to increase commitment, and (4) to increase fun, friendship, and sensuality thereby boosting positive bonding. To achieve PREP's goals, the program educates couples on positive approaches to effectively deal with the negative aspects of relationships (Renick et al. 1992; Stanley et al. 2001). For example, PREP teaches couples the Speaker-Listener technique to help reduce communication problems (Stanley et al. 1999).

PREP is a 12-h program with flexibility in format (e.g., six 2-h sessions, weekend, or 1 day with two follow-up sessions; Stanley et al. 1999). PREP providers not only have the flexibility to choose the format but also have the flexibility to choose which sessions/lessons to place more or less emphasis on and to choose the examples and stories that would be most relevant to the couple they are serving (Markman et al. 2004). Each session provides the couple with information followed by an opportunity to practice the skills discussed (Stanley et al. 1999). The PREP leaders provide the couple with feedback during these practice sessions, which helps the couple to further acquire those skills.

During the first hour, communication is discussed in the context of safety and structure, and the Intent-Impact Model of communication is presented. During the second hour, the Speaker-Listener technique is taught. The third hour involves couples learning to give feedback to each other with continued focus on good listening skills. During the fourth and fifth hours, hidden agendas and expectations about the relationship are discussed. The sixth hour deals with the role of fun in the couple's relationship to help maintain stability. The seventh hour focuses on conflict resolution skills. During the eighth hour, team-building issues are introduced to help promote commitment and intimacy between the couple. The ninth and tenth hours deal with spiritual values and how these values impact the relationship. During the 11th hour, the physical relationship is discussed in regards to sensual communication and sexual dysfunction. The final hour focuses on combining the skills learned and teaching the couple how to successfully incorporate them at home (Renick et al. 1992).

PREP leaders must attend a training seminar that presents the PREP material as well as the research and theoretical concepts the program is based on. Renick et al. (1992) noted, "With the proper training, clergy may integrate the skills taught to couples through PREP into their own traditions of premarital counseling" (p. 142). Obtaining the proper training is increasingly becoming more feasible because of the large number of opportunities provided by conferences and workshops. Markman et al. (2004) found that once clergy are trained in PREP, they will provide at least part of the program in the marriage preparation they provide. In addition, Markman et al. (2004) found that a 3-day training seminar is adequate to give clergy the confidence to use the PREP program.

Research has shown that PREP influences short-term marital outcomes. Stanley et al. (2001) found that couples who participated in PREP showed gains in positive communication and problem-solving skills with a decline in negative communication directly after the intervention. Studies by Markman et al. (1988) and Schilling et al. (2003) found similar results. These studies suggest that couples that participate in PREP have an early advantage in regards to interaction outcomes and relationship quality compared to couples who receive more traditional premarital education (Stanley et al. 2001) and that couples are indeed learning the skills taught in the PREP program (Markman et al. 1988).

In addition to short-term outcomes, research has shown PREP to be influential in regards to long-term marital outcomes. For example, Markman et al. (1988) found at the 3-year follow-up that the divorce rate was lower for couples that participated in PREP compared to the control group. Similarly, Markman et al. (1993) found that, even at the 5-year follow-up, PREP couples had a significantly lower divorce rate. In addition, PREP couples maintained relationship satisfaction as well as experienced fewer problems and less sexual dissatisfaction compared to control couples (Markman et al. 1988). Markman et al. (1993) found that PREP gave couples an advantage in communication and conflict resolution skills as much as 4 years later. Specifically, the researchers found PREP couples to have increased communication skills, positive affect, problem-solving skills, and support while they decreased negative communication, withdrawal, denial, dominance, negative affect, conflict, and physical violence (Markman et al. 1993). Similar results were obtained in Germany (see Hahlweg et al. 1998). These research findings suggest that the improvement in relationship skills associated with PREP may be the key to long-term prevention of divorce (Markman et al. 1988).

One advantage of PREP is that it has the option of Christian and Jewish versions, which incorporate theological perspectives. Concepts from the Christian version of the program also are presented in book format in *A Lasting Promise: A Christian Guide to Fighting for Your Marriage* (Stanley et al. 1998).

PREPARE The PREPARE program requires the engaged couple to complete the PREPARE inventory, described above, followed by participation in four to eight feedback sessions where the facilitator teaches the couple essential relationship skills (Life Innovations 2009; Olson and Olson 1999). As discussed earlier, pastors that use PREPARE must attend a workshop to be trained how to correctly administer and use the program (Olson and Olson 1999).

Six couple exercises were added to the inventory to expand PREPARE into a more comprehensive skills-based program for marriage preparation (Olson and Olson 1999). The goals of these exercises are to help the couple in the following areas: (1) relationship strengths and growth areas, (2) communication skills, (3) conflict resolution, (4) family of origin, (5) financial management, and (6) personal, couple, and family goal development (Knutson and Olson 2003). The couples are given the *Building a Strong Marriage* workbook to help couples complete these exercises (Larson et al. 1995; Knutson and Olson 2003; Olson and Olson 1999). During the first exercise, the couple shares their relationship strengths as well as areas they need to work on, thereby creating awareness and better understanding of each other's views. The second exercise involves teaching the couple assertiveness and active listening skills. During the third exercise, the couple learns the Ten Step Model to conflict resolution. In the fourth exercise, the couple receives feedback on family-of-origin issues using the Couple and Family Map, and the fifth exercise involves the couple completing a budget worksheet and setting financial goals. During the final exercise, the couple develops and shares goals for each person, the couple, and the family. They also develop an action plan using the CHANGE model to help accomplish these goals (Olson and Olson 1999).

The PREPARE program is based on the belief that the premarital relationship can predict the quality of the future marital relationship. Therefore, if relationship factors that affect quality can be identified and improved, the quality of the marriage relationship also will be improved (Fowers and Olson 1986). As Fowers and Olson (1986) stated, "Adequate predictive information is the cornerstone of prevention efforts" (¶ 6). Based on this assumption and those factors that have been identified in research as predictors of marital quality and stability, the PREPARE inventory assesses 85 % of these identified premarital relationship factors (Larson et al. 1995).

Knutson and Olson (2003) evaluated the effectiveness of the PREPARE program by comparing couples that received an average of four feedback sessions after completing the inventory with a control group and with couples that took the inventory but had no feedback. Both PREPARE groups significantly increased scores on the Couple Satisfaction Scale, while there was no change in the control group. Additionally, both PREPARE groups also made gains in several relationship skills and other relationship areas including relationship expectations, communication, financial management, children and parenting, family and friends, couple closeness and flexibility, and spiritual beliefs. Of the highest-risk couples, 83 % moved to a more positive couple type (Knutson and Olson 2003).

The combined individual scores and the Couple Positive Agreement score from the questionnaire can discriminate in 91 % of cases between those that will have successful marriages and those that will end in divorce (Fowers and Olson 1986). Furthermore, these combined scores also can discriminate in over 80 % of the cases between couples that are satisfied or dissatisfied with their marriage. Larsen and Olson (1989) found similar results regarding PREPARE's predictive capability: couples were accurately discriminated in 84 % of the cases. These findings support the predictive validity of the PREPARE assessment and its use as a preventive tool (Fowers and Olson 1986; Larsen and Olson 1989).

Based on an engaged couple's PREPARE scores, Fowers and Olson (1992) found a typology to emerge where the couple could be classified as vitalized, harmonious, traditional, or conflicted. This typology is helpful to premarital education providers because it allows for a more focused intervention plan that is directed by the couple's specific needs (Fowers et al. 1996; Fowers and Olson 1992).

Engaged Encounter Engaged Encounter (EE) is a community-based premarital workshop (Silliman and Schumm 2000) in a weekend format that provides a total of 21 h of marriage preparation (Callaway 1993). The program is an outgrowth of Marriage Encounter, which originated in the Catholic Church in 1968, reportedly has been attended by more than 5 million couples in more than 97 countries, and has expanded to numerous Jewish and Christian organizations (Worldwide Marriage Encounter 2010). Limited research has indicated that Marriage Encounter has been popular and effective (Elin 1999).

Engaged Encounter generally is implemented by two or three married couples and a priest. Communication, marriage attitudes, finances, partner expectations, problem-solving strategies, sexuality, and spirituality are the topics covered in EE, with communication receiving the most emphasis (Blumberg 1991; Callaway

1993). EE is "an approach that focuses on exposing couples to sensitive issues with suggestions for change" (Blumberg 1991, p. 12). Topics are first covered by the leaders in a lecture format where the leaders also provide personal examples of coping and dealing with these issues. Then the topics are covered again during a structured sharing time between the engaged couple with exercises involving oral and written communication designed to increase intimacy (Callaway 1993). Partners complete the exercises separately and then discuss the exercises together (Blumberg 1991; Pino 1982).

There has been little empirical research to study the effectiveness of EE, but anecdotal evidence and the program's wide popularity indicate that it is beneficial for many couples. When compared to an information-only-based premarital education program, Callaway (1993) found that EE is more beneficial. However, Callaway's (1993) study also discovered that some participants thought EE to be too long, repetitive, and boring. Callaway hypothesized that these shortcomings could be the result of a discrepancy between the program's format and the participants' learning styles. Blumberg (1991) found that, although EE encourages couple communication, EE was not as effective as PREP in improving couples' communication skills. In addition, Blumberg (1991) discovered that EE couples did not increase their relationship satisfaction after the premarital program.

Partnering with Other Pastors and Educators

Clergy and other wedding officiants in more than 200 communities in 43 states have established Community Marriage Policies (CMPs), setting minimum standards for marriage preparation for any couple whose weddings they perform (Marriage Savers 2007, 2009; McManus 1995). Typically a CMP will include six core elements, including the following related to marriage preparation: (1) require a minimum of 4 months marriage preparation; (2) require a premarital inventory; (3) meet with an older, solidly married Mentor Couple; and (4) cooperate with other congregations to share resources. Some CMPs include other optional elements such as promoting chastity outside of marriage, encouraging a courtship of at least a year, and providing post-marital sessions for newlyweds.

Evaluated counties with CMPs and found that those counties had a decline in the divorce rate nearly twice that of counties established as controls. Several years ago I had the opportunity to initiate a CMP, and I found the experience to be very profitable. As we worked together to write our document and provide community resources, I learned from other pastors and lay leaders, and we encouraged one another to keep marriage preparation a high priority in our community.

Our Research

We have referred to our national sample several times in this chapter. Because there was so little accurate or recent information about this important topic, we conducted a national survey to gather information about the attitudes and practices of pastors related to marriage preparation. I have described the survey below, and more detailed information is available on request.

Method

The sampling frame was based on the *2000 Religious Congregations and Membership Survey* in the Association of Religious Data Archives (2002), which provided information on 149 religious groups, including the number of congregations and adherents for each. Adherents were defined as all full members, their children, and others who regularly attend services. The categories of congregations included evangelical Protestants, mainline Protestants, orthodox, and other groups. The "other" category included both Christian and non-Christian traditions such as Judaism, Islam, Church of Jesus Christ of Latter-day Saints, and Church of Christ, Scientist.

A limitation of the *2000 Religious Congregations and Membership Survey* data is that 14 religious bodies reporting more than 100,000 members to the Yearbook of American and Canadian Churches did not participate in the survey's data collection. In particular, no historically African American denominations participated (e.g., African Methodist Episcopal Church, National Baptist Convention USA Incorporated, or Church of God in Christ).

Our survey was limited to clergy from the three largest religious groups in the United States, based on the number of adherents in each: Roman Catholic (43.9%), evangelical Protestant (28.3%), and mainline Protestant (18.5%). We excluded the orthodox category, which was too small (0.7%) for statistical analysis, and the "other" category (8.7%), which we deemed too heterogeneous for meaningful comparisons.

In order to make statistically meaningful comparisons among denominations, we further limited the sampling frame to the 15 Christian denominations with the largest number of congregations. We used stratified random sampling to select 2000 congregations. The rationale for basing the sample on congregations rather than clergy was threefold: (1) our interest was in premarital education provided in the context of the congregational setting, (2) it was more feasible to construct an exhaustive list from which to draw the sample, and (3) congregational addresses are more stable than clergy addresses. The number of participants selected from each denomination was calculated using the ratio of the number of congregations within that denomination to the total number of congregations in the sampling frame. Therefore, 46.5% of this study's sample was composed of evangelical Protestant congregations ($n=930$), 42% mainline Protestants ($n=840$), and 11.5% Roman Catholic ($n=230$).

Of the 2000 congregations surveyed, there were 820 responses, a response rate of 41 %. Of the 820 returned responses, 793 (96.7 %) were usable for data analysis. Clergy who responded tended to be male (91.2 %), married (84.0 %), Caucasian (90.3 %), evangelical Protestant (49.8 %), and a senior pastor (93.0 %). The mean age was 53.1 years (*SD*=10.9), the mean years in ministry was 23.1 (*SD*=13.0), and the mean tenure in the clergy's current position was 8.32 years (*SD*=8.10). Clergy who responded typically had a master's degree (53.0 %) with 2.01 (*SD*=2.38) college or seminary courses related to marriage preparation as well as 2.48 (*SD*=3.53) related continuing education opportunities. Although the mean of active congregational members was 429.1, half of the congregations had fewer than 150 members.

The Questionnaire

The 4-page, 126-item, self-report questionnaire was modified from the "Oklahoma Clergy Involvement in Marriage Preparation" questionnaire (Wilmoth 2005). The instrument included seven sections: demographics, structural requirements set by clergy for marriage preparation, content, resources, value and effectiveness, hindrances, and community marriage initiatives. We distributed the questionnaire by mail, and participants whose email addresses were available also had the opportunity to complete the survey online.

To discover what structural requirements clergy set for marriage preparation, participants were asked to indicate on a Likert-type scale, ranging from 0 (*Never Require*) to 4 (*Always Require*), how often they require each of the following structural components: preparation/waiting period before the wedding, premarital couple inventory, meetings or sessions with pastor, group premarital class/education/enrichment, mentor or sponsor couples, homework, church membership, premarital sexual abstinence, and meetings/sessions after the wedding. The Requirements Scale (range: 0–36, $\alpha=0.71$) was constructed by summing each of nine individual items.

In addition, if clergy required a preparation/waiting period before the wedding, they were asked the length of the waiting period in months. If clergy required completion of a premarital couple inventory, the participant was asked to identify which one they required. If clergy required meetings or sessions with the pastor, respondents were asked the number of sessions required as well as the length of time in minutes per session. If clergy required homework, the participants were asked to indicate the number of assignments given. Finally, if meetings or sessions after the wedding were required, the clergy were asked to list the number of sessions required and how many months after the wedding the sessions took place.

To discover what content areas were covered in clergy-provided marriage preparation, participants were asked how effectively they deal with each of the following content areas: the wedding ceremony, realistic expectations, roles, children/parenting, career, personality/temperament, relationship to God, communication, conflict resolution, problem-solving, family of origin, finances/budgeting, in-law relationships, friends, sexual relations, family planning, spiritual dimensions of marriage, and legal issues.

To determine the format clergy use in marriage preparation, participants were asked to check which of the following best describes their approach to marriage preparation: (1) information-based, which focused on helping someone understand a concept, and (2) skills-based, which not only promotes understanding but also provides the opportunity to practice learned skills.

Study Conclusions

Consistent with previous research (e.g., Sullivan 2001; Wilmoth 2005), this study found that clergy-provided marriage preparation consists of approximately four 1-h sessions even though Stahmann and Hiebert (1997) recommended five to seven sessions for counseling to be beneficial. In addition, this study found that sessions after the wedding are one of the least required components of premarital education even though Buckner and Salt (1985) and Murray (2005) recommended providing these booster sessions to help identify and address both problems and joys of married life.

Also, this study found that most clergy require some kind of premarital assessment. PREPARE and FOCCUS, which are two out of the three assessments that Larson et al. (2002) stated could be confidently used in marriage preparation, were the instruments most frequently used by clergy. However, this study also found that a significant number of clergy continue to utilize assessments that may not be appropriate for marriage preparation (see Larson et al. 1995; Wilmoth and Smyser 2010).

Although recent research has suggested the effectiveness of using mentor couples in marriage preparation (e.g., Sandstrom 2004), this study found that mentoring was the least required component of clergy-provided premarital education. This finding suggests that even though mentors could offer insight and support to newly-married couples, clergy do not perceive their potential effectiveness or do not know how to implement such a program.

Additionally, this study found that only a fourth of clergy reported using a skills-based format for marriage preparation even though Halford et al. (2003) found skills-based premarital education to be useful in influencing marital outcomes. Given that the skills-based approach to marriage preparation is the only method that has reliably demonstrated effectiveness (see Hawkins et al. 2004a), this finding suggests that most clergy are still using approaches that have not proved effective.

In regards to topics covered in the premarital education program, this study found that clergy do not effectively cover or address family-of-origin issues, which research has shown to be a significant factor in determining marital quality and stability (see Larson and Holman 1994). Other important areas that researchers have suggested be included in premarital education but that clergy reported being less effective at addressing were conflict resolution and problem-solving (see Bradbury et al. 2000).

Although the response rate for this study was reasonably high, the rate of response could have been hindered by the length of the instrument. In addition, the results are subject to all the limitations of self-report questionnaires. Generalizability also was reduced by restricting the sample to evangelical Protestant, mainline Protestant, and Roman Catholic clergy and by using a database that did not include historically African American denominations. Future research should investigate whether these findings would be replicated among clergy from other religious traditions.

Conclusion

I suggest that clergy have not only the opportunity but also the obligation to provide quality marriage preparation to the couples in their congregations. The research literature makes it clear that marital conflict and divorce frequently have a devastating and lasting effect on the couple and their children. Marital disruption also has a direct impact on religious congregations since families are less likely to stay connected to their church after divorce. Investing in these marriages can counteract the cultural message that marriage is trivial and transient, and the investment can yield dividends for churches and families that continue to grow across generations.

It is significant that the large study of couples in Oklahoma and neighboring states found that couples with premarital education experienced a 30% decline in the likelihood of divorce over 5 years (Stanley et al. 2006). However, I believe that this evidence for the effectiveness of marriage preparation is even more remarkable when you consider that this study did not measure what kind of premarital education the couples received. If any sort of program makes this big a difference, certainly we can expect that quality, evidenced-based marriage preparation can help couples have healthy, lasting, God-honoring marriages.

Based on the research, clergy should consider including several specific components in the marriage preparation they provide:

- Begin at least 6 months before the wedding.
- Include at least six sessions.
- Follow up several months after the wedding.
- Utilize one of the three validated premarital assessment questionnaires.
- Pair premarital couples with mentor couples.
- Use a skills-based approach to communication, conflict resolution, and problem solving.
- Address important topics such as family-of-origin influences, sexual relationships, parenting, and finances.

Researchers also have suggested that clergy can provide a dimension to marriage preparation that goes beyond what most therapists or educators can offer. Teaching couples how to communicate, solve problems, and manage conflict can help couples face challenges with skill and confidence; giving accurate, relevant information about finances, family of origin, and sex can help them avoid potential pitfalls. Yet, however important skills and information might be, a successful marriage is primarily a matter of the heart. Clergy can go beyond talking about the importance of commitment, faithfulness, and kindness and point individuals to spiritual resources that can transform relationships.

As a former pastor, I know something about the demands of ministry. Very few clergy can do all the things that research suggests might be helpful. I'd like to recommend some principles that I believe will help you use your time productively and be more effective when you prepare couples for marriage.

First, *invest in yourself.* Clergy often express concerns about their lack of expertise and sometimes feel they need to say to couples, "Do as I say, not as I do." Couples cannot learn relationship skills simply by being told what to do: They need to see examples and then practice those skills. By receiving training in a curriculum such as PREP or Couple Communication, you can confidently say, "Let me show you what to do." The appendix provides websites for several research-based curricula.

Second, *tailor your marriage preparation* to the unique needs of each couple. No two couples will have identical strengths and challenges. It will be much more efficient—and effective—to focus on the areas that would be most helpful for a particular couple. An inventory such as PREPARE is one of the best ways to determine which areas to emphasize. (Contact information for the three most appropriate questionnaires is in the appendix.) Not only does this kind of instrument help you know the needs of the couple, but it also provides useful tools to deal with important issues. Again, an upfront investment in your preparation can help you use your time and energy more effectively.

Third, *share the load.* Depending on your interests and resources, you may be better off to delegate some or (almost) all of the marriage preparation to one or more colleagues. For example, there may be someone else on your staff or in your congregation who could help the couple set financial goals and learn how to use a budget. I also believe that using mentor couples is a great idea. Although there's little research on the effectiveness of marriage mentoring, there is much anecdotal evidence that this is an idea that works. Just as important, it is a method of discipleship with strong biblical support. The appendix lists some of the programs that provide resources for an effective mentoring program.

Preparing couples for marriage is a ministry that can have powerful, long-lasting benefits. This is a ministry that needs to be done and to be done well. I urge you to make a commitment to providing marriage preparation, a ministry that changes lives, marriages, and families.

Appendix

Websites for Selected Resources

The following Internet sites are examples of programs or resources related to marriage preparation. This list is not exhaustive, but it includes some of the best-known sources.

Curricula Couple Communication: http://www.couplecommunication.com

Engaged Encounter

Catholic: http://www.engagedencounter.org/
United Methodist: http://www.encounter.org/ee.htm

The Marriage Garden: http://www.uaex.edu/health-living/personal-family-well-being/couples/

Married and Loving It: http://marriedandlovingit.org/wp/

PREP: www.PrepInc.com

Relationship Enhancement: www.nire.org

Premarital Assessment Questionnaires PREPARE: www.prepare-enrich.com

FOCCUS: www.foccusinc.com

RELATE: www.relate-institute.org

Mentor Training Programs Marriage Mentoring: 12 Conversations for Building Strong Marriages, Ed Gray: www.12conversations.com

Marriage Savers, Mike & Harriet McManus: www.marriagesavers.org

PREPARE/ENRICH Customized Version Marriage Mentor Program, David Olson et al., www.prepare-enrich.com

The Complete Guide to Marriage Mentoring, Les & Leslie Parrott: http://www.marriagementoring.com

General information National Healthy Marriage Resource Center: www. http://www.healthymarriageinfo.org/

Smart Marriages: www.smartmarriages.com/app/Directory.BrowsePrograms

References

Amato, P. R. (2007). Divorce and the well-being of adults and children. *National Council on Family Relations Report, 52,* F3–F4, F18.

Amato, P. R., & Cheadle, J. (2005). The long reach of divorce: Divorce and child well-being across three generations. *Journal of Marriage and Family, 67,* 191–206.

Amato, P. R., & DeBoer, D. D. (2001). The transmission of marital instability across generations: Relationship skills or commitment to marriage? *Journal of Marriage and Family, 63*(4), 1038–1051.

Association of Religious Data Archives. (2002). Religious congregations and membership in the United States, 2000. From the Association of Statisticians of American Religious Bodies and the Association of Religion Data Archives web site. http://www.thearda.com/mapsReports/reports/US_2000.asp. Accessed 6 Oct 2008.

Barlow, J. L. (1999). A new model for premarital counseling within the church. *Pastoral Psychology, 48,* 3–9.

Biblarz, T. J., & Gottainer, G. (2000). Family structure and children's success: A comparison of widowed and divorced single-mother families. *Journal of Marriage and the Family, 62,* 533–548.

Blumberg, S. L. (1991). *Premarital intervention programs: A comparison study*. Doctoral dissertation, University of Denver.

Booth, A., & Amato, P. R. (2001). Parental predivorce relations and offspring postdivorce well-being. *Journal of Marriage and Family, 63,* 197–212.

Bradbury, T. N., Fincham, F. D., & Beach, S. R. H. (2000). Research on the nature and determinants of marital satisfaction: A decade in review. *Journal of Marriage and the Family, 62*(4), 964–980.

Buckner, L. P., & Salts, C. J. (1985). A premarital assessment program. *Family Relations, 34,* 513–520.

Buikema, J. K. (2001). *The preparation of pastors in premarital counseling.* Ames: Iowa State University.

Burnett, C. K. (2004). *PreMarital inventory*. Inver Grove Heights: Intercommunications.

Busby, D. M., Gardner, B. C., & Taniguchi, N. (2005). The family of origin parachute model: Landing safely in adult romantic relationships. *Family Relations, 54*(2), 254–264.

Busby, D. M., Ivey, D. C., Harris, S. M., & Ates, C. (2007). Self-directed, therapist-directed, and assessment-based interventions for premarital couples. *Family Relations, 56*(3), 279–290.

Callaway, M. E. (1993). *A study of a marriage preparation programs*. Doctoral dissertation, University of Rhode Island.

Carroll, J. S., & Doherty, W. J. (2003). Evaluating the effectiveness of premarital prevention programs: A meta-analytic review of outcome research. *Family Relations, 52*(2), 105–118.

Center for Disease Control and Prevention. (22 December 2009). Marriage divorce. From the Center for Disease Control and National Center for Health Statistics website. http://www.cdc.gov/nchs/fastats/divorce.htm. Accessed 20 Jan 2013.

Cherlin, A. J., Chase-Lansdale, P. L., & McRae, C. (1998). Effects of parental divorce on mental health throughout the life course. *American Sociological Review, 63,* 239–249.

Clements, M. L., Stanley, S. M., & Markman, H. J. (2004). Before they said "I do": Discriminating among marital outcomes over 13 years. *Journal of Marriage and Family, 66*(3), 613–626.

Doherty, W. J., & Anderson, J. R. (2004). Community marriage initiatives. *Family Relations, 53*(5), 425–432.

Elin, R. J. (1999). Marriage encounter: A positive preventive enrichment program. In R. Berger & M. T. Hannah (Eds.), *Preventive approaches in couples therapy* (pp. 55–72). Philadelphia: Brunner/Mazel.

Ellis, B. J., Bates, J. E., Dodge, K. A., Fergusson, D. M., Horwood, L. J., Pettit, G. S., et al. (2003). Does father absence place daughters at special risk for early sexual activity and teenage pregnancy? *Child Development, 74*(3), 801–821.

Fagan, P. F., Patterson, R. W., & Rector, R. E. (2002). *Marriage and welfare reform: The overwhelming evidence that marriage education works* (No. 1606). Washington, DC: The Heritage Foundation.

Forste, R., & Tanfer, K. (1996). Sexual exclusivity among dating, cohabiting, and married women. *Journal of Marriage & Family, 58*(1), 33–47.

Fowers, B. J., & Olson, D. H. (1986). Predicting marital success with PREPARE: A predictive validity study. *Journal of Marital and Family Therapy, 12*(4), 403–413.

Fowers, B. J., & Olson, D. H. (1992). Four types of premarital couples: An empirical typology based on PREPARE. *Journal of Family Psychology, 6*(1), 10–21.

Fowers, B. J., Montel, K. H., & Olson, D. H. (1996). Predicting marital success for premarital couple types based on PREPARE. *Journal of Marital and Family Therapy, 22*(1), 103–119.

Glenn, N. D. (2005). *With this ring: A national survey on marriage in America*. Washington, DC: National Fatherhood Initiative.

Gordon, L. (1996). *Training manual and curriculum guide* (Available from PAIRS International, 1152 North University Drive, Suite 203, Pembroke Pines, FL 33024).

Guerney, B. G., Jr. (1977). *Relationship enhancement: Skills-training programs for therapy, problem prevention and enrichment*. San Francisco: Jossey-Bass.

Hahlweg, K., Markman, H. J., Thurmaier, F., Engl, J., & Eckert, V. (1998). Prevention of marital distress: Results of a German prospective longitudinal study. *Journal of Family Psychology, 12*(4), 543–556.

Halford, W. K. (2004). The future of couple relationship education: Suggestions on how it can make a difference. *Family Relations, 53*(5): 559–566.

Halford, W. K., Markman, H. J., Kline, G. H., & Stanley, S. M. (2003). Best practice in couple relationship education. *Journal of Marital and Family Therapy, 29*(3), 385–406.

Halford, W. K., Moore, E., Wilson, K. L., Farrugia, C., & Dyer, C. (2004). Benefits of flexible delivery relationship education: An evaluation of the Couple CARE program. *Family Relations, 53*(5), 469–476.

Halford, W. K., Markman, H. J., & Stanley, S. (2008). Strengthening couples' relationships with education: Social policy and public health perspectives. *Journal of Family Psychology, 22*(3), 497–505.

Hammer, A. L. (1987). *The Myers-Briggs type indicator relationship report*. Palo Alto: Counseling Psychologists Press.

Hawkins, A. J., Carroll, J. S., Doherty, W. J., & Willoughby, B. (2004a). A comprehensive framework for marriage education. *Family Relations, 53*(5), 547–558.

Hawkins, A. J., Carroll, J. S., Doherty, W. J., & Willoughby, B. (2004b). A comprehensive framework for marriage education. From the Administration for Children and Families web site. http://www.acf.hhs.gov/programs/opre/strengthen/compreh_frmwk/reports/comp_frmwk/comp_frmwk_title.html. Accessed 20 Jan 2013.

Hawkins, A. J., Blanchard, V. L., Baldwin, S. A., & Fawcett, E. B. (2008). Does marriage and relationship education work? A meta-analytic study. *Journal of Consulting and Clinical Psychology, 76*(5), 723–734.

Hetherington, E. M., & Stanley-Hagan, M. (1999). The adjustment of children with divorced parents: A risk and resiliency perspective. *Journal of Child Psychology & Psychiatry & Allied Disciplines, 40*(1), 129 (Retrieved from EBSCO*host*).

Holman, T. B., Larson, J. H., & Harmer, S. L. (1994). The development and predictive validity of a new premarital assessment instrument: The preparation for marriage questionnaire. *Family Relations, 43*(1), 46–52.

Institute for American Values. (2000). *The marriage movement: A statement of principles*. New York: Institute for American Values.

Jeynes, W. H. (2000). The effects of several of the most common family structures on the academic achievement of eighth graders. *Marriage & Family Review, 30,* 73–97.

Jeynes, W. H. (2001a). The effects of recent parental divorce on their children's consumption of alcohol. *Journal of Youth and Adolescence, 30*(3), 305–319.

Jeynes, W. H. (2001b). The effects of recent parental divorce on their children's consumption of marijuana and cocaine. *Journal of Divorce & Remarriage, 35,* 43–65.

Jeynes, W. H. (2001c). The effects of recent parental divorce on their children's sexual attitudes and behavior. *Journal of Divorce & Remarriage, 35,* 115–133.

Kennedy, S., & Bumpass, L. (2008). Cohabitation and children's living arrangements: New estimates from the United States. *Demographic Research. 19*(47). http://www.demographic-research.org/Volumes/Vol19/47/. Accessed 14 July 2009.

Knutson, L., & Olson, D. H. (2003). Effectiveness of PREPARE program with premarital couples in community settings. *Marriage and Family: A Christian Journal, 6*(4), 529–546.

L'Abate, L. (1999). Structured enrichment and distance writing for couples. In R. Berger & M. T. Hannah (Eds.), *Preventive approaches in couples therapy* (pp. 106–124). Philadelphia: Brunner/Mazel.

Larsen, A. S., & Olson, D. H. (1989). Predicting marital satisfaction using PREPARE: A replication study. *Journal of Marital and Family Therapy, 15*(3), 311–322.

Larson, J. H., & Holman, T. B. (1994). Premarital predictors of marital quality and stability. *Family Relations, 43*(2), 228–237.

Larson, J. H., Holman, T. B., Klein, D. M., Busby, D. M., Stahmann, R. F., & Peterson, D. (1995). A review of comprehensive questionnaires used in premarital education and counseling. *Family Relations, 44,* 245–252.

Larson, J. H., Taggart-Reedy, M., & Wilson, S. M. (2001). The effects of perceived dysfunctional family-of-origin rules on the dating relationships of young adults. *Contemporary Family Therapy: An International Journal, 23*(4), 489–512.

Larson, J. H., Newell, K., Topham, G., & Nichols, S. (2002). A review of three comprehensive premarital assessment questionnaires. *Journal of Marital and Family Therapy, 28*(2), 233–239.

Larson, J. H., Vatter, R. S., Galbraith, R. C., Holman, T. B., & Stahmann, R. F. (2007). The relationship evaluation (RELATE) with therapist-assisted interpretation: Short-term effects on premarital relationships. *Journal of Marital and Family Therapy, 33*(3), 364–374.

Life Innovations. (2009). PREPARE-ENRICH Program. PREPARE-ENRICH web site: https://www.prepare-enrich.com. Accessed 30 Mar 2009.

Mace, D. R., & Mace, V. (1974). *We can have better marriages*. Nashville: Abingdon.

Markey, B., & Micheletto, M. (1997). *Instructor manual for FOCCUS.* Omaha: Archdiocese of Omaha.

Markman, H. J., Floyd, F. J., Stanley, S. M., & Storaasli, R. D. (1988). Prevention of marital distress: A longitudinal investigation. *Journal of Consulting and Clinical Psychology, 56*(2), 210–217.

Markman, H. J., Renick, M. J., Floyd, F. J., Stanley, S. M., & Clements, M. (1993). Preventing marital distress through communication and conflict management training: A 4- and 5-year follow-up. *Journal of Consulting and Clinical Psychology, 61,* 70–77.

Markman, H. J., Whitton, S. W., Kline, G. H., Stanley, S. M., Thompson, H., St. Peters, M., et al. (2004). Use of an empirically based marriage education program by religious organizations: Results of a dissemination trial. *Family Relations, 53*(5), 504–512.

Marriage Savers. (2007). *Marriage savers report card 2007*. Potomac: Author.

Marriage Savers. (2009). CMPs: Where are they? Community Marriage Policy, Marriage Savers web site. http://www.communitymarriagepolicy.org/sitecmp/Locations/locationlist.htm. Accessed 30 Mar 2009.

McManus, M. J. (1995). *Marriage savers: Helping your family and friends avoid divorce*. Grand Rapids: Zondervan.

McManus, M. (2001). Couple mentoring: How to save nine of ten troubled marriages. *Ethics & Religion,* (Column) *1051,* 1–2.

Miller, S. L., Miller, P. A., Nunnally, E. W., & Wackman, D. B. (1992). *Couple communication instructor manual.* Denver-Littleton: Interpersonal Communication Programs.

Murray, C. E. (2005). Prevention work: A professional responsibility for marriage and family counselors. *The Family Journal: Counseling and Therapy for Couples and Families, 13,* 27–34.

Myers, S. M. (1996). An interactive model of religiosity inheritance: The importance of family context. *American Sociological Review, 61,* 858–866.

National Healthy Marriage Resource Center. (2010). Relationships and marriage curricula. National Healthy Marriage Resource Center website. http://www.healthymarriageinfo.org/curricula/index.cfm. Accessed 20 Jan 2013.

Olson, D. H., & Olson, A. K. (1999). PREPARE/ENRICH Program: Version 2000. In R. Berger & M. T. Hannah (Eds.), *Preventive approaches in couples therapy* (pp. 196–216). Philadelphia: Brunner/Mazel.

Olson, D. H., Fournier, D. H., & Druckman, J. M. (1986). *Counselor's manual for PREPARE-ENRICH*. Minneapolis: Life Innovations.

Ooms, T., & Wilson, P. (2004). The challenges of offering relationship and marriage education to low-income populations. *Family Relations, 53*(5), 440–447.

Osborne, C., & McLanahan, S. (2007). Partnership instability and child well-being. *Journal of Marriage and Family, 69*(4), 1065–1083.

Parrott, L., & Parrott, L., (1995). *Saving your marriage before it starts*. Grand Rapids: Zondervan Publishing House.

Phillips, T. M., Wall, S. K., Li, C., & Phillips, L. E. (2009). Memories of the past and expectations of the future: Young adults in romantic relationships. *Journal of Family & Consumer Sciences, 101*, 23–27.

Pino, C. (1982). Development and assessment of personalized programs for marriage preparation and enrichment. *Family Perspective, 16*, 33–39.

RELATE Institute. (2009). RELATE Evaluations. RELATE Institute web site: http://www.relate-institute.org/About/Questionnaires/Default.aspx. Accessed 20 Jan 2013.

Renick, M. J., Blumberg, S. L., & Markman, H. J. (1992). The prevention and relationship enhancement program (PREP): An empirically based preventive intervention program for couples. *Family Relations, 41*(2), 141–147.

Roberts, W., & Wright, H. N. (1978). *Before you say "I Do."* Eugene: Harvest House Publishers.

Roisman, G. I., Madsen, S. D., Hennighausen, K. H., Sroufe, L. A., & Collins, W. A. (2001). The coherence of dyadic behavior across parent-child and romantic relationships as mediated by the internalized representation of experience. *Attachment & Human Development, 3*(2), 156–172.

Russell, M. N., & Lyster, R. F. (1992). Marriage preparation: Factors associated with consumer satisfaction. *Family Relations, 41*(4), 446–451.

Sanders, M. R., Halford, W. K., & Behrens, B. C. (1999). Parental divorce and premarital couple communication. *Journal of Family Psychology, 13*(1), 60–74.

Sandstrom, G. D. (2004). *The effect of marriage mentoring when utilized in a premarital program*. Doctoral dissertation, Capella University. (UMI No. 3129597).

Scafidi, B. (2008). *The taxpayer costs of divorce and unwed childbearing: First-ever estimates for the nation and all fifty states*. New York: Georgia Family Council and Institute for American Values.

Schilling, E. A., Baucom, D. H., Burnett, C. K., Allen, E. S., & Ragland, L. (2003). Altering the course of marriage: The effect of PREP communication skills acquisition on couples' risk of becoming maritally distressed. *Journal of Family Psychology, 17*(1), 41–53.

Schoen, R., & Canudas-Romo, V. (2006). Timing effects on divorce: 20th century experience in the United States. *Journal of Marriage and Family, 68*(3), 749–758.

Schramm, D. G. (2006). Individual and social costs of divorce in Utah. *Journal of Family and Economic Issues, 27*(1), 133–151.

Schumm, W. R., Walker, A. B., Nazarinia, R. R., West, D. A., Atwell, C., Bartko, A., et al. (2010). Predicting the short- and long-term helpfulness of premarital counseling: The critical role of counseling quality. *Journal of Couple and Relationship Therapy, 9*, 1–15.

Silliman, B., & Schumm, W. R. (2000). Marriage preparation programs: A literature review. *The Family Journal: Counseling and Therapy for Couples and Families, 8*(2), 133–142.

Silliman, B., Stanley, S. M., Coffin, W., Markman, H. J., & Jordan, P. L. (2002). Preventive interventions for couples. In H. A. Liddle, D. A. Santisteban, R. F. Levant, & J. H. Bray (Eds.), *Family psychology: Science-based interventions* (pp. 123–146). Washington, DC: American Psychological Association.

Simon, R. W. (2002). Revisiting the relationship among gender, marital status, and mental health. *American Journal of Sociology, 107*(4), 1065–1096.

Stahmann, R. F., & Hiebert, W. J. (1997). *Premarital and remarital counseling: The professional's handbook*. San Francisco: Jossey-Bass.

Stanley, S. M. (1997). What's Important in Preparation for Marriage? *Marriage & Family: A Christian Journal, 1*(1), 54–60.

Stanley, S. M. (2001). Making a case for premarital education. *Family Relations, 50*, 272–280.

Stanley, S. M., Markman, H. J., St. Peters, M., & Leber, B. D. (1995). Strengthening marriages and preventing divorce: New directions in prevention research. *Family Relations, 44,* 392–401.

Stanley, S., Trathen, D., McCain, S., & Bryan, M. (1998). *A lasting promise: A Christian guide to fighting for your marriage*. San Francisco: Jossey-Bass Publishers.

Stanley, S. M., Blumberg, S. L., & Markman, H. J. (1999). Helping couples fight for their marriages: The PREP approach. In R. Berger & M. T. Hannah (Eds.), *Preventive approaches in couples therapy* (pp. 279–303). Philadelphia: Brunner/Mazel.

Stanley, S. M., Markman, H. J., Prado, L. M., Olmos-Gallo, P. A., Tonelli, L., St. Peters, M., et al. (2001). Community-based premarital prevention: Clergy and lay leaders on the front lines. *Family Relations, 50,* 67–76.

Stanley, S. M., Amato, P. R., Johnson, C. A., & Markman, H. J. (2006). Premarital education, marital quality, and marital stability: Findings from a large, random household survey. *Journal of Family Psychology, 20*(1), 117–126.

Sullivan, P. O. (2001). Clergy's training in and the use of premarital counseling. *Dissertation Abstracts International: Section B: The Sciences and Engineering, 61*(7–B), 3863 (UMI No. 9981451).

Taylor, R. M., & Morrison, L. P. (1984). *Taylor-Johnson temperament analysis manual*. Los Angeles: Psychological Publications.

Tomcikova, Z., Geckova, A. M., Orosova, O., van Dijk, J. P., Reijneveld, S. A. (2009). Parental divorce and adolescent drunkenness: Role of socioeconomic position, psychological well-being and social support. *European Addiction Research, 15,* 202–208.

Trathen, D. W. (1995). *A comparison of the effectiveness of two Christian premarital counseling programs (skills and information-based) utilized by Evangelical Protestant churches*. Doctoral dissertation, University of Denver (UMI No. 9532956).

United States Conference of Catholic Bishops. (2008). Getting married in the Catholic church. For Your Marriage web site: http://www.foryourmarriage.org/interior_template.asp?id=20398749. Accessed 4 Sept 2009.

Wages, S. A. (2003). *A formative and summative evaluation of a marriage preparation program using mentor couples*. Doctoral disseration, Florida State University.

Whitton, S. W., Rhoades, G. K., Stanley, S. M., & Markman, H. J. (2008). Effects of parental divorce on marital commitment and confidence. *Journal of Family Psychology, 22,* 789–793.

Wilcox, W. B., Doherty, W. J., Fisher, H., Galston, W. A., Glenn, N. D., Gottman, J., et al. (2005). *Why marriage matters: Twenty-six conclusions for the social sciences* (2nd ed.). New York: Institute for American Values.

Williams, L. M. (1992). Premarital counseling: A needs assessment among engaged individuals. *Contemporary Family Therapy, 14*(6), 505–518.

Williams, L. M. (2003). Communication training, marriage enrichment and premarital counseling. In L. L. Hecker & J. L. Wetchler (Eds.), *An introduction to marriage and family therapy* (pp. 337–368). Binghamton: Haworth Clinical Practice Press.

Williams, L., & Jurich, J. (1995). Predicting marital success after five years: Assessing the predictive validity of FOCCUS. *Journal of Marital and Family Therapy, 21*(2), 141–153.

Williams, L. M., Riley, L. A., Risch, G. S., & Van Dyke, D. T. (1999). An empirical approach to designing marriage preparation programs. *The American Journal of Family Therapy, 27*(3), 271–283.

Wilmoth, J. D. (2005). *Involvement of Oklahoma clergy in providing marriage preparation*. Doctoral dissertation, Oklahoma State University.

Wilmoth, J. D., & Fournier, D. G. (2009). Barriers to providing marriage preparation. *The Journal of Family and Community Ministries, 22*(4), 31–41.

Wilmoth, J. D., & Smyser, S. L. (2007). *Premarital requirements and perceived effectiveness of clergy*. Poster session presented at the annual meeting of the National Council on Family Relations, Pittsburgh.

Wilmoth, J. D., & Smyser, S. L. (2010). Use of premarital assessment questionnaires by clergy in marriage preparation. *Journal of Couple and Relationship Therapy, 9,* 252–267.

Worldwide Marriage Encounter. (2010). History of Worldwide Marriage Encounter. Worldwide Marriage Encounter website: http://www.wwme.org/history-of-worldwide-marriage-encounter.html. Accessed 20 Jan 2013.

Yu, T., Pettit, G. S., Lansford, J. E., Dodge, K. A., & Bates, J. E. (2010). The interactive effects of marital conflict and divorce on parent-adult children's relationships. *Journal of Marriage and Family, 72*, 282–292.

Dr. Joe D. Wilmoth PhD is an associate professor of human development and family studies at Mississippi State University, where his research focuses on aging, families, and religion. Before his academic career, he served in multiple church ministry positions. As a pastor he founded a nonprofit community organization focused on strengthening marriages.

Worldview, Christian Maturity, and Young Adulthood: The What, When, Where, and How of Education after High School

Dick M. Carpenter II

Abstract The years directly following high school graduation play a significant part in the realization of Christian maturity. During this time, children begin to take ownership over most aspects of their life, including their spirituality. For many, this process unfolds simultaneously with post-secondary education in colleges or universities that can strengthen the faith system of the student's childhood or divert her/his attention to a different pursuit. Consequently, children in their late teens need the guidance of parents to help them find the environment that will best enable them to grow in their Christian maturity, develop a Christ-centered worldview, and acquire the skills necessary to succeed personally and professionally. To that end, this chapter begins by defining Christian maturity and the development of worldview. In such context, the chapter discusses the values inherent in modern (or postmodern) universities and the influence colleges play in a person's life. Finally, the chapter provides details, advantages, and disadvantages of various choices after high school and guidance on discerning the best option.

Keywords Worldview · Life after high school · Christian maturity · Post-secondary education

Throughout the life of a child, one desire of Christian parents remains constant—the hope that their child will come to a saving knowledge of Jesus Christ, which will eventually flourish into a life of Christian maturity. Even as children transition into adulthood, this desire remains. For as every parent of adult children knows, parenting does not cease after children graduate from high school and enter the adult world; it just takes on a new dimension.

The years directly following high school graduation play a significant part in the realization of Christian maturity. During this time, children begin to take ownership over most aspects of their life, including their spirituality. Through testing and trying, challenges and questioning, young adults form and habituate belief systems

D. M. Carpenter II (✉)
Dept of Education, University of Colorado, 1420 Austin Bluffs Pkwy., Colorado Springs, CO 80918, USA
e-mail: dmcarpenter@gmail.com

W. Jeynes, E. Martinez (eds.), *Ministering Spiritually to Families*,
DOI 10.1007/978-3-319-13302-7_7

and behaviors. For many, this process unfolds simultaneously with post-secondary education in colleges or universities that can strengthen the faith system of the student's childhood or divert her/his attention to a different pursuit.

Consequently, the what, when, where, and how of life after high school is a vital decision that Christian parents are ill-advised to leave simply to the whims of their teenage children or the determination of convenience and cost. Instead, children in their late teens need the guidance of parents to help them find the environment that will best enable them to grow in their Christian maturity, develop a Christ-centered worldview, and acquire the skills necessary to succeed personally and professionally.

The role of parents is particularly important given the unique nature of each individual and the special knowledge of that nature parents possess. Each child has a distinct temperament and personality that must be carefully matched to a school that will be right for him or her. This means Christian parents should take inventory of their child's maturity level—emotionally, socially, academically, and spiritually—in order to find the best post-secondary fit (Bennett n. d.). This requires a clear understanding of Christian maturity and worldview and either a realistic understanding of the dominant values in today's colleges and universities or practical knowledge of how to discern a post-secondary institution's prevailing ideologies in order to match a child's present state with his or her social, emotional, spiritual, and professional needs.

To that end, this chapter begins by defining Christian maturity and the development of worldview. In such context, the chapter discusses the values inherent in modern (or post-modern) universities and the influence colleges play in a person's life. Finally, the chapter provides details, advantages, and disadvantages of various choices after high school and guidance on discerning the best option.

Christian Maturity

Like the general concept of maturity, Christian maturity can be thought of as a developmental process during which an individual passes through multiple stages of knowledge, belief, and action (assuming growth, of course). Gibson (2004, p. 298) proposes a four-stage model of Christian maturity, displayed in Fig. 1. At Level 1, much like the immature child in relationship to his or her parents, accommodation to God's rules grows out of fear of punishment (hell) or hope for reward (heaven). Therefore, a Christian's motivation for responding to God at this level of development is driven by self-interest. The desire to imitate and please a central, godly figure in one's life reflects the movement toward a second level of spiritual maturity. The concern of believers at this level is how they are perceived by an influential Christian in their life as fulfilling divine laws.

Level 3 maturity recognizes a person does not have beliefs of his or her own until those beliefs undergo challenge. Therefore, individuals reach a third level of spiritual development when they internalize the Christian worldview, which grows out of a personal commitment to Christ. The evidence of such internalization is the

Four Levels of Christian Maturity

Level 1	Level 2	Level 3	Level 4
Accommodation to God's Law out of fear of punishment or hope of reward.	Imitation of godly exemplars with growing respect for and obedience to the Ten Commandments.	Personal, principle centered commitment to Christian worldview.	Movement beyond focus on individual piety to the active promotion of corporate piety and the redemption of creation's sin-stained structures.
Source of Authority: Self-centered	Source of Authority: Other-centered	Source of Authority: Principle-centered	Source of Authority: Kingdom-centered

Fig. 1 Four levels of Christian maturity

repeated demonstration of behavior consistent with Christian law and worldview in the absence of a "reinforcer" (Gibson 2004).

At Level 4 maturity, individuals move beyond a focus on individual piety to actively promoting corporate piety. The person who reaches this stage of spiritual maturity moves beyond internalization of principles to taking concrete action to promote "the liberation of persons and societies from all that prevents them from living an authentic existence in justice and shared community" (Bangkok Consultation 1973, p. 37). As such, the individual takes action on internalized principles to minister to society and the world. More concretely, the fourth level of spiritual development is attained by men and women who share and act on a vision to fulfill the Great Commission, to foster brotherhood and sisterhood, to house the homeless, feed the poor and embrace the sick, to speak out against inequality, to challenge oppressive economic systems, and so on. Here, the source of authority is Kingdom-centered (Gibson 2004).

Attaining Level 4 maturity requires an internalized commitment to the Christian worldview. This commitment comes not just from intellectual knowledge but also from an examination of core beliefs, an examination that leaves open the possibility of believing in something other than Christian principles. Indeed, as Gibson (2004) suggests, Christ calls for such an examination process and internalized commitment to following Him in John 6:42–58, when many chose to depart from Him. According to Halstead (1995), this process includes questioning assumptions, engaging in debate, and grappling with conflicting worldviews. For as Hall (1977) posits, surrounded by people of differing worldview, it is unlikely that individuals can rely upon padded answers for believing what they do.

What's Worldview?

This requires, of course, knowing what worldview is. According to McKenzie (1991), Reich et al. (1994), and others (Astley and Francis 2002; Ladson-Billings 2000; Shahjahan 2005) worldview is how one interprets the world around her after reflecting on her experience in and knowledge of it. It is what dictates people's decisions, how they define reality, and how they see themselves and others (Carpenter 2001).

Some of the more commonly recognized worldviews, among the panoply, include Marxism, which offers a total and definitive interpretation of human reality that is atheistic, materialist, and dialectical; liberalist-pluralist, the theories of reality of which are agnostic, individualistic, and tied for their moral legitimacy to the notions of human rights and respect for social contracts; and humanism, which is atheistic, seeing humanity as the apex of development and looking to the self-perfecting of humanity, including the founding of morality, by the use of reason (Plunkett 1990). Although each of these has had, and continues to have a presence in colleges and universities, for many years academia was dominated by the worldview of modernism, which subscribes to the centrality of reason, the belief in progress, the virtues of individualism, and faith in the scientific method (Bloland 2005).

But in recent decades, the academy, indeed the culture at large, has seen a transformation from modernism to postmodernism (Bloland 2005). In the worldview of modernism, culture and self-identity are viewed more or less as stable, and colleges focus on educating for citizenship, preparing for jobs, and facilitating personal growth and development. Postmodernism, on the other hand, subscribes to the idea of multiple, socially-created realities, malleable identities, shifting conceptions of self over time, and multiple truths. Postmodern higher education contributes to this by challenging prevailing tenets (modernist and otherwise) and encouraging students to do likewise, most fundamentally by prompting them to question who they are and what they believe.

At odds with postmodernism, indeed, one of the historically prevailing tenets challenged by it, is the Christian worldview, which teaches that reality is not created by us but by a Creator, in whose image mankind is made and to whom it is accountable (Gibson 2004). Consequently, human nature is predictable, and truth is known, fixed, and written on the hearts of all humanity (Holy Bible, Romans 2:15).

To the mature believer, this definition, and even this discussion of worldview, borders on simplistic, but as Kanitz (2005) and other Christian professors recognize, students—including those from Christian homes—need to be taught (a) about the concept of worldview, (b) to recognize various worldviews around them, (c) to realize their own worldview, and (d) to see how their worldview is shaped by the views around them. Indeed, Kanitz observes that Christian college students often see Christian thought as just one of many perspectives and not necessarily a correct or true one. Dumestre (1995) echoes this observation in his discussion of the rather shallow knowledge Christians generally hold of their faith principles, a lack of knowledge that can only lead to an undeveloped and malleable worldview.

Life After High School

This dynamic further emphasizes the need for Christian parents to help guide their children in choosing a college or university in their growth toward spiritual maturity. The college years are a time when students not only equip themselves for a vocation, but a period when they formulate convictions about faith, values, and worldview (Bennett n. d.; Kuh 2002). Significant changes in moral reasoning and reflective judgment are common between the first and senior years of college (Baxter Magoida 1992). Faculty and courses most certainly contribute to this (Astin 1993; Pascarella and Terenzini 1991), but so do other factors of the environment, including peers, activities, work, sports, and so forth (Hammond and Hunter 1984; Kuh 2002).

In many colleges and universities, this influence is hostile toward spirituality generally (Shahjahan 2005) and toward a Christian worldview specifically. For faculty and students alike, faith, moral education, and spirituality have been marginalized in most areas of university activity, from student life to curricula (Bok 1982, 1990; Colby et al. 2003; Glanzer et al. 2004; Hoekema 1994; Long 1992; Reuben 2000; Wilshire 1990). Instead university life is dominated by a host of worldviews, such as those listed above, antagonistic toward the Christian worldview (Johnson 1995; Shahjahan 2005), an observation going back more than six decades (Nash 1944).

Thus, it is important for Christian parents to evaluate honestly and critically their child's state of maturity, both in general and as a Christian to determine the best fitting post-secondary option. For some children, particularly those in the early stages of Christian maturity, this may mean a Christian college or university that will provide a much needed foundation in Christian worldview along with education for a productive civic and economic life. For others, likely those in more advanced stages of Christian maturity, an environment that will challenge and sharpen their beliefs may prove a better fit. This assumes, of course, that a child will pursue post-secondary education. For some, college or university matriculation after high school may not be the wisest choice. Instead, pursuing employment opportunities may be a better option, given a child's academic trajectory or level of personal and emotional maturity. Therefore, it is important to consider *all* the various options when evaluating a child's needs.

Work or Service

As Bennett (n. d.) observes, from God's perspective, success in life is related to character and not necessarily to intellect or college degrees. God rewards honest, hard-working people who have succeeded in the critical areas of life, whether they have a college education or not. If a young person is not a serious student or is not sure what vocational field he wants to pursue, it may be best to consider rejecting or delaying the college decision until the potential student has matured. During this time the child could work in the field he or she is considering. Another option would be to encourage the him/her to work with a Christian ministry in order to mature spiritually and further strengthen character skills that will help the student succeed, no matter what educational or vocational choice he or she makes. A year's wait—often called a "gap year" (Martin 2010)—at this stage in life can make a significant difference in a student's attitude and academic performance.

Community College

Community colleges are often a good option for the student who is struggling academically or is undecided about her educational or vocational future. They provide an opportunity for a student to mature a year or two before entering a larger college or a university. They also offer the added benefit of being more economical and allowing for more parental involvement. Time to grow in emotional maturity, more parental involvement, and more time in a home church could also facilitate the opportunity to realize greater Christian maturity.

Secular Institutions

As discussed above, secular colleges may be a good alternative for more mature Christian students. They offer broader vocational choices and often cost much less than Christian colleges. Many offer excellent opportunities for students to grow in their faith and develop evangelism and discipleship skills in the refining fire of a challenging academic and social environment (Bennett n. d.; Hammond and Hunter 1984; Veith 1998). To grow and thrive in such an environment, however, students will quickly need to settle into a vibrant church that has a campus ministry or participate in an interdenominational campus ministry (Bennett n. d.; Hammond and Hunter 1984).

For reasons of necessity or choice, most students from Christian homes will end up in a secular university. It is therefore important that students and parents consider how to arrange an educational program that will result in optimal vocational training and spiritual growth. This is not an impossible task, but it will require work on the part of the student and parents.

Christian College or University

As Wilhoit and Dettoni (1998) acknowledge, "Christians do not emerge from the spiritual experience of being born again as full and complete Christians but as child-like Christians, who, like human children, have all the potential for growing into complete and mature adults but need to be nurtured and guided" (p. 28). Thus, for the young person who would benefit from a college or university education but also needs to grow in Christian maturity, a Christian college or university is an important option. And the choices are many and diverse. As Hammond and Hunter (1984) observes, there are several hundred Bible colleges and seminaries and approximately 100 private Evangelical liberal arts colleges and universities.

These institutions are typically populated by faculty who passionately believe in a call to integrate faith and learning for students, which includes helping students develop a vibrant, holistic Christian worldview (Kanitz 2005). This often comes through close relationships developed between faculty and students. Because classes at these institutions are typically smaller, they facilitate greater interaction and more opportunities to ask questions. Informal discussions at a professor's home or at a restaurant are not unusual.

Not all Christian colleges or universities are created equal, of course, which means the resources dedicated to teaching students about worldviews or facilitating Christian maturity differ from one institution to another. In general, the more evangelical the institution, the more likely it is to offer or require that students take worldview-related courses (Fisher 1995; Glanzer et al. 2004). Glanzer et al. note that such institutions are more likely to influence character development than less evangelical institutions.

Discerning the Best Option

To be sure, the distinctions made above between institutional types are not always as simple as written. Despite calling themselves Christian institutions, some colleges or universities are essentially ChINO—Christian in Name Only. Likewise, secular universities vary in their levels of animus toward the Christian worldview. Thus, parents and students should endeavor to determine an institution's climate as part of the decision-making process. Although seemingly difficult, colleges and universities provide a host of indicators to the discerning eye. Generally, these indicators can be grouped into three categories: "print" material, people associated with the campus, and the campus tour (Carpenter 2001).

"Print" Material

Some research can begin on the Web.

- Visit the campus's website, and give it a critical look. What is featured and prominent on the pages? Who is on the faculty? How does the institution describe itself on its "about" page?
- Visit professors' webpages in your child's prospective major and generally. Read resumes, vitas, or bios. What types of works have they written? Scan their syllabi. What do they teach in their courses?

- Visit the student life webpage. Check out the calendar of events. What activities and festivals does the school sponsor? Do they host a speaker's series? Who do they invite to speak? What kinds of student clubs are listed? For Christian schools the ratio of evangelical vs. ecumenical groups can indicate the schools' evangelical nature. For secular schools, more extreme secular groups indicate a more liberal environment. A good mixture of Christian and secular groups can indicate a more tolerant environment for conservatives or Christians.
- Visit websites dedicated to reviewing institutions and faculty. One of the more popular is ratemyprofessors.com, where students rate their professor and include detailed comments about the courses and the faculty.

Hardcopy media also provides insightful information.

- Catalogs and handbooks are an excellent source of information (Fisher 1995). These publications usually contain church affiliation (if applicable), university mission statements, core values, statements of faith (for religious schools), student behavior policies, and general school policies (Glanzer et al. 2004). What courses are required of all students or of students within a major in which your child is interested? A college's requirements of its students are those subjects or skills that it believes are so vital that every student ought to learn them (Fisher 1995).
- Scan the schedule of courses. A college's courses and curriculum are arguably its most significant statement about what it seeks to teach its students (Fisher 1995). It is a reflection of the values that really drive the institution and receive the time, attention, and resources of the college's faculty and students.
- Check out departmental publications like brochures, annual reports, and academic magazines or journals. What do brochures or annual reports feature or value? What types of research do magazines or journals contain?
- Even applications reveal a school's worldview. Analyze the essay questions students have to complete. These can often point to what the institution values. Likewise, the types of essay questions Christian schools require indicate their evangelical nature.
- Scrutinize other application materials, such as scholarship and financial aid information. To whom do they distribute their funds? What criteria do they use to award money?
- Seek out magazine surveys, like the *U.S. News and World Report.* Other surveys rank schools on different criteria, including student life, party life, sexual activity, drug use, etc. Often these surveys reflect a school's reputation, which they likely have earned.
- Check out handbooks and other publications that include descriptions of various institutions. One of the better known is "Choosing the Right College" (Beer 2007), but other helpful books include The Templeton Foundation's "Colleges that Encourage Character Development" and Peterson's "Christian Colleges and Universities."

People Associated with the Campus

People on or associated with campuses provide great insight directly and indirectly.

- Ask admissions counselors, who spoke at recent commencements? What is the political background of the student body or faculty? Who are prominent alums or faculty? Are some Christians or conservatives?
- Be certain to visit with faculty. Ask professors what research they are working on. What do they value? How is the curriculum structured? Why is it structured that way? What is the purpose behind what is taught?
- How do religious schools and professors integrate faith into the courses and curricula? Solid Christian schools integrate faith into every aspect of life on campus, including the classroom.
- Talk to students, including former ones. What is taught in classes? How do students and faculty treat the Christian worldview? Is there room for discussion or debate related to worldview?

The Campus Tour

All campuses offer tours for prospective students and families, and most tours are highly organized to spotlight the best features of the campus. To really discern what the institution is about, pay attention to and make plans to spend "unscripted" time looking for the following.

- Look at a college's bulletin boards. What is advertised? What kinds of activities are held on campus?
- Read the student newspaper. What are they writing about? What are the campus's hot issues?
- What kind of student and faculty art is prevalent? What are people talking about on campus? What kinds of music do you hear while walking through dorms?
- While visiting professors websites at a secular institution, note if any are Christians. Make appointments to visit them while on campus. Ask them about the environment on campus, its people, their values, etc. If a search of the website is unproductive in identifying Christian faculty, check with local churches or student ministries such as Campus Crusade for Christ, Intervarsity Christian Fellowship, or The Navigators. Student ministries are often required to have a faculty advisor in order to be an officially recognized student organization (Bennett n. d.). While you are at it, ask representatives from those ministries about the institution.
- Talk to students on campus and ask open-ended questions like, "What do you like most about the campus?" and "Who is your favorite professor, and why?" (Bennett n. d.).

Resources

Life in the Information Age (Castells 1999) means an abundance of resources available to help make the best decision for life after high school, many of which are online. Although some are designed for young people, they nonetheless provide invaluable information for parents as well.

World View

True U: This online worldview project is a creation of Focus on the Family and provides excellent and accessible apologetics training (http://www.mytruthproject.org/truthproject/trueu/home.html).

- Leadership U: A creation of Campus Crusade for Life, this website provides a host of information on worldview, issues, and other related topics (http://www.leaderu.com/).

College Life

- Intercollegiate Studies Institute (ISI): This non-sectarian, non-partisan organization seeks to "further in successive generations of college students a better understanding of the values and institutions that sustain a free and humane society." They publish the aforementioned "Choosing the Right College" and offer numerous resources on their website (http://www.isi.org/).
- Intervarsity (http://www.intervarsity.org/), Campus Crusade for Christ (http://www.ccci.org), and Navigators (http://www.navigators.org/us/): Although there are others, these three represent the best known college ministries in the country.
- Boundless: This webzine is a publication of Focus on the Family that targets college-aged readers. In addition to general content, numerous articles address worldview, college life, and staying Christian on secular campuses (http://www.boundless.org).

List of Christian Colleges and Universities

- Council for Christian Colleges and Universities (CCCU): In addition to the handbooks listed above, CCCU provides a list of Christian colleges and universities with links to each one (http://www.cccu.org/).

Conclusion

The decision of life after high school often represents a critical juncture in the emotional, civic, economic, and spiritual life and maturity of a young person. Although cost and convenience often play a significant, if not the most important part in determining a child's post-secondary options, the importance of the years immediately following high school should not be left only to cost and convenience. Parents should also consider their child's needs related to spiritual development and include that in the decision making process by:

1. critically and honestly evaluating their child's present level of Christian maturity;
2. understanding their own and their child's worldview;
3. considering all post-secondary options, ranging from work or service to matriculation at a Christian college or university;
4. aligning those options with their child's emotional, professional, and spiritual needs; and
5. doing the research necessary to choose the specific opportunity or institution that best meets their child's needs.

One challenging aspect in this process is a child's increasing independence from parents in making decisions about his or her life. Because life immediately after high school typically means almost complete autonomy, it is tempting for parents to defer in large measure to their child in this decision. And it may not be unusual for children to try to isolate their parents from the process. The latter might be exacerbated when the criterion by which decisions are made about post-secondary options differ between child and parent, as could be the case, for example, when a child favors a college for its social life and parents see the school as a bad fit given their child's spiritual (im)maturity.

All of this points to the importance of early, detailed, honest, and frank discussions between parents and children about priorities and needs, goals and plans for the future, and the process that will be used for decision making. Through it all, children will likely learn more about themselves, Christian life and maturity, and the decisions and processes necessary in adult life. For their part, parents have the privilege of guiding their children into a new phase of life and laying a foundation for a different relationship with their soon-to-be adult children. And all involved will likely grow in their knowledge and beliefs as they consider their Christian faith and worldview in light of the beliefs and priorities of different post-secondary institutions and opportunities and their accompanying worldviews.

References

Astin, A. W. (1993). *What matters in college: Four critical years revisited.* San Francisco: Jossey Bass.

Astley, J., & Francis, L. J. (2002). Christian education and openness: An empirical investigation among undergraduates. *Religious Education, 97*(1), 4–22.

Bangkok Consultation. (1973). Salvation isn't the same today. *Christianity Today, 17,* 37–39.
Baxter Magoida, M. (1992). *Knowing and reasoning in college: Gender related patterns in students' intellectual development.* San Francisco: Jossey Bass.
Beer, J. (2007). *Choosing the right college.* Wilmington: ISI Books.
Bennett, C. (n. d.). Choosing a college or university. http://www.leaderu.com/choosingcollege/choosingacollege.html. Accessed 24 Feb 2007.
Bloland, H. G. (2005). Whatever happened to postmodernism in higher education? No requiem in the new millennium. *Journal of Higher Education, 76*(2), 121–150.
Bok, D. (1982). *Beyond the ivory tower: Social responsibilities of the modern university.* Cambridge: Harvard University Press.
Bok, D. (1990). *Universities and the future of America.* Durham: Duke University Press.
Carpenter, D. M. (2001). All views are not created equal. http://www.boundless.org/2001/features/a0000551.html. Accessed 24 Feb 2007.
Castells, M. (1999). *The information age: Economy, society, and culture* (Vol. 1, 2, and 3). Malden: Blackwell.
Colby, A., Ehrlich, T., Beaumont, E., & Stephens, J. (2003). *Educating citizens: Preparing America's undergraduates for lives of moral responsibility.* San Francisco: Jossey-Bass.
Dumestre, M. J. (1995). Postfundamentalism and the Christian intentional learning community. *Religious Education, 90*(2), 190–207.
Fisher, A. (1995). Religious and moral education at three kinds of liberal arts colleges: A comparison of curricula in Presbyterian, evangelical, and religiously unaffiliated liberal arts colleges. *Religious Education, 90*(1), 30–49.
Gibson, T. S. (2004). Proposed levels of Christian spiritual maturity. *Journal of Psychology and Theology, 32*(4), 295–304.
Glanzer, P. L., Ream, T. C., Villarreal, P., & Davis, E. (2004). The teaching of ethics in Christian higher education: An examination of general education requirements. *JGE: The Journal of General Education, 53*(3–4), 184–200.
Hall, E. (1977). *Beyond culture.* Garden City: Anchor/Doubleday.
Halstead, J. M. (1995). Should schools reinforce children's religious identity? *Religious Education, 90*(3/4), 360–377.
Hammond, P. E., & Hunter, J. D. (1984). On maintaining plausibility: The worldview of evangelical college students. *Journal for the Scientific Study of Religion, 23*(3), 221–238.
Hoekema, D. (1994). *Campus rules and moral community.* Lanham: Rowman and Littlefield.
Johnson, R. L. (1995). The university question revisited. *Journal of Ecumenical Studies, 32,* 521–525.
Kanitz, L. (2005). Improving Christian worldview pedagogy: Going beyond mere Christianity. *Christian Higher Education, 4,* 99–108.
Kuh, G. (2002). Do environments matter? A comparative analysis of the impress of different types of colleges and universities on character [Electronic Version], 2. http://www.collegevalues.org/articles.cfm. Accessed 1 June 2003.
Ladson-Billings, G. (2000). Racialized discourses and ethnic epistemologies. In N. Denzin & Y. Lincoln (Eds.), *Handbook of qualitative research* (pp. 257–278). London: Sage.
Long, E. (1992). *Higher education as a moral enterprise.* Washington: Georgetown University Press.
Martin, A. J. (2010). Should students have a gap year? Motivation and performance factors relevant to time out after completing school. *Journal of Educational Psychology, 102*(3), 561–576.
McKenzie, L. (1991). *Adult education and worldview construction.* Malabar: Krieger.
Nash, A. S. (1944). *The university and the modern world.* New York: Macmillan.
Pascarella, E. T., & Terenzini, P. T. (1991). *How college affects students: Findings and insights from twenty years of research.* San Francisco: Jossey Bass.
Plunkett, D. (1990). *Secular and spiritual values: grounds for hope in education* London: Routledge.

Reich, K. H., Oser, F. K., & Valentin, P. (1994). Knowing why I now know better: Children's and youth's explanations of their worldview changes. *Journal of Research on Adolescnece, 4*(1), 151–173.

Reuben, J. (2000). The university and its discontents. *The Hedgehog Review, 2,* 72–91.

Shahjahan, R. A. (2005). Spirituality in the academy: Reclaiming from the margins and evoking a transformative way of knowing the world. *International Journal of Qualitative Studies in Education, 18*(6), 685–711.

Veith, G. E. (1998). Surviving a hostile professor. http://www.boundless.org/1999/features/a0000001.html. Accessed 24 Feb 2007

Wilhoit, J., & Dettoni, J. (Eds.). (1998). *Nurture that is Christian: Developmental perspectives on Christian education.* Grand Rapids: Baker.

Wilshire, B. (1990). *The moral collapse of the university: Professionalism, purity, and alienation.* Albany: State University of New York Press.

Dick M. Carpenter II PhD is a professor of leadership, research, and foundations at the University of Colorado Colorado Springs and former education policy analyst at Focus on the Family, an international Christian ministry headquartered in Colorado, USA.

Scriptural Views of Parenting

William Jeynes

Abstract The author presents biblical principles that are designed to help mothers and fathers be more effective parents. The chapter first examines a real centerpiece of faith-filled parenting, which is living by what is true and yet demonstrating loving sensitivity. Balance along a number of dimensions is a real emphasis of the chapter. The author also examines the notion that one can demonstrate better parenting skills for children of certain ages versus others and how the parent can adjust to become a more effective parent at some of the ages that are more challenging. One of the most interesting aspects of the chapter is the section that examines how out of a desire to set a virtuous example for the youth, a parent can actually spoil a child. The call again is to one of a loving and character-based balance.

Keywords Family · Parenting · Ministry · Faith · Spirituality · Religion · Christian · Children

The Essence of Long-Term Faith-Filled Parenting

Parenting practices should change as the age of the children progresses (Jeynes 2005a, b). This is one of the most underemphasized aspects of parenting. On the one hand it is true that, "Jesus Christ is the same yesterday, today, and forever" (Holy Bible, NIV, Hebrews 13:8 1979). Therefore, the general principles that parents act by should remain biblical and those principles naturally do not change (Dobson 2007; Hetzendorfer 2009; Montague 2011; Strobel and Strobel 2010). Beyond this, however, Christ acted using a wonderful sensitivity toward people, depending on their level of spiritual development (Clinton and Ohischlager 2002; Kruschwitz 2001). There is no more important a practice to apply this principle

W. Jeynes (✉)
Witherspoon Institute, Princeton, NJ, USA
e-mail: whjharvard@post.harvard.edu

California State University, Long Beach, 6572 Red Coach Drive Huntington Beach, CA 92647, USA

W. Jeynes, E. Martinez (eds.), *Ministering Spiritually to Families*,
DOI 10.1007/978-3-319-13302-7_8

to than parenting. The Bible is very sensitive to the various stages of a person's development that they go through (Cloud and Townsend 2001; Jeynes 2005d; Kruschwitz 2001). In fact, this element of the Word of God is one of the most overlooked and yet explicit teachings of Scripture (Barber 2010; Barclay 2010; Jeynes 2010c). The verses listed below provide a valuable overview of this sensitivity to age and one's stage in life, that Scripture provides.

> Behold, children are a heritage from the Lord, the fruit of the womb a reward. Like arrows in the hand of a warrior are the children of one's youth. Blessed is the man who fills his quiver with them! Psalms 127: 3, 4. (Holy Bible, NIV 1979)

> For you formed my inward parts; you knitted me together in my mother's womb. I praise you, for I am fearfully and wonderfully made. Wonderful are your works; my soul knows it very well. My frame was not hidden from you, when I was being made in secret, intricately woven in the depths of the earth. Your eyes saw my unformed substance; in your book were written, every one of them, the days that were formed for me, when as yet there was none of them. Psalm 139: 13–16. (Holy Bible, NIV 1979)

> Like newborn babies, crave pure spiritual milk, so that by it you may grow up in your salvation, now that you have tasted that the Lord is good. I Peter 2: 2–3. (Holy Bible, NIV 1979)

> Only take care, and keep your soul diligently, lest you forget the things that your eyes of seen, and lest they depart from your heart all the days of your life. Make them known to your children and your children's children. Deuteronomy 4:9. (Holy Bible, NIV 1979)

> Impress them on your children. Talk about them when you sit at home and when you walk along the road, when you lie down and when you get up. Deuteronomy 6:7. (Holy Bible, NIV 1979)

> My son, keep your father's commands and do not forsake your mother's teaching. Proverbs 6:20. (Holy Bible, NIV 1979)

> Discipline your son, and he will give you rest; he will give delight to your heart. Proverbs 29: 17. (Holy Bible, NIV 1979)

> Train up a child in the way he should go; even when he is old he will not depart from it. Proverbs 22: 6. (Holy Bible, NIV 1979)

> Fathers, do not exasperate your children; instead bring them up in the training and instruction of the Lord. Ephesians 6:4. (Holy Bible, NIV 1979)

> Fathers, do not provoke your children, lest they become discouraged. Colossians 3:21. (Holy Bible, NIV 1979)

> When I was a child, I talked like a child, I thought like a child, I reasoned like a child. When I became a man, I put my childish ways behind me. I Corinthians 13:11. (Holy Bible, NIV 1979)

> All your children shall be taught by the Lord, and great shall be the peace of your children. Isaiah 54:13. (Holy Bible, NIV 1979)

The Gentle Balance in Parenting

The teaching of Scripture is that the best believing parents combine solid biblical principles coupled with a reliance on the Holy Spirit to provide the ambience of love and flexibility in the home (DeMuth 2006; Piper 2011; Post 2000; Selvaggio and Meath 2008). This is why for believers to engage in efficacious parenting, it is absolutely essential that they have a strong knowledge of- and reliance on- the truths of God's Word (Dallman 2007; Jeynes 2009b, 2010c). It is also vital that they depend on the Holy Spirit, so that they can appropriately respond to God's promptings regarding how best to apply these truths (Jeynes 2009a; Micklethwait and Wooldridge 2009; Montague 2011). God provides His Spirit, in part, to provide counsel and guidance regarding how best to apply these principles. It is therefore vital to understand that the best type of parenting does not emerge *only* out of the knowledge of God's Word or out of a dependence on the Holy Spirit. Rather, the two must occur concurrently (Piper 2011). The declaration of Ephesians 6:17 is particularly enlightening along these lines. It states, "Take the helmet of salvation and the sword of the Spirit, which is the Word of God."

It is a profound truth in Scripture that the realm of God's Word and Spirit are not seen as separate entities but rather as acting in unison, i.e., "…the sword of the Spirit, which is the Word of God (Holy Bible, NIV, Ephesians 6:17 1979).

Parenting with the Stages of Childhood in Mind

It is important to understand the significance of the stages that children frequently go through (McLanahan and Sandefur 1994; Nord 2010; Palm and Fagan 2008; Popenoe 2000). What the vital application is for our lives is to understand that just because we are an efficacious parent when the child is at a certain age, does not automatically mean that we are effective at other stages (Jeynes 2007b). Most parents can sense, more or less, whether they are being effective during different chapters in their children's lives. Often mothers and fathers begin being relatively pleased with their early "performance" in rearing children (Wallerstein 2005; Wallerstein and Lewis 1998). But then at a certain juncture or at multiple times they become less enthralled with their parenting skills (Altschul 2011; Arnold 2007; Jeynes 2002b, 2003b). Some parents are taken aback, when suddenly they realize their ability to raise their children seems to have decreased. They ask themselves, "What happened? What have we started doing wrong?" But the reality of the matter is that in nearly every case, the mother and father have not suddenly become awful caregivers. Rather, what they have not been cognizant of is that being an effective parent requires that one periodically make adjustments to the ongoing age and maturity changes in their children (Baehr 1998; Borruel 2002; Brooks and Goldstein 2001; Chapman et al. 2008). That is, it is quite possible and even common to be a much better parent when the children are at one age than when they are at another.

When at child is a baby, toddler, five years old, ten years old, or fifteen tears old their needs are different versus other ages (Brooks and Goldstein 2001; Chapman et al. 2008; Evertson and Emmer 2009; Palm and Fagan 2008). It is essential that mothers and fathers sensitize themselves to the varying needs that youth possess at different ages. Through all the years of their upbringing, young need to have a sense that their parents love them (Jeynes 2011a, b, 2012c; Swindoll 1998; Wallace 2001). Similarly, offspring also require some expression of structure throughout their developing years (Becker 1981; Strom 2002). Nevertheless, how children need that love and especially that structure expressed varies over time. It is this latter fact to which parents needs to be sensitive. When children are very young they need a high degree of structure and an adoring and consistent expression of love (Jeynes 2012d). But what it is so vital for parents to understand is that over time mothers and fathers should: (a) gradually reduce certain expressions of structure, (b) introduce other developmentally-sensitive aspects of structure, (c) show love in ways that the child will receive, which may or may not be the ways that the parents are used to showing love; and (d) show love in ways that are appropriate for the developmental stage through which the child is passing (Cervone and Shoda 1999; Murray 2001; Vangelisti 2004). It is valuable to examine each of these points individually.

a. *Gradually Reduce Certain Expressions of Structure*- There is no question that as children grow and learn more about how to function in life, to whatever extent they show themselves able and trustworthy, they need to be given more "room." In other words, as one's young successfully pass certain landmarks in their lives and demonstrate that they are trustworthy and true, part of their reward should be that parents should show some degree of acknowledgement and reward for this advancement. A considerable part of that acknowledgement and reward should be granting the youth added "mobility" and "room for development." If children do not believe that they are periodically being granted more room, they wonder whether their parents truly believe in, trust in, and have confidence in them. A major reason why children in the teen years frequently rebel against their caregivers is because they feel restricted to a degree that is out of proportion to what is appropriate for their age level (McPherson 2002; Thompson 2006; Tripp 2001). And indeed, if parents do not allow steadily increasing autonomy as their young march toward adulthood, it almost invites some degree of adolescent rebellion (McPherson 2002; Thompson 2006; Tripp 2001). Parents need to be sensitive to the fact that there is a reasonable expectation among their children that if they are faithful to make certain advances in their lives and make certain achievements, they ought to be granted some greater autonomy (Jeynes 2010d).
b. *Introduce Other Developmentally-Sensitive Aspects of Structure*- Clearly structure must not decrease in every way as children get older (Jeynes 2012a, b; McPherson 2002; Thompson 2006; Tripp 2001). For example, when a family is blessed with babies and toddlers there is no reason to communicate alcohol consumption restrictions on the young within your home. That should occur when the child is old enough to be aware of alcohol and its availability as a consumption option (Jeynes 2002c). It is now well documented that young people thrive

the most in an atmosphere that concurrently offers a high degree of encouraging love and a great deal of supportive structure (Jeynes 1999, 2011c). One of those attributes in operation is not sufficient without the other. They both need to work in harmony with each other and as a means of complementing the other (Jeynes 1999; McPherson 2002; Thompson 2006; Tripp 2001).

In providing structure in the home, it is important that the parents distinguish between what is necessary and unnecessary structure. That is, it is important that one "minor on the minors" and "major on the majors." That is, one should place a great deal of emphasis on what is, in the larger context of things, important areas of discipline and less emphasis on items of lesser import (McPherson 2002; Thompson 2006; Tripp 2001). In other words, there is a sense in which mothers and fathers need to choose their battles in dealing with children. To not do so would be to invite unnecessary conflict. To distinguish between what is important and unimportant is not only productive in the short-run, but also in the long-run. After years have transpired, one's children will then be able to look back in retrospect and understand that any disagreements over too much structure involved salient issues designed to protect the child and were not over inane issues that were unnecessary and not well thought out (Worthington 2000; Wright and Oliver 1999). How children view these issues is important both at the time of the event and in the long-term (Jeynes 2003b; Wallace 2001; Worthington 2000; Wright and Oliver 1999).

c. *Show Love in Ways that the Child Will Receive, Which May or May not be the Ways that the Parents Are Used to Showing Love*- A myriad of teens are convinced that their mothers and fathers do not love them (Jeynes 2006a). This conclusion is really an unfortunate shame, because in the vast majority of cases the parents do love them (McPherson 2002; Thompson 2006; Tripp 2001). To the extent that this is the case, why is it that so many teens are convinced that their caregivers really do not love them? The primary reason why this is the case is because they define love as being cared for the way they want to be cared for and this usually involves granting them some degree of carte blanche in doing whatever they desire to do (Worthington 2000; Wright and Oliver 1999). In the very limited purview of most teenagers, if a person does not love them the way they want to be loved, then it really is not love at all. Teens possess a very limited ability to define as love anything different than the way they want to be treated. The research literature is teeming with evidence that this scenario is much more likely to occur in homes in which a child has been spoiled into procuring an attitude that he or she must be treated a certain way (Worthington 2000; Wright and Oliver 1999). Nevertheless, it is also quite possible for a youth to develop this perspective even when the family members have done nothing to encourage this type of narcissistic orientation (McPherson 2002; Minith 2004; Worthington 2000; Wright and Oliver 1999). This is largely because a plethora of parents raise their children to exhibit this kind of spoiled behavior and these are the parents that spend time with their children.

The reality is that we now live in a society in which peers have a level of influence upon our children that is likely unprecedented in the nation's history. Peers have always had an impact, perhaps more than we would care to admit (Jeynes 2000). For example, Benjamin Franklin wrote a letter in the 1700s that declared that one of the primary reasons that so many individuals wanted to become to New England and the Mid-Atlantic states was because there were so many God-fearing youth who set good examples for other young people (Jeynes and Beuttler 2012). Even hundreds of years ago, peer pressure had more of an impact than many are willing to acknowledge. But what we often fail to fathom is that, even as Benjamin Franklin's letter suggests, peer pressure can actually be a positive force rather than just a negative one (Jeynes 2010a). Having stated this fact, however, the reality is that in contemporary society the effects of peer pressure are largely negative and the sheer number of children in modern society raised to embrace a self-centered attitude can do a great deal of harm to our children, even if they are raised in a healthy home (Jeynes 1999; Jeynes and Robinson 2010). Today, young people adopt a narcissistic attitude in part because of the peers with whom they associate (Powell 2009; Szabo 2004; Tripp 2008).

The fact that youth today are often self-centered and often are that way because of their distasteful personal associations, does not mean that parents need to throw up their hands in capitulation. Rather, parents would be prudent if they understood that creating a more harmonious environment for raising teenagers is not simply about creating an atmosphere in which love exists, but also one in which it is perceived by all involved that love exists (Chapman et al. 2008; Meyer 2002). In other words, mothers and fathers should not only take inventory of their lives to make sure that they are loving their children in the best way, but also honestly ask the question of the extent to which that love is perceived by the youth. And then if one's love is not interpreted as such the way that one would like, he or she should ask what steps can be taken to improve that perception.

Herein lies where parents frequently make a mistake. Just as youth often have a glaring weakness in their inability to identify love for what it is, when it is not expressed in the form they desire, parents often have a fault in that they love people in the way in which they themselves are accustomed and do not ask the pertinent question of how the other person wants to be love (Chapman et al. 2008). Naturally, it would be unwise to always love people they way they want to be loved (Chapman et al. 2008). Sometimes what the other person wants is not good for them at all. Nevertheless, it is wise to be sentient of the ways that people desire to be loved so that parents can at least make certain adjustments. Even teenagers have the capacity to be realistic. For the most part, they do not demand or expect their fathers and mothers to love them in every way that they would desire. They do, however, expect some of those manifestations to come their way. Therefore, the more that parents can adapt their expressions of love to consider the way that their teens best receive love, the more likely teens are to have affirmed that their fathers and mothers love them (Chapman et al. 2008).

Why a parent should love his or her children, at least in some ways, in expressions that youth desire and will receive is because if one does this, the child is more likely to understand that the other expressions of parental love, albeit not perhaps the manifestations these young people might prefer, are genuine nevertheless. That is a huge accomplishment in parent-adolescent relationships.

d. *Show Love in Ways that are Appropriate for the Developmental Stage through which the Child is Passing*- The most effective parents are those that maintain biblical principles and values but also with constant sensitivity to the Lord, adapt to the chapters through which children pass in their lives (Dobson 2007; Hetzendorfer 2009; Piper 2011). There is no question that some expressions of love work best for children at some ages, but fall short when a child becomes older (Cloud and Townsend 2001; Kruschwitz 2001). Because they are in such close proximity to the situation, parents may not be able to identify this fact at the household level. Therefore, let us examine an example from the school level. Let us say that a student was behaving especially impressively and the teacher wanted to reward that obedience. If that student was in kindergarten, the teacher might offer him or her to sit next to the teacher at lunch. Most students of that age would be ecstatic over such an offer. In contrast, however, if the teacher made that offer to a seventh or eighth grade student, the reaction would be entirely different and would not be embraced so easily.

Taking Seriously the Stages That Children Go Through

The Importance of a Foundation

Human beings all go through stages or chapters in their lives (Cloud and Townsend 2001; Kruschwitz 2001; Wallerstein and Lewis 1998). This fact has been emphasized substantially enough by preachers and even by self-help psychologists so that most individuals are cognizant of this fact. Interestingly enough, this was one of the first post-conversion principles that I learned. This truism quickly became so axiomatic to me that the very first book that I wrote (which was not the first to be released, but later came out as "Stages I" and "Stages II"). The more believers can concurrently apply the eternal truths of God and yet appreciate the stages that children journey through, the more effective parents they will be (Cloud and Townsend 2001; Kruschwitz 2001; Piper 2011). So much of what the Christian life is all about is simultaneously growing in our understanding of God and human beings. On a personal level, we grow in Christ the more we come to fathom who God is and who God has made us to be in Christ (Jeynes 2006a). Therefore, the likelihood of being an effective parent is enhanced not merely by having greater intimacy with God, but also anticipating and responding appropriately to the various stages that children go through (Cloud and Townsend 2001; Kruschwitz 2001; Piper 2011).

Ironically, the first stage that it is important for parents to be sensitive to is the pre-birth stage. That is, it is wise indeed for parents to begin- praying for the child, having a family devotional, and interacting with the child even before the baby is born. This stage is the foundational stage, the ultimate opportunity to establish the groundwork on which the remainder if the youth's life will be built. At this time, if this child is the first born of the parents, it is an opportunity for the mother and father to establish a regular family devotional time (Dallman 2007; Piper 2011). It is a chance to initiate a practice of praying for the salvation of the child, which should be first and foremost on the parents' priority list. Another precious practice is singing to the child in the womb every single day. My wife and I chose two songs that we daily sang to our children in the womb. With each of our three children we chose to sing them two different songs (e.g., Amazing Grace, Blessed Assurance, and so forth). As they matured in the womb and we could feel their movement, we distinctly noticed that they were much more likely to be active in the womb when we sang to them. In fact, all our children very clearly recognized the two songs that were distinct to them. In almost every case, in their first few months after birth once our children would hear one of these two songs they would immediately stop crying. We would also read the Bible to them and talk with them with my lips right up to my wife Hyelee's belly. Once again, when we engaged in these thoroughly enjoyable disciplines (which was at least once a day), we noticed a distinctively enhanced level of activity in the womb, on their part.

Aside from the benefits mentioned above, one of the most tangible benefits that appeared to emerge after their birth is that our children appeared much more interactive and had higher activity levels after their birth than it seemed was evident in other babies of similar ages. They all seemed very desirous of interacting with my wife and me. As it was, even before our children were born, my wife and I decided that we were going to spend a significant amount of time interacting with our children throughout their lives, including their early days. When it became evident, however, just how desirous our newborns, babies, and toddlers were of communicating with us, it encouraged us to interact with them that much more. In other words, the trend toward greater levels of communication with our children in the early formative years, appeared to build upon itself without the need for forced effort on our part (Arnold 2007; Borruel 2002). My wife and I both believe that it was largely due to this high level of interaction that our babies all uttered their first word at around 6 or 7 months.

Freedom Tower Analogy

In those early formative years, it is vital that two trends be established that hopefully will always remain with the children. That is, it is extremely important the children realize that they are operating in a loving, secure, and supportive environment (Jeynes 1999, 2003a, b). What the children sense from us as their parents in the first two years or so will set the stage for all developments that follow (Arnold 2007; Borruel 2002). Those first two years form the foundation of the remainder of the child's life. It is much like when construction workers are building a skyscraper. When the Freedom Tower was built, the builders laid the foundation of the building by constantly digging and building 12 stories beneath the level of the ground. During this time, from the perspective of the casual onlooker, little progress was seemingly being made on the construction of the Freedom Tower. In reality, however, one can argue that the building of the foundation is the most crucial phase of the entire construction product. A physical building is only as strong as its foundation. The same may be said about raising children (Jeynes 2007a, 2010a). Although at such a young age, when it may seem impossible for children to let a parent know the extent he or she are making an impression on them, this is nevertheless perhaps the most important stage at all (Jeynes 2006b). Once the foundation is laid, people may love or dislike this approach. But its contribution is undeniable.

The First Two Years of a Child's Life and Love and Structure

The salience of the foundation being what it is, it is vital that parents understand that if there is to be any time that they love their children, the first couple of years of the child's life are of paramount importance (Kostenberger and Jones 2004; Mahoney 2010). The primary reason is simple: these first two years form the foundation of a child's existence (Kostenberger and Jones 2004; Mahoney 2010). One of the reasons why adults frequently have a hard time understanding just how crucial this period is finds its roots in the fact that the overwhelming number of people find it difficult to remember that far back in their journey of human experiences (Kullberg 1996). But if one cares to take a step back for a moment from current reality, it does not take much creativity to realize that those first two years are when one discovers just how the world works and gets an overall sense of whether the world is a desirable place to live. One of the reasons why parents, grandparents, aunts, and uncles take so much pleasure in being with the young children in their family is because everything seems new to them. Parents would be wise if they remembered that just as this sense of newness is what makes young children special, it is also what makes them vulnerable. During the first very vulnerable first two years of a child's life, it is crucial that he or she feel loved and develop a sense of growing up in a secure but also structured environment. It would be foolish indeed to raise a child either with an abundance of love, but a dearth of discipline and similarly it would be equally capricious to train a child focusing only on structure with no real demonstration of heart-felt love (Jeynes 2006b, 2010a). In order for there to be a healthy environment in which children can grow, both qualities need to exist simultaneously (Jeynes 2005c). If there is no structure, the children will become self-centered even to the place of narcissism. On the other hand, if any expression of love is evanescent, the child will tend to develop a rigid and judgmental mentality.

As important as these first two years are, some secular psychologists make a major mistake when they put too much focus on the first two years of a child's life (Doinick 1998; Egan 2002). And indeed this is especially true of Freudian psychiatrists who almost worship the idea of fixation at certain points of development, that are, in their view, crucial in life (Doinick 1998; Egan 2002). One can argue that it is the Freudian psychiatrists who suffer from fixation even more than the ones that they examine life (Doinick 1998; Egan 2002). One example of their literal obsession with these early formative years is a case I personally am familiar with of a man and woman who were divorced. The husband still wanted to save the marriage and would give his wife, who was the one filing for divorce, frequent phone calls begging her to reconsider and work on the marriage together to try to keep them together. My purpose in mentioning this is not to in any way condone the wife's actions in filing for divorce. Indeed, the Bible declares that, God "hates divorce" (Holy Bible, NIV Malachi 2:16 1979). Nevertheless, the wife became stressed out by her husband's insistence that if they both had a determination to work on the marriage, a stronger relationship would result. As a result, the wife consulted a Freudian psychiatrist to help her deal emotionally with the issue. If filing for the divorce was a mistake, so was appealing to this Freudian psychiatrist. She conveyed her problem with her Freudian psychologist and he focused not any set of recent events, but rather the situation she had faced she was an infant. His key question to her was, "When you were a child, did your parents give you a pacifier?" When she replied, "No," he responded that this was the central part of the problem. That is, her parents had not given her a pacifier when she was younger and that she had never successfully overcome that. The solution was to find items that she could suck on in her life today that would help her overcome this fixation. In spite of her protests asserting that it was recent events that had caused her such emotional strain, her Freudian psychiatrist insisted that returning to a life of sucking, whether it was on cigarettes, gum, or even an occasional pacifier was the key. She decided to follow the psychiatrist's advice, believing that she had no reasonable alternative. And after months of following his advice, she felt that she became considerably more emotionally distressed and psychologically imbalanced. In the end, she concluded that seeing the Freudian psychiatrist had done her considerably more harm than good. She testified later that she believed that she was psychologically healthy until she went to the Freudian counselor and it was after that point that she really began to develop emotional problems, simply because he was so off the mark in terms of identifying what her central problem actually was (Doinick 1998; Egan 2002).

Children at Ages 3–5

In contrast to this Freudian approach, then, Christian parents are to have greater respect for the passage of time (Piper 2011). They understand that only a small percentage of current problems faced by individuals originate with forces that were at work when a child is between the ages of zero and two (Hallett 1998; Jeynes 2002c). A plethora of challenges can be manifested at any time, whether an individual be in his childhood, his adolescent years, be a young adult, middle-aged, or a senior citizen (Cloud and Townsend 2001). As important as development during the first two years of life is, it is also true that the ages of 3–5 are vital as well (Cloud and Townsend 2001). This is the period during which youngsters consistently explore their surroundings at an amazing rate. They still need the supportive love that we addressed before, but the difference now is that the love and support fulfills something of a different function. Whereas before that love gave them a good sense about the world as a whole, now it helps give them the security to go out into the world to explore and try new things. Even during these relatively early years, as incipient as they may be, it is vital that parents understand that these young children are not to be treated as babies. Rather, these children need to be encouraged to begin to connect with and understand the world around them. They need to be taught that although the primary relationships at this stage are still with mom and dad, there are other interactions both with peers and relatives that they should pursue. My wife and I once met a mother who breastfed her child until he was nearly finished with elementary school. This would probably represent one of the more extreme examples of not appreciating the changes that children go through, even at this age.

Parental Adjustments with Dealing with Children Five and Above

It should be mentioned, however, that although part of being a good parent means, anticipating and responding appropriately to the various stages that children go through this can translate into different actions at different times (Wright and Oliver 1999). For example, thus far we have been examining the need to appreciate that children change and, in fact, need to change as they get older. There are two truths that should be noted at this juncture. First, sometimes the reverse can be true. For example, sometimes the politicians or forces that be in our society attempt to force children to change faster than is probably healthy for them or at a rate far beyond what would be considered desirable or normal. For example, sometimes teachers will force children to address issues of sexuality in kindergarten or the early grades, well before children even know what intercourse is (Jeynes 2007a; Tuch 2000). A number of studies suggest that such presumptuous- and agenda-tinged techniques can damage children (Baumrind et al. 2010; Shears et al. 2008; Steinberg et al. 2006). In fact, there is a considerable amount of research that indicates that some children may not be prepared to enter school at the time that conformity dictates that they should (Datar 2006; Ede 2004). Second, there is a sense that many day modern institutions may artificially slow the intellectual, emotional, and spiritual development of children (Hirsch 1999; Jeynes 2002a; Sykes 1996). Some have even argued that the idea of teenager is a modern day construct that artificially delays entrance by youth into adulthood (Pickhardt 2011; Salvatore 2013). They argue that by the time youth are in the 13–16 age range they generally have the physical stature of adults and that a myriad of societies in the past celebrated one or more of these years as representing that transition (Pickhardt 2011; Salvatore 2013). They assert that to not embrace this time for what it really is creates an unnatural friction in society between what the youth desire to become, i.e., more adult-like and the insistence by society that, for the most part, they remain in the cocoon of being children (Pickhardt 2011; Salvatore 2013). In the minds of many, it is this society- and government-imposed resistance to a rapid development into maturity that creates frustration in the youth and causes an unnecessarily high level of rebellion against their parents (Hirsch 1999; Salvatore 2013; Sykes 1996). Maturity is discouraged and an elongated childhood is imposed and the result is, in today's lingo, "arrested development." It is therefore wise for parents to consider the messages that government and society sometimes send to see if they are any way undermining the potential of their children. Put another way, parents must not assume that larger society works in a way that is conducive to the overall benefit of most children. In fact, there are countless times in which societal forces, e.g., unions and university presidents, are more focused on how their situation can be ameliorated rather than what is good for those that they represent, and that they sometimes have almost no regard what is best for the nation as a whole (Hirsch 1999; Sykes 1996).

The reality just stared makes parenting during the adolescent years of one's children, generally the most difficult. Nevertheless, if the mother and father commit themselves to applying the principles addressed earlier in this chapter, long-term fruit can still emerge, in spite of the obstacles.

Parenting Over the Life Course

Parenting, unlike just about every occupation under the sun, really has no retirement age. Yes indeed, there is a very real sense that once the child is an adult, the parent needs to back off and have much more of a "laissez faire" attitude toward parenting than was previously plausible and advisable. But as parents we are always there, whether this means to simply serve as an example, confidant, consoler, and so forth. As a testimony to this fact, many sons engage in immoral behavior after their father dies, when during the time that their father was alive they were able to fight off the tantalizing tentacles of temptation (Lamb 1997). Tiger Woods is one example of an individual who succumbed to his weaknesses much more after his father passed on than he did while his father was still alive.

The Wrestling Match Between Being a Strong Example and Spoiling the Children

There is a topic that few really want to talk about and, in fact, most people want to pretend really does not exist. That is, the tension that exists between attempting to be a strong example for children and spoiling them. Innumerable parents run into problems raising children because they fail to acknowledge this problem either totally or at least to some extent. For example, many parents spend their lives sacrificing for their children. To a large degree this is very healthy, but there are two warning flags that go up as an indication that it is being overdone (Ehrensaft 1997; Kindlon 2001; Sigman 2009). First, when the marriage is suffering because too much emphasis is placed on the children, e.g., the husband and wife rarely have time with each other and the needs of one or both of the spouses are not being met because the children are perceived as more important than the spouse (Ehrensaft 1997; Kindlon 2001; Sigman 2009). Second, when the children themselves almost never sacrifice for others, because they are only accustomed to people serving their needs (Ehrensaft 1997; Kindlon 2001; Sigman 2009). With this example in mind, and many others like it, it is therefore quite possible to raise a family with some of the most Christ-like examples possible and yet raise a group of children that is narcissistic and spoiled. There are a number of examples in the Bible of people who were men or women of God, but whose children fell well short of expectations (Barber 2010). Believers make a mistake indeed if they assume that every time that took place it was due to some inadequacy in the parenting of the mother and father. It is likely that there were times when this was the case, but we can hardly assume that this was the situation each and every time. There are a variety of reasons why children may not turn out as well as expected and poor parenting is one of them, but there are various and sundry other reasons as well.

If one looks at the Word of God, it is clear that there are certain examples of poor parenting that yielded children that did not walk in the ways of the Lord the way that they should have. Moreover, there are numerous admonitions in the Bible, particularly in Proverbs and in the Pentateuch (the first five books of the Old Testament) of the consequences of not rearing children in a scriptural way. Clearly, David did not spend enough time with Absalom at a crucial time and this contributed to at least some of Absalom's rebellious behavior. Isaac, partially due to his failing eyes and health, seemed detached from interactions with Jacob. God gave Eli a stern rebuke for not giving proper oversight to his sons. Samuel's sons were not as completely self-centered as Eli's sons, but it is quite patent that they were corrupt. Nevertheless, there are also a number of times in which strong believing fathers had spoiled and narcissistic children and Scripture is not clear regarding what were the reasons why. Hezekiah was a wonderful example of walking righteously before the Lord, but his son Manasseh certainly was not. The same pattern also holds with Josiah. In each case, Scripture is not clear on the reasons why and both of these kings were the beneficiaries of lavish praise from God. In fact, given that God extolled the virtues of Hezekiah and Josiah to a profound degree, specifically declaring that these men were in a class by themselves in terms of the quality of kings that followed David, and apparently did not rebuke them for insufficient acts of fatherhood, it becomes much more difficult to make the case that Hezekiah and Josiah were poor fathers.

In reality, virtually every human being acknowledges that although coming from an unrighteous or dysfunctional family environment increases the chances that children will not turn out as holy and right before God, there are also many spoiled and self-centered children that come from loving Christ-centered homes. And part of the reason such results are quite possible stems from the fact that there exists this tension between attempting to be a strong example for children and spoiling them. The reality then is that fathers and mothers need to demonstrate a balance (Ehrensaft 1997; Kindlon 2001; Sigman 2009). On the one hand, parents need to be very cognizant of the need to set a solid spiritual example for their children. On the other hand, this example must not be to the place that virtually all acts of love and sacrifice are initiated by the parent and the child is always on the receiving end. Yes, the father and mother can, as the need arises, set that example of sacrificing their bed and allowing their guests to stay in their bed. But it is also true that to be efficacious parents, they should give occasional opportunities for children sacrifice their beds for guests as well. In this way, the children are not always on the observing or receiving end of a sacrifice, but are at times given opportunity to apply what they have learned from their parents (Ehrensaft 1997; Kindlon 2001; Sigman 2009). Such an approach increases the chances that parental holiness will yield a similar result in the children (Piper 2011).

We presently live in a society in which countless parents are doing for children what the youngsters really need to be doing for themselves or at least largely for themselves (Ehrensaft 1997; Kindlon 2001; Sigman 2009). These days parents buy their children cars, pay for the gas that goes in their car, purchase their automobile insurance, a variety of luxury items, and so forth. In addition, mothers and fathers commonly complete their children's homework and in some of the extreme cases hire professors and tutors to write the students' application essays in order to get into a better college (Ehrensaft 1997; Kindlon 2001; Sigman 2009). When their children get in trouble because of irresponsible behavior, sloth, inane planning, or inveterate selfishness, these parents often bail their children out. In many respects there is a real irony to the fact that many world leaders, economists, social scientists, and people generally are raising real concerns about the number of bailouts that are taking place around the world, especially in Western Europe and the United States (McDonald and Robinson 2009). Countless economists and social scientists find it totally enigmatic how so many millions of people in these areas of the world could have developed an attitude in which they think that they can take all kinds of unwarranted risks, engage in activities that are totally decoupled from every vestige of logic, and live existences that are very precarious, with little concern about what consequences might result from their careless and irresponsible behaviors of today (McDonald and Robinson 2009). And indeed it is mind-boggling. This sense of entitlement pervades many aspects of Western society that was once well known for practicing the Protestant work ethic.

These days it appears that most of the major socioeconomic- and demographic-groups believe that society somehow "owes" them and they therefore possess an attitude of entitlement concerning many facets in their lives (Block 2013; McDonald and Robinson 2009). Numerous wealthy people tend to have the attitude that they really do not care about the welfare of other people, but rather feel that gifts that helped make them wealthy entitle them to a plenteous lifestyle (Block 2013). A copious number of Wall Street executives have shown that at times their concerns for others is almost non-existent; and rather these executives are focused in lining their own pockets. There are nearly 50 million people on food stamps, who believe that the government somehow owes them a living (Block 2013). And indeed, when I see these people purchase items in the grocery store, they usually buy better meat than our family can afford. And yet our tax dollars are supporting them. The middle class is paying the bills resulting from the profligate- and irresponsible- living of many Americans. I recall meeting some Chinese societal leaders who commented that the U.S. is a great place to be poor, because the government takes such good care of them and a great place to be rich. But they also added that it as a horrible place to be middle class, because they were the ones bailing out the rich and the poor, for their self-centered behavior.

Within this context, if fathers and mothers remember that their goal is to teach their children "how to fly in life," rather than spoiling them and show some "tough love," their efforts may not be appreciated initially, but likely will be in the long run. If the parents put on an emphasis on teaching love, responsibility, respect, diligence, perseverance, dedication, and loyalty not only by their examples, but also in terms of what they teach their children both in their words and the deeds they encourage, the young can learn to become mature adults. What is important to realize, that many people do not understand, is that just as words are not enough to guide behavior neither is setting an example. Young people need to be taught what the example means for them in the context of their daily lives. That is, they need to follow that example or else the example is of limited merit. The best example one can set for one's children is one that is explained and contagious (Jeynes 2009a).

The Body of Research and Parenting

We live in an era in which many people are convinced that parents really do not have the influence on children that they did in generations past (Jeynes 2011a, 2012d). Alternatively, the argument goes that it is peers and the media that impact youth to the greatest degree (Baehr 1998; Jeynes 2010b, 2011c). The interesting reality, however, is that as tangible and common as these perceptions are, the body of research indicates that parents do still enjoy a greater effect on their children than these rival forces (Jeynes 2011b). Admittedly, these other factors do have more of an impact than they once did. Moreover, with the development and dispersion of more sources of influence than existed decades ago, one can make an argument that parental influence is not as potent as it once was. And clearly, there is some real justification for this belief. However, that dilution is probably a good deal less than the media often makes it out to be. And indeed, there are several good reasons to believe that the decline of parental influence is exaggerated. First, one needs to recall that most of the reports about the diminished role of the parent comes from media outlets. It must therefore be remembered that the media benefits personally if their role is highlighted and the family role is underemphasized. The media is therefore a biased source of information, because those who serve in this industry have every reason to magnify their influence. The media only increases the influence it has on children by emphasizing it and at times bombastically exaggerating the role that it plays in helping shape children's lives (Baehr 1998; Price and Dahl 2012).

Second, much of the media is run by people who are in rebellion against the "establishment" and there is no more palpable example of the establishment in the minds of youth than parents. A myriad of media experts have pointed out the fact that those in Hollywood, in particular, but in other media outlets as well, often portray older people as inept, ignorant, and clueless (Baehr 1998). In contrast, contemporary shows describe youth as insightful, wise, and bright (Baehr 1998). Quite a number of commentators have attributed this to the fact that many of those in Hollywood desire to usurp control from the traditional institutional pillars of society that heretofore have had a puissant role in establishing the morals, ethics, and valued practices of society (Robinson and Jeynes 2010). Once again, the bias is clear and there is every reason for the Hollywood crowd to become almost maudlin in their exaggeration of how media affects children and how little parents do. To be sure, Hollywood, the internet, and other media expressions have a measurable impact on youth (Price and Dahl 2012). Nevertheless, it is one thing to assert that these influences are poignant and real and it is another thing to belittle the prominent role that family plays in the development of the next generation.

Third, the reality is that when asked, children still name their parents as the most important influence on their lives. As much as youth might surf the internet and watch television for an interminable number of hours, they are still aware that it is parents who are the primary human influence in their lives. Fourth, those who argue that the role of family is declining in influence in children's lives often measure this so-called descent purely by the amount of time children spend engaged in particular activities (Price and Dahl 2012). But these studies fail to fully consider that children are not stupid. They are usually aware that it is those that raise them who are supposed to have the most dynamic influence in their lives. They are usually able to discern between fact and faction, as well as understand the difference between reality and fantasy. Therefore, the young often internalize the effects of the spiritual and emotional investments of their father and mother.

The Advantages to Children of Close Relationships with Their Parents

There are some very notable advantages that accrue to youth, when they have a close relationship with their parents. First, there is a greater dedication among members of the family to each other. Although there are exceptions, as a general rule a person can only love an individual insofar as one knows that individual. Strong relationships make interpersonal knowledge possible and from there, love can spawn. Second, children in close relationships with their parents are less likely to engage in harmful behaviors, e.g., the consumption of illegal drugs and excessive amounts of alcohol. Young men in gangs are almost always fatherless (Lamb 1997; Popenoe 2000). Close relationships with fathers and mothers make it less likely that youth will look for surrogate parents elsewhere and substantially reduce the chances for ongoing emotional wounds that so often create addictions to drugs and alcohol. Children with close relationships with their parents also perform better than school and are more likely to succeed in their future marriages and in life in general (McLanahan and Sandefur 1994; Wallerstein 2005). For the parents the investment of love in their children is worth the result; and for children a positive response to this investment of love is worth the reward.

References

Altschul, I. (2011). Parental involvement and the academic achievement of Mexican American youths: What kinds of involvement in youth's education matter most. *Social Work Research, 35*(3), 159–170.

Arnold, L. B. (2007). *Family communication: Theory and research*. Boston: Allyn & Bacon.

Baehr, T. (1998). *The media-wise family*. Colorado Springs: Victor Publishing.

Barber, C. J. (2010). *Profiles of the patriarchs: Jacob*. Eugene: Wipf and Stock Publishers.

Barclay, W. (2010). *Forgiveness: What the Bible tells us about forgiveness*. Edinburgh: Saint Andrew.

Baumrind, D., Larzelere, R. E., & Owens, E. B. (2010). Effects of preschool parents' power assertive patterns and practices on adolescent development. *Parenting: Science and Practice, 10*(3), 157–201.

Becker, G. (1981). *Treatise on the family*. Cambridge: Harvard University Press.

Block, P. (2013). *Stewardship: Choosing service over self-interest*. San Francisco: Berrett-Koehler.

Borruel, T. W. (2002). The ten p's of parent communication. A strategy for staff development. *Child Care Information Exchange, 143*(1), 54–57.

Brooks, R. B., & Goldstein, S. (2001). *Raising resilient children: Fostering strength, hope, and optimism in your child*. Lincolnwood: Contemporary Books.

Cervone, D., & Shoda, Y. (1999). *The coherence of personality: Social-cognitive bases of consistency, variability, and organization*. New York: Guilford.

Chapman, G. D., Campbell, R., & Fabry, C. (2008). *The five love languages of children*. Carol Stream: Oasis.

Clinton, T. E., & Ohischlager, G. W. (2002). *Competent Christian counseling*. Colorado Springs: Waterbrook.

Cloud, H., & Townsend, J. S. (2001). *How people grow: What the Bible reveals about personal growth*. Grand Rapids: Zondervan.

Dallman, C. A. (2007). *One-minute Bible devotions*. Lincolnwood: Publications International.

Datar, A. (2006). Does delaying kindergarten entrance give children a head start? *Economics of Education Review, 25*(1), 43–62.

DeMuth, M. E. (2006). *Building the Christian family you never had*. Colorado Springs: Westbrook.

Dobson, J. C. (2007). *Life on the edge: The next generation's guide to a meaningful future*. Carol Stream: Tyndale House.

Doinick, E. (1998). *Madness on the couch: Blaming the victim in the heydey of psychoanalysis*. New York: Simon & Schuster.

Ede, A. (2004). Is my children really too young for kindergarten? *Childhood Education, 80*(4), 207–208.

Egan, K. (2002). *Getting it wrong from the beginning*. New Haven: Yale University Press.

Ehrensaft, D. (1997). *Spoiling childhood: How well-meaning parents are giving children too much—but not what they need*. New York: Guilford Press.

Evertson, C. M., & Emmer, E. T. (2009). *Classroom management for elementary teachers*. Upper Saddle River: Pearson.

Hallett, G. (1998). *Priorities and Christian ethics*. Cambridge: Cambridge University Press.

Hetzendorfer, R. (2009). *The pastoral counseling handbook*. Nashville: Beacon Hill.

Hirsch, E.D. (1999). *The schools we need: And why we don't have them*. Norwell: Anchor.

Holy Bible (1979). *Holy Bible*, New International Version. Nashville: Thomas Nelson.

Jeynes, W. (1999). The effects of religious commitment on the academic achievement of black and Hispanic children. *Urban Education, 34*(4), 458–479.

Jeynes, W. (2000). Assessing school choice: A balanced perspective. *Cambridge Journal of Education, 30*(2), 223–241.

Jeynes, W. (2002a). A meta-analysis of the effects of attending religious schools and religiosity on black and Hispanic academic achievement. *Education and Urban Society, 35*(1), 27–49.

Jeynes, W. (2002b). *Divorce, family structure, and the academic success of children*. New York: Haworth Press and Taylor & Francis.
Jeynes, W. (2002c). The relationship between the consumption of various drugs by adolescents and their academic achievement. *The American Journal of Drug and Alcohol Abuse, 28*(1), 1–21.
Jeynes, W. (2003a). A meta-analysis: The effects of parental involvement on minority children's academic achievement. *Education and Urban Society, 35*(2), 202–218.
Jeynes, W. (2003b). The effects of black and Hispanic twelfth graders living in intact families and being religious on their academic achievement. *Urban Education, 38*(1), 35–57.
Jeynes, W. (2005a). Parental involvement and student achievement: A meta-analysis. *Family involvement research digest, harvard family research project*. Cambridge: Harvard Family Research Project.
Jeynes, W. (2005b). A meta-analysis of the relation of parental involvement to urban elementary school student academic achievement. *Urban Education, 40*(3), 237–269.
Jeynes, W. (2005c). Effects of parental involvement and family structure on the academic achievement of adolescents. *Marriage and Family Review, 37*(3), 99–117.
Jeynes, W. (2005d). The relationship between urban students attending religious revival services and academic and social outcomes. *Education and Urban Society, 38*(1), 3–20.
Jeynes, W. (2006a). *A hand not shortened*. Greenwich: Information Age.
Jeynes, W. (2006b). Standardized tests and the true meaning of kindergarten and preschool. *Teachers College Record, 108*(10), 1937–1959.
Jeynes, W. (2007a). *American educational history: School, society, and the common good*. Thousand Oaks: Sage.
Jeynes, W. (2007b). The relationship between parental involvement and urban secondary school academic achievement: A meta-analysis. *Urban Education, 42*(1), 82–110.
Jeynes, W. (2009a). *Getting closer to God*. Charlotte: Information Age.
Jeynes, W. (2009b). The relationship between Bible literacy and academic achievement, and school behavior. *Education and Urban Society, 41*(4), 419–436.
Jeynes, W. (2010a). *A call for character education and prayer in the schools*. Westport: Praeger.
Jeynes, W. (2010b). Religiosity, religious schools, and their relationship with the achievement gap: A research synthesis and meta-analysis. *Journal of Negro Education, 79*(3), 263–279.
Jeynes, W. (2010c). The relationship between Bible literacy and academic and behavioral outcomes in urban areas: A meta-analysis. *Education and Urban Society, 42*(5), 522–544.
Jeynes, W. (2010d). The salience of the subtle aspects of parental involvement and encouraging that involvement: Implications for school-based programs. *Teachers College Record, 112*(3), 747–774.
Jeynes, W. (2011a). Help families by fostering parental involvement. *Phi Delta Kappan, 93*(3), 38–39.
Jeynes, W. (2011b). *Parental involvement & academic success*. New York: Taylor & Francis/Routledge.
Jeynes, W. (2011c). Race, racism & Darwinism. *Education and Urban Society, 43*(5), 535–559.
Jeynes, W. (2012a). A meta-analysis on the effects and contributions of public, public charter, and religious schools on student outcomes. *Peabody Journal of Education, 87*(3), 305–335.
Jeynes, W. (2012b). A meta-analysis of the efficacy of different types of parental involvement programs for urban students. *Urban Education, 47*(4), 706–742.
Jeynes, W. (2012c). Character instruction in Protestant education throughout history. In W. Jeynes & D. Robinson (Eds.), *The international handbook of protestant education*. (pp. 3–24) London: Springer.
Jeynes, W. (2012d). Reaching out to make a difference. *Phi Delta Kappan, 93*(6), 80.
Jeynes, W., & Robinson, D. (2010). Character education in Christian higher education: A historic analysis and contemporary challenge (Part I). *Christian Higher Education, 9*(4), 295–315.
Jeynes, W., & Beuttler, F. (2012). What public and private schools can learn from one another. *Peabody Journal of Education, 87*(3), 285–304.
Kindlon, D. (2001). *Too much of a good thing: Raising children of character in an indulgent age*. New York: Hyperion.

Kostenberger, A. J., & Jones, D. W. (2004). *God, marriage & family: Rebuilding the biblical foundation*. Wheaton: Crossway Books.
Kruschwitz, R. B. (2001). *Forgiveness*. Waco: Baylor University.
Kullberg, K. M. (1996). *Finding god at Harvard: Spiritual journeys of thinking Christians*. Grand Rapids: Zondervan.
Lamb, M. (1997). *The role of the father in child development*. New York: Wiley.
Mahoney, A. (2010). Religion in families, 1999–2009: A relational Spirituality framework. *Journal of Marriage and Family, 72*(4), 805–827.
McDonald, L. G., & Robinson, P. (2009). *A colossal failure of common sense*. New York: Crown.
McLanahan, S. & Sandefur, G. (1994). *Growing up with a single parent: What hurts, what helps*. Cambridge: Harvard University Press.
McPherson, J. (2002). *How to parent your teen without losing your mind*. Nashville: Broadman & Holman.
Meyer, J. (2002). *Making marriage work: The advice you need for a lifetime of happiness*. New York: Warner Faith.
Micklethwait, J., & Wooldridge, A. (2009). *God is back: How the global revival of faith is changing the world*. New York: Penguin.
Minith, F. B. (2004). *In pursuit of happiness: Choices that can change your life*. Grand Rapids: Fleming H. Revell.
Montague, G. T. (2011). *First Corinthians*. Grand Rapids: Baker Academic.
Murray, J. (2001). *Love, marriage, and family in the Middle Ages*. Peterborough: Broadview.
Nord, W. (2010). *Does God make a difference*. New York: Oxford University Press.
Palm, G., & Fagan, J. (2008). Father involvement in early childhood programs: Review of the literature. *Early Child Development and Care, 178*(7/8), 745–759.
Pickhardt, C. E. (2011). *Boomerang kids: A revealing look at why many of our children are failing on their own, and how parents can help*. Naperville: Sourcebooks.
Piper, J. (2011). *Desiring God: Meditations of a Christian hedonist*. Colorado Springs: Multnomah.
Popenoe, D. (2000). Life without father. In Daniels, C. R. (Ed.), *Lost fathers: The politics of fatherless in America*. (pp. 33–49). New York: St. Martin's.
Post, S. G. (2000). *More lasting unions: Christianity, the family, and society*. Grand Rapids: Eerdmans.
Powell, K. E. (2009). *Friends and peer pressure*. Ventura: Regal.
Price, J. & Dahl, G. B. (2012). Using natural experiments to study the impact of media on the family. *Family Relations, 61*(3), 363–373.
Robinson, D., & Jeynes, W. (2010). Character education in Christian higher education: A historic analysis and contemporary challenge (Part II). *Christian Higher Education, 9*(4), 316–335.
Salvatore, C. (2013). *Arrested adult offenders: A study of delayed transitions To adulthood*. El Paso: LFB Scholarly Publishing.
Selvaggio, A. T., & Meath, K. (2008). *A proverbs driven life: Timeless wisdom for your Work, wealth, and relationships*. Wapwallopen: Shepherd.
Shears, J. K., Whiteside-Mansell, L., & McKelvey, L. (2008). Assessing mothers' and Fathers' authoritarian attitudes: The psychometric properties of a brief survey. *Social Work Research, 32*(3), 179–184.
Sigman, A. (2009). *The spoilt generation: Why restoring authority will make our children and society happier*. London: Piakus.
Steinberg, L., Blatt-Eisengart, I., & Caufman, E. (2006). Patterns of competence and adjustment among adolescents from authoritative, authoritarian, indulgent, and neglectful homes: A replication in a sample of serious juvenile offenders. *Journal of Research on Adolescence, 16*(1), 47–58.
Strobel, L., & Strobel, L. (2010). *Surviving a spiritual mismatch in marriage*. Grand Rapids: Zondervan.
Strom, B. (2002). Communicator virtue and vice: Neglected constructs of relational communication. *Atlantic Journal of Communication, 10*(1), 84–103.

Swindoll, C. R. (1998). *Joseph: A man of integrity and forgiveness: Profiles in Character*. Nashville: Word Publishers.
Sykes, C. (1996). *Dumbing down our kids: Why American children feel good about themselves but can't read, write, or odd*. New York: St. Martins.
Szabo, C. (2004). *Peer pressure*. Nashville: Abington.
Thompson, J. A. (2006). *Parenting teens: A field guide*. Colorado Springs: Cook Communications.
Tripp, P. D. (2001). *Age of opportunity: A biblical guide to parenting teens*. Phillipsburg: P & R Publishing.
Tripp, P. D. (2008). *Peer pressure: Warning signs and giving new direction*. Greensboro: New Growth Press.
Tuch, R. (2000). *The single woman-married man syndrome*. Northvale: Aronson.
Vangelisti, A. L. (2004). *Handbook of family communication*. Mahwah: Erlbaum.
Wallace, R. S. (2001). *The story of Joseph and the family of Jacob*. Grand Rapids: W.B. Eerdmans.
Wallerstein, J. S. (2005). Growing up in a divorced family. *Clinical Social Work Journal, 33*(4), 401–418.
Wallerstein, J. S., & Lewis, J. (1998). The long-term impact of divorce on children: A first report from a 25-year study. *Family and Conciliation Courts Review, 36*(3), 368–383.
Worthington, E. Jr. (2000). *Christian marital counseling: Eight approaches to helping couples*. Eugene: Wipf and Stock.
Wright, H. N., & Oliver, G. J. (1999). *Raising kids to love Jesus*. Ventura: Regal.

William Jeynes William Jeynes has served in counseling ministry for over 34 years and in academics for 23 years. He and his wife have counseled thousands of families over the years and he has three degrees in Psychology and Counseling and a fourth in a related field. He is a Professor at California State University, Long Beach and a Senior Fellow on the Family at the Witherspoon Institute in Princeton, New Jersey. He graduated first in his class at Harvard University and also graduated from the University of Chicago, where he received the Rosenberger Award for the most outstanding student in his cohort. Bill has ministered in churches in every inhabited continent and in nearly every state in the country. He has spoken a number of times at Yoido Full Gospel Church in Korea, the largest church in the world. He has spoken on family and faith issues for the White House, the U.S. Department of Justice, the U.S. Department of Education, and the U.S. Department of Health & Human Services. He has spoken for both the G. W. Bush and Obama administrations. He has spoken for foreign and UN leaders, Harvard University, Cambridge University, Oxford University, Columbia University, Duke University, Notre Dame University, and the Harvard Family Research Project. His four-point family and economic proposal given to the Acting President of Korea was passed and became the foundation for their economic and family policy to arise from the Asian Economic Crisis of 1997–1998. He has about 140 academic publications, including 12 books on family and faith issues.

Dr. Jeynes has been interviewed or quoted by the Washington Post, the Los Angeles Times, The Wall Street Journal, the New York Times, the London Times, the Associated Press (AP), CBS, NBC, ABC, FOX, public radio, Al Jazeera and many other news sources. His work has been cited and quoted numerous times by the U.S. Congress, the British Parliament, the EU, and many State Supreme Courts across the United States. Dr. Jeynes has been listed in Who's Who in the World for each of the last nine years and received a Distinguished Scholar Award the California State Senate, the California State Assembly, and his university. He formerly taught at USC and the University of Chicago. Bill has been married for over 28 years and has three wonderful children.

The Impact of Family Religiosity for Latina/o Youth: Building a Case for Personal and Academic Enhancement through Faith

René Antrop-González, Tomás Garrett and William Vélez

Abstract This chapter presents two overarching themes. First, it describes the dual role of religiosity and its impact on academic achievement according to the experiences of ten poor Puerto Rican students schooled in a large comprehensive urban high school in the United States. These students' theorizing regarding the impact of their religiosity on their high academic achievement is especially important because, unlike the large majority of studies that have examined the effects of religiosity on academic achievement through quantitative analyses, this study focuses on the lived experiences and voices of urban high school youth of color. Second, we discuss the implications of these findings in relation to families in the hopes that they can encourage schools to seriously look to faith communities and places of worship as important partners in the educative process. Faith based communities have the vast potential to encourage their youth to remain engaged in them in order to reduce their likelihood of making problematic decisions that could hinder their academic achievement. Likewise, the expectation is that schools will also work like places of faith, as they strive to being intimately connected to the education of urban youth of color.

Keywords Latina/o students · Puerto Rican students · Urban education · Religiosity · Social capital · High achievers

Introduction

Latina/o high achievers are largely invisible in traditional, public urban high schools and in educational research. More specifically, the impact of religiosity on the academic achievement of these high achievers and their implications for

R. Antrop-González (✉)
School of Education, Dalton State College, Brown, 309, Dalton, GA 30720, USA
e-mail: rantropgonzalez@daltonstate.edu

T. Garrett · W. Vélez
College of Letters and Science, University of Wisconsin-Milwaukee, Bolton Hall, 728, P.O. Box 413, Milwaukee, WI 53201, USA
e-mail: velez@uwm.edu

W. Jeynes, E. Martinez (eds.), *Ministering Spiritually to Families*,
DOI 10.1007/978-3-319-13302-7_9

ministering to families is rarely discussed. Consequently, over the last three decades, numerous scholars have written about the connections between the academic *underachievement* of Puerto Rican colonial subjects educated in the United States and socioeconomic/academic barriers like internal and direct colonialism, single-parent households, poverty, culturally irrelevant curricula, and the non-academic tracking these students face within traditional public urban schools on a continual basis (Díaz 1998; Nieto 1998, 2000; Spring 1994). Although the above-mentioned scholarship is important, it places overdue emphasis on the academic underachievement of these students.

To counteract the overabundance of scholarly literature that discusses reasons why Puerto Rican students are pushed out of school and/or academically underachieve, we felt it was important to ask the following question: What factors do poor urban Puerto Rican students, enrolled in traditional urban high schools, attribute to their academic success in spite of the previously mentioned socioeconomic and sociopolitical barriers? As a result of our larger conversations with these students, we discovered that all of them credited their religiosity as having a positive impact on their high academic achievement. Furthermore, these students theorized how their religiosity played an important dual role in their academic and personal lives.

Therefore, the purpose of this chapter is twofold. First, we describe the dual role of religiosity and its impact on academic achievement according to the experiences of ten poor Puerto Rican students schooled in a large comprehensive urban high school in the United States. These students' theorizing regarding the impact of their religiosity on their high academic achievement is especially important because, unlike the large majority of studies that have examined the effects of religiosity on academic achievement through quantitative analyses (see Flores-González (2002) for exceptions), our particular study focuses on the lived experiences and voices of urban high school youth of color. Second, we discuss the implications of these findings in relation to families in the hopes that they can encourage schools to seriously look to faith communities and places of worship as important partners in the educative process. Faith based communities have the vast potential to encourage their youth to remain engaged in them in order to reduce their likelihood of making problematic decisions that could hinder their academic achievement. Likewise, the expectation is that schools will also work to view themselves and work like places of faith, as they strive to being intimately connected in the education of urban youth, particularly those of color (Scheurich 1998).

Scholarship on Religion and Academic Achievement

Scholars have recently produced research that serves to deconstruct, reconstruct, and transcend the scholarship on academic underachievement by examining the myriad ways in which religiosity foments the high academic achievement of urban youth of color (Flores-González 2002; Jeynes 2003a, b, c; Park 2001; Sikkink and Hernández 2003). This research is especially important, because it has paid particular attention to the ways in which individual religious beliefs, rather than institutional ones (i.e., religious schools), have positively impacted the academic achievement of urban youth of color. William Jeynes (2003a, pp. 37–38; emphasis mine) comments:

> In terms of examining the effects of religious commitment, part of the reason for the dearth of studies in this area of endeavor results from the fact that researchers have generally examined the effects of religion on academic achievement from the macrolevel, that is, they have primarily investigated the effects of *religious schools* on academic achievement. One can argue, however, that the *individual religious beliefs* of students are just as important as, and perhaps more important than, the beliefs of the educational institution that they attend.

Furthermore, religiosity by way of active participation in church related activities has been found to be an important source of social capital for two reasons. First, church membership provides mentoring relations between adults and youth that instill positive attitudes, values, and behaviors that promote school success and serve as protective measures against oppositional youth behaviors like gang membership, drug use, and truancy. Second, participating in church activities like retreats and conventions facilitates intergenerational closure (Sikkink and Hernández 2003). Intergenerational closure is valuable, because it helps these students, through the relationships they have with their friends and their friends' parents, gain access to important resources like advice, mentorship, and other positive help-seeking behaviors that encourage them to pursue and maintain their high academic achievement.

Kaye Cook interviewed African American high school students living in poverty and found they credited their high academic achievement with their religious commitment. They specifically mentioned the notion that "God has my back," which meant they felt protected from anti-school influences like gang membership, drug use, and the need to engage in sexually promiscuous behaviors. Additionally, these high achieving students discussed the importance their community-based churches played in their lives. These churches served not only religious functions but social ones, as youth and adults engaged one another in mentoring relationships. These mentoring relationships made it possible for the youth in this study to receive counseling in times of personal crisis and to receive important information like how to apply for financial aid in college and receive tutoring for college entrance examinations, such as the SAT and ACT.

Nilda Flores-González (1999, 2002) used role identity theory to explain the multiple ways in which urban high schools inequitably structure opportunities for Puerto Rican students by influencing whether they adopt either a "school kid" or "street kid" identity. The high achieving Puerto Rican students whom she interviewed and classified as having a "school kid" identity were more likely to be sheltered in safe social niches with other school kids and encouraged by school staff to actively participate in extracurricular activities like athletic teams, church-related activities, and academic-based school clubs. These extracurricular activities also enabled these students to set themselves apart from the "street kids." Moreover, these school kids were more likely to view post-secondary education as a way through which they could become a member of the middle class.

On the contrary, the low achieving Puerto Rican students who she found adopted a "street kid" identity found it difficult to situate themselves within school oriented peer social networks and the school staff neither encouraged nor facilitated these students' participation in school related activities. Hence, the self-concept that children and young adults develop reflects their images of their future and what they hope to become, and thus guides their actions in schools and other social institutions. Additionally, unlike the schooling experiences of high achieving African-American students in previous studies (Fordham and Ogbu 1986), the high achieving Puerto Rican students interviewed by Flores-González (1999, 2002) voiced a strong Puerto Rican ethnic identity, revealing that they neither perceived themselves nor were perceived by other school peers as "acting White."

William Jeynes (2003a, b, c) found that the individual religious commitment of African American and Latina/o urban high school students enabled them to outperform their nonreligious school peers. Furthermore, he found that living in intact families was also a major contributor to the high academic achievement of these students. He goes on to suggest that religiosity was important for these students' academic success because they were much less likely to engage in drug and/or alcohol abuse and sexually active behavior. Finally, Jeynes specifically points out the positive relationship between religiosity and an internal locus of control, because Christianity stresses the fact that the spirit of God often resides not only outside the believer but also from within. Likewise, Hae-Seong Park (2001) found that religiousness had a profound positive effect on the academic achievement of African American, Latina/o, Asian, and White high school students. Like Jeynes (2003a, b, c) and Park (2001), David Sikkink and Edwin Hernández (2003) found that religiosity had a positive impact on the academic achievement of urban Latina/o high school students because of the high degrees of social capital that were inherent within churches and church-sponsored activities like youth groups. These activities enabled these students to find their places within safe peer niches where they were sheltered from the same types of behaviors as mentioned before like substance abuse and teenage pregnancy.

Finally, while these recent studies have done much to advance the exploration of religiosity and its effects on the academic achievement of urban youth of color, most of them have been conducted through quantitative analyses. This study, however, acknowledges the voices of Puerto Rican students as they speak to the power that religiosity has had on their high academic achievement in spite of the socioeconomic/sociopolitical hardships they constantly face and the alienating nature of large, comprehensive urban high schools.

Methods

Research Question

This study was guided by the principal research question, "According to the experiences of Puerto Rican 11th and 12th grade students who are enrolled in a traditional comprehensive urban high school, what factors are linked to their high academic achievement?

Setting and Participants

This study was conducted at University High School (a pseudonym), a large comprehensive high school located in a large Midwestern city, during the 2001–2002 academic year. This high school enrolls 1500 students from grades 9 to 12 of which 55 % fall below the federal poverty line. Approximately 70 % of the high school's students are of color with 15 % of these students being Puerto Rican. This school is regarded as one of only two of the district's best high schools, because its curriculum offers many advanced placement and honors level courses and because 70 % of its graduates go on to pursue some sort of postsecondary education. As a result, this high school attracts many students of color from around the city because of its reputation as a college preparatory high school. Moreover, we selected this high school for the study precisely because of this reputation.

The students recruited for this study had to meet three criteria that would help us purposefully select students who could best speak about their schooling and home experiences and how these impacted their high academic achievement. First, they had to be enrolled in grades 11 or 12, because the majority of Puerto Rican students drop out of school by the 10th grade (Nieto 1998). Second, the students had to have a cumulative GPA of 3.0 or higher, because we determined this GPA to be indicative of a high achieving student. Third, the students could not have dropped out of school at any time, because we wanted this study to focus on non-dropouts. Using these three criteria, a Puerto Rican guidance counselor at the school facilitated the recruitment and selection process of the participants, because she knew the Latina/o students well. A total of ten students met these three criteria, and they all agreed to participate after we explained the purpose of the study to them.

Data Collection

In the philosophical tradition and method of phenomenology, our primary data collection tool consisted of in-depth interviews. Phenomenology attempts to "examine the *meaning of experiences* for individuals" (Creswell 1998, p. 86; original emphasis). Because the main data collection tool of phenomenology is the in-depth interview (Merriam 1998; Tesch 1994), we structured our conversations with each student using the three-interview series (Seidman 1998). Each of the three semi-structured interviews lasted approximately 1 h and was spaced 1 week apart. All interviews were audiotaped and transcribed verbatim.

The first interview, called the "focused life history" interview, elicited the students' descriptions regarding their family backgrounds and previous schooling experiences. The second interview, known as the "details of experience" interview, focused on each student's current schooling experiences. Thus, they were asked questions meant to elicit rich descriptions of their current relationships with teachers, their peers, other school staff, and community members. Finally, the purpose of the third "reflection on the meaning" interview was to have each student compare and contrast their previous and current school and home experiences and discuss their future life aspirations.

Data Analysis

The objective of the phenomenological data analysis process is to identify and examine recurring meaning units, which are the "the smallest segments of texts that are understandable by themselves" (Tesch 1994, p. 148). Moreover, phenomenological researchers "do not establish categories, but aim at discovering the 'themes' in the data" (Tesch 1994, p. 148). Thus, our data analysis consisted of reading and analyzing all the interviews to discover meaningful recurring themes, and the ways in which our participants linked them to their high academic achievement. When these recurring themes were discovered within the interview data, we proceeded to color code them and place them into distinct themes. Hence, using the inductive process of narrowing data enabled us to collapse participants' experiences under major categories. Consequently, religiosity and its positive dual role on the high academic achievement of the Puerto Rican students we spoke with emerged as a central theme in the data analysis process.

Validity, Reliability, and Trustworthiness

The interview protocols we constructed did not contain questions pertaining to religiosity and/or religious commitment. Rather, we asked general questions such as, "Whom or what do you attribute to your high academic achievement?" In other words, we did not expect students to address these issues and how they impacted our participants' academic achievement. It was not until religiosity and/or religious commitment emerged as a recurring theme did we delve into the research literature that had previously, specifically, and similarly addressed this connection. Upon our further investigation pertaining to this literature, we discovered that similar work had been conducted through a quantitative research paradigm (Jeynes 2003a, b, c; Park 2001) and through qualitative and/or mixed methods (Cook 2000; Flores-González 1999, 2000, 2002; Sikkink and Hernández 2003). As evidenced, these studies reflect a recent, growing trend that explores the area of religiousness and academic achievement. Finally, it should be noted that when we conducted interviews with participants, we did not reveal our personal religious beliefs during the duration of the project.

Trustworthiness in this study was assured in several ways like the simultaneous tape recording and note taking of all interviews to check for inconsistencies in the data. Additionally, we triangulated our data; for example, we also recorded our observation of participants in a journal that was maintained throughout the duration of the research process and compared them to how students described their schooling experiences during the interviews. Additionally, credibility was enhanced in this study in two ways. First, we asked colleagues to "peer examine" (Merriam 1998) the interview transcripts to determine if all possible themes had been discovered. Second, we conducted member checks by asking participants to read the personal profiles we constructed for them and to examine the findings to ensure that we had not misinterpreted their experiences. The discovery of findings was also partly facilitated by our personal experiences as marginalized students educated in public schools and our previous research knowledge concerning the factors that had the potential to influence the low and high academic achievement of Puerto Rican urban high school students.

General Participant Profile

Of the ten Puerto Rican high achievers who shared their experiences with us, seven were female and three were male. Likewise, seven of the students reported being of the Catholic faith and three reported being Pentecostal. All had a grade point average (GPA) of 3.0 or higher. Additionally, all of them were enrolled in advanced placement (AP) or honors classes, and they all considered themselves to be English-dominant bilinguals. Moreover, all of the students commented that their parents had either dropped out of high school or had not had a college experience.

The Influence of Religiosity on the High Academic Achievement of Puerto Rican Urban High School Youth: A Dual Role

External Components of Religiosity: Examining Religiosity and Extracurricular Activities as Sources of Social Capital

Many of the students we interviewed voiced a connection between their high academic achievement and their ties to a religious organization and/or other extracurricular activities. When asked which religious faith or church they professed or belonged to, our participants stated they were either Catholic or Pentecostal. They also mentioned that the main benefit of participating in these activities consisted of targeted recreational activities for youth that steered them away from anti-school, oppositional youth culture like gang membership and truancy. These activities also contributed to high degrees of social capital through the community/social networks that facilitated their access to school-related resources like homework help and mentorship. Daniel commented:

> Growing up my mom always took me and my sister to church and she always had us involved in youth groups as far as you know, Sunday school and we went on trips with our church groups and that always helped me keep on a straight path.

In addition to his church involvement, Daniel's participation on athletic teams also played a major role in his high school career, because it helped him gain much access to positive help-seeking resources like information regarding college, mentorship from his teammates' parents, and access to computers at his friends' homes.

This intergenerational closure (Carbonaro1998), comprised of Daniel's friends and their parents, proved to be valuable for Daniel, because he now is very confident that he has the information that he needs to become successful in college, get a job after graduation, and obtain a middle class lifestyle. He commented:

> A lot of my friends who I play with on the teams are a lot better off than me. Like, David's parents live out in the suburbs and both his parents are college psychology professors and make a lot of money. They both have been a great influence on me because they've talked to me about what I need to get into college and be successful in college. They helped me make the decision on which university to apply to. I like their advice because I see that they have become successful. I want to follow their examples and also have a big house and nice cars like them one day.

As evidenced in recent studies (Flores-González 1999, 2002; Hébert and Reis 1999), several of our participants suggested that multicultural peer networks consisting of other high achieving urban youth were valuable assets that influenced their academic achievement. Cecilia remarked that she valued her church involvement and its impact on her academic achievement because of the multicultural peer networks she belonged to. These networks were highly conducive to supportive relationships and to her strong sense of belonging. In fact, although the majority of the students were English dominant bilinguals, they spoke about their multicultural approach in their school peer networks, as they expressed the importance of their friendships with Latinas/os and other friends of color like African Americans and Mexican Americans.

> Ever since I was in the ninth grade, I have been going to church regularly. I also sing in the church choir. The people at church have always been friendly and supportive of me. I feel like I really belong. I have also met a lot of people at church. I have a lot of friends from different backgrounds. I have Hispanic, White, Asian, and Black friends. We all treat each other as friends and we keep each other in line. I really think going to church has helped me become a better student.

Estrella also talked about her involvement in a church and connected it with her high academic achievement. Like Cecilia, she was able to participate in church activities with peer networks consisting of other Latina/o youth. She also felt that these friendships and her participation in religious-based activities had a positive impact on her academic achievement. She remarked:

> I'm involved in church very much. I have lots of friends of church in church. We do lots of things together. We do retreats and we invite other youths to come. We also evangelize together. We want other youths to know God and Jesus. There are also lots of camps in the summer and conventions in the Midwest. There are lots of Latinos that get together for these conventions and we have lots of fun. I really think that these church things have helped me be a good student.

While Daniel, Cecilia, and Estrella talked about the importance of receiving mentorship and informational resources through their social networks at church, several students specifically mentioned the influence of God in their scholastic lives through an internal locus of control framework.

Internal Components of Religiosity: Examining Personal Faith as Internal Locus of Control

This particular finding is consistent with recent research (Cook 2000; Jeynes 2003b, c), which shows that religious people are more likely to have an internal locus of control because they feel the spirit of God resides within them and steers them to positive things like high academic achievement. Rachel commented:

> God has helped me become a good student. He has helped me keep focused. I know he helps me do the best I can in school.

Likewise, Limari also commented:

> God had helped me become a good student because He has been with me through all my struggles.

While these participants credited their high academic achievement with their participation to church and school-related activities, other participants spoke about their involvement with community-based agencies and how it facilitated their engagement with school and meeting people from different walks of life. Alexia stated:

> I do all kinds of work with people in the community. I work with the Private Industry Council and help people get jobs. I also work with the Historical Society. These jobs keep me busy and focused on school and help me meet lots of interesting people.

Just like the recent research that shows religiosity (Jeynes 2003a; Park 2001; Sikkink and Hernández 2003) and participation in extracurricular activities (Flores-González 1999, 2002; Hébert and Reis 1999) have a positive impact on academic achievement for students of color, our participants also suggested that involvement in church and other school and community-based extracurricular activities served an important dual function. First, church involvement served as a protective measure by discouraging them from participating in oppositional youth culture (i.e., gang life and truancy), because it impinges on their scholastic endeavors. Second, involvement in these kinds of activities also contributed to their high degrees of social capital through the intergenerational closure between these students, their friends, and their friends' parents. This high degree of intergenerational closure was valuable, because it insured that these students gained access to important resources like good advice through adult mentorship and other positive help-seeking behaviors that encouraged them to pursue academic excellence and a school kid identity (Flores-González 2002).

Finally, the students we interviewed manifested the inextricably connected and important ways in which the external and internal components of religiosity influenced their academic achievement in positive ways. Thus, both components are of extreme value and serve as motivational tools for youth of color who are schooled in urban centers where only approximately 45 % of Latina/o youth graduate from high schools across the United States (Flores-González 2002).

Limitations of the Study and Implications for Further Research

This study had several limitations. First, our sample size was small, and we only interviewed students from one high school who were either in the 11th or 12th grades, which prevents us from making broad generalizations regarding the impact of religiosity on the academic achievement of urban youth. We also limited our study to students who came from working class backgrounds. Moreover, we exclusively employed a qualitative research paradigm to this study. Consequently, further research is needed in order to provide additional and/or deeper insights within this area of inquiry. Possible examples of such research include employing mixed methods studies at multiple school sites across grade levels and across geographically diverse areas in the United States. Additionally, it would be interesting to explore the similarities and differences, if any, regarding the impact of religiosity on academic achievement taking into account students who come from various socioeconomic backgrounds. Lastly, it would be interesting to note whether these experiences vary or remain constant among Latina/o students who come from other ethnic groups (i.e. Central and South American, Cuban, Mexican-origin, etc.).

School Based Implications for Family Religiosity and its Impact on Personal and Academic Enhancement

The Puerto Rican urban high school students we interviewed taught us the dual role and importance religiosity had on their academic achievement. The first component within this dual role consisted of the students' acquisition of social capital that made it possible for them to receive important information about college from adults in church and receive mentoring and counseling from them within their places of faith in times of personal crisis. The second component of this dual role involved the notion of an internal locus of control. This internal locus of control was manifested through students expressing that God resided within them and, thus, steered them on a straight path, which resulted in large part to their academic success.

Interestingly enough, it became evident to us that these students succeeded academically *in spite of school* and thanks to their places of faith and belief in God. In other words, their academic success was due to factors *outside* of school and contingent on their family religiosity. Moreover, it became apparent through these students' schooling experiences and our additional informal conversations with them that their religiosity provided several important things that their school did not, and acted as a mitigating zone between their worlds inside and outside of school. Hence, it is important that school officials continue to support their students' desire to continually attend their places of worship and build meaningful relationships with trusted, responsible adults within them. These adults can provide important information to youth that will enable them to continue on their paths of academic success. Additionally, school based adults also have the powerful potential of facilitating their Latina/o students' engagement with school.

For example, many of the students we spoke with mentioned the absence of culturally relevant courses that take into account their daily lived experiences and, hence, the home and community-based funds of knowledge they already bring to school (Moll et al. 1992). Another shortcoming students voiced was that many of their teachers held them to low academic expectations by virtue of their ethnic background and, thus, did not make the extra effort to academically push them, offer special tutoring, and/or provide advice on where to go to find academic services within and/or outside school. Moreover, all the students we spoke with deemed most of their teachers as "uncaring" precisely because of the lack of support and encouragement they received from them.

Thus, it is crucial that school officials look to parents/caregivers as knowledgeable allies who can share culturally relevant resources with their youth's/s' teachers. Needless to say, teachers must also be willing to humbly learn from their students' parents/caregivers. Furthermore, urban teachers must also be willing to conduct their own research regarding the racial/ethnic and linguistic realities of their students and the communities in which they are situated. All too often, many urban teachers are unwilling and/or are constrained to conduct this kind of research and/or do not view their students' parents/caregivers as knowledgeable partners in education.

Furthermore, it is important that educators, teacher trainers, and policy makers also acknowledge and value the advantageous impact of participation in faith communities on academic achievement. Faith workers, particularly those of color, also have the potential to play significant roles in encouraging schools to examine the various ways in which their students' lives are acknowledged and affirmed both inside and outside schools. Above all, it is crucial that schools strive to become *sanctuaries* (Antrop-González 2003). Schools become sanctuaries when students and teachers are engaged in highly meaningful interpersonal relationships, affirm their students' racial/ethnic and linguistic backgrounds, possess culturally relevant curricula (Ladson-Billings 1995), and serve as psychologically and physically safe spaces where students are free to become the holders and creators of knowledge with their teachers (Delgado-Bernal 2002). While the school as sanctuary model (Antrop-González 2003) largely describes the aforementioned conditions as they take place within school, what happens outside the school doors becomes just as important, if not more so.

Hence, faith communities and urban schools alike should encourage broader partnerships between themselves and other community based agencies that have an authentic interest in the well-being of urban youth, particularly youth of color. Through these types of faith-school-community partnerships, urban schools can further reinforce the social and cultural capital urban students already possess and use in their homes and communities and which our students need to graduate from high school, enter college, and eventually obtain a career that will increase their life chances and structures of opportunities. Rather than talk down to parents/caregivers, schools can find ways to welcome families into the school community and offer them opportunities to become an integral part of the decision making process.

Teachers, administrators, and other staff members can also venture out and explore their students' communities, learn from them, and bring this community-based knowledge with their students into the classroom to develop and implement much more relevant curriculum (Delgado-Gaitán 2004; Espinoza-Herold 2003; Kuykendall 1991; Moll et al. 1992). Because students are savvy and can detect when school staff may be intimidated based on who they are racially/ethnically and where they come from (i.e., economically challenged and ignored neighborhoods), it is of the utmost importance that teachers not only have passion for their subject matter but also for establishing high quality, meaningful interpersonal relationships with their students, families, and community-based institutions (Antrop-González and De Jesús 2006; Valenzuela 1999).

In sum, faith based institutions and the activities they sponsor have the vast potential to encourage and foster the adoption of "school kid" identities (Flores-González 2002), which can result in greater academic success and higher life chances for urban youth of color. Our student participants rightfully looked to their faith for the many things that their schools failed to provide them. Hence, more urban schools need to "step up to the plate" and also become sanctuaries for their students and communities while partnering with faith communities. Furthermore, these powerful school-family-community sanctuary partnerships would also have the vast potential to enable much more urban youth to academically succeed precisely because their schools would have the wisdom to do what their students' places of faith do already—serve as sanctuaries of hope and guidance for urban youth.

Practical Advice for Latina/o Parents/Caregivers and Students for Family Religiosity and its Impact on Personal and Academic Enhancement

While the previous section described school based implications for family religiosity and its impact on personal and academic enhancement, this section describes practical advice for Latina/o parents/caregivers and students regarding the impact of family religiosity and its impact on personal and academic enhancement. In other words, this section is intended to offer pieces of advice to Latina/o families regarding the extent to which their religiosity can serve as a powerful anchor and moral compass for their academic achievement. The first piece of advice we offer involves strongly encouraging Latina/o parents/caregivers to pass on and share their academically successful youth's/s' experience and knowledge with other young Latinas/os who may need help with navigating the world of troubled urban schools.

Through sharing their experience and knowledge as well as their youth's/s' with other young Latinas/os, strong community relationships have the potential to grow in the spirit of mentorship based on religiosity and its positive effects on personal and academic enhancement. Furthermore, these important faith based relationships serve as mitigating buffers between highly nurturing Latina/o home cultures and ineffective urban school cultures and/or negative influences, such as gang membership and/or alcohol/drug abuse and/or problematic sexual behaviors on the part of some adults and/or youth across racial/ethnic and socioeconomic groups.

A second point of advice we offer is the strongly encouraging religious families to openly and frankly discuss with school agents the important roles their faith plays in their personal and academic lives. Hence, while many urban schools may strongly and rightfully encourage their youth to participate in extracurricular activities like sports and academic clubs, emphasis on participation in faith based activities must also be stressed to school officials who may often feel discouraged or hesitant about discussing the advantages of faith based activities for youth due to explicit and/or implicit rules and/or expectations about discussing such things with students. Perhaps if enough school officials are made aware of the numerous benefits of faith based influences on the personal and academic identities of youth of color, they will begin to also keep at bay their reluctance to discuss the importance of religious faith in their life endeavors.

Lastly, it is imperative that Latina/o parents/caregivers and their youth continue to support their religious communities and reinforce avid participation in them. In addition to the high quality, meaningful relationships these communities foment, they also provide potentially ample opportunities for youth leadership development in addition to the important, continued development of one's moral compass. It is our hope that these points of advice, if followed with vigor, will guide our Latina/o youth towards high quality lives of personal and academic enhancement marked by passion and caring with/for their peers in addition to their societies at large.

Authors' Notes

This research project was funded by generous grants through the University of Wisconsin System Institute on Race and Ethnicity, the University of Wisconsin-Milwaukee Graduate School, and the University of Wisconsin-Milwaukee Institute for Excellence in Urban Education Initiative.

References

Antrop-González, R. (2003). "This school is my sanctuary:" The Dr. Pedro Albizu Campos alternative high school. *Journal of the Center for Puerto Rican Studies, 15*(2), 232–255.

Antrop-González, R., & De Jesús, A. (2006). Toward a theory of *critical care* in urban small school reform: Examining structures and pedagogies of caring in two Latino community-based schools. *International Journal of Qualitative Studies in Education, 19*(4), 409–433.

Cook, K. V. (2000). "You have to have somebody watching your back, and if that's God, then that's mighty big": The church's role in the resilience of inner-city youth. *Adolescence, 35,* 717–730.

Creswell, J. W. (1998). *Qualitative inquiry and research design: Choosing among five traditions*. Thousand Oaks: Sage.

Delgado-Bernal, D. (2002). Critical race theory, Latino critical theory, and critical raced-gendered epistemologies: Recognizing students of color as holders and creators of knowledge. *Qualitative Inquiry, 8*(1), 105–126.

Delgado-Gaitán, C. (2004). *Involving Latino families in schools: Raising student achievement through home-school partnerships*. Thousand Oaks: Corwin Press.

Díaz, E. I. (1998). Perceived factors influencing the academic underachievement of talented students of Puerto Rican descent. *Gifted Child Quarterly, 42*(2), 105–122.

Espinoza-Herold, M. (2003). *Issues in Latino education: Race, school culture, and the politics of academic success*. New York: Allyn and Bacon.

Flores-González, N. (1999). Puerto Rican high achievers: An example of ethnic and academic identity compatibility. *Anthropology and Education Quarterly, 30*(3), 343–362.

Flores-González, N. (2000). The structuring of extracurricular opportunities and Latino student retention. *Journal of Poverty, 4,* 85–108.

Flores-González, N. (2002). *School kids/street kids: Identity development in Latino students*. New York: Teachers College Press.

Fordham, S., & Ogbu, J. (1986). Black students' school success: Coping with the "burden of 'acting White.' *Urban Review, 18*(3), 176–206.

Hèbert, T., & Reis, S. (1999). Culturally diverse high-achieving students in an urban high school. *Urban Education, 34*(4), 428–457.

Jeynes, W. (2003a). The effects of Black and Hispanic 12th graders living in intact families and being religious on their academic achievement. *Urban Education, 38*(1), 35–57.

Jeynes, W. (2003b). The effects of religious commitment on the academic achievement of urban and other children. *Education and Urban Society, 36*(1), 44–62.

Jeynes, W. (2003c). *Religion, education, and academic success*. Charlotte: Information Age Publishing.

Kuykendall, C. (1991). *From rage to hope: Strategies for reclaiming Black and Hispanic students*. Indiana: National Educational Service.

Ladson-Billings, G. (1995). Toward a theory of culturally relevant pedagogy. *American Educational Research Journal, 32*(3), 465–491.

Merriam, S. B. (1998). *Qualitative research design and case study applications in education*. Hoboken: Jossey-Bass.

Moll, L. C., Amanti, C., Neff, D., & González, N. (1992). Funds of knowledge for teaching: Using a qualitative approach to connect homes and classrooms. *Theory into Practice, 31*(2), 132–141.

Nieto, S. (1998). Fact and fiction: Stories of Puerto Ricans in U.S. schools. *Harvard Educational Review, 68*(2), 133–163.

Nieto, S. (2000). *Puerto Rican students in U.S. schools: Sociocultural, political, and historical studies in education*. New York: Lawrence Erlbaum Associates.

Park, H. S. (2001). Religiousness as a predictor of academic performance among high school students. *Journal of Research on Christian Education, 10*(2), 361–378.

Scheurich, J. J. (1998). Highly successful and loving elementary schools populated mainly by low-SES children of color. *Urban Education, 33*(4), 451–491.

Seidman, I. (1998). *Interviewing as qualitative research: A guide for researchers in education and the social sciences*. New York: Teachers College Press.

Sikkink, D., & Hernández, E. I. (2003). Religion matters: Predicting schooling success among Latino youth. Interim reports. IRVol20031, (Jan): 49, For full text: http://www.nd.edu/~latino/research/pubs/Sikkink_paper.pdf. Accessed 10 July 2009.

Spring, J. (1994). *Deculturalization and the struggle for equality: A brief history of the education of dominated cultures in the United States*. New York: McGraw-Hill.

Tesch, R. (1994). The contribution of a qualitative method: Phenomenological research. In M. Lagenbach, C. Vaughn, & L. Aagaard (Eds.), *An introduction to educational research* (pp. 143–157). Boston: Allyn & Bacon.

Valenzuela, A. (1999). *Subtractive schooling: U.S.-Mexican youth and the politics of caring*. New York: SUNY Press.

Prof. René Antrop-González is Professor and Goizueta Foundation Chair in Education at Dalton State College in Dalton, Georgia. His research interests are African American and Latina/o sociology of education and urban education.

Tomás Garrett is an independent researcher with an interest in Latina/o sociology of education.

Prof. William Vélez is Professor of Sociology and Latino Studies at the University of Wisconsin-Milwaukee. His research interest is Latina/o sociology of education.

Christian Principles for Ministering to Families with Children with Disabilities

Mary Poplin

Abstract The principles of Judeo-Christian thought offer a higher rationality from which to see, understand and minister with those who have disabilities and with those who love them. It begins with a view of the human person's highest and most real identity, which goes far beyond our disabilities and the utilitarian abilities valued by our secular culture. This view from "above" offers us God's perspective, which is larger, greater and more creative than current law, theory and/or practice admits. It begins with a view of the "disabled", first and foremost, as a beloved and essential member of God's very diverse family in which we are all like cells in Christ's body on earth. Operating from this perspective we are all offered an exquisite opportunity to increase in wholeness and holiness.

Keywords Family · Ministry · Faith · Spirituality · Religion · Christian · Disabled · Children

> Being a Christian, I first learned this word Beloved from the story of the baptism of Jesus of Nazareth. "No sooner had Jesus come up out of the water than he saw the heavens torn apart and the Spirit, like a dove, descending on him. And a voice came from heaven: 'You are my Son, the Beloved; my favor rests on you.'" For many years I had read these words and even reflected on them in sermons and lectures…Our many conversations led me to the inner conviction that the words "You are my Beloved" revealed the most intimate truth about all human beings. (Nouwen 2002 p. 30)

From the very beginning, early pioneers of work with disabled youngsters, such as Edward Seguin (1907), Maria Montessori, Louis Guggenbuhl, Thomas Gallaudet, Anne Sullivan, Helen Keller, had a deep and abiding sense that God loves and is equally present to the strong and the weak. This quote from 1857 reveals the strong presence of Christian faith in the early work of these pioneers.

> Dr. Guggenbuhl deemed it wise to infuse into their dawning minds the knowledge and the love of a higher Being, to teach them something of the power and goodness of God. The result, he assures us, has been highly satisfactory; the mind, too feeble for earthly lore, too weak to grasp the simplest facts of science, has yet comprehended something of the love of the All-Father, and lifted up to him its imperfect but plaintive supplication….God has so

M. Poplin (✉)
Graduate School of Education, Claremont Graduate University, 150 East Tenth Street, Claremont, CA 91711, USA
e-mail: Mary.Poplin@cgu.edu

W. Jeynes, E. Martinez (eds.), *Ministering Spiritually to Families*,
DOI 10.1007/978-3-319-13302-7_10

> willed it, that the mightiest intellect which strives unavailingly to comprehend the wisdom and glory of his creation, and the feeblest intelligence which knows only and instinctively his love, shall alike find in that love their highest solace and delight. (The Atlantic Monthly, Volume 1 1857)

In the Christian spiritual realm even the concepts of strong and weak are rarely what they appear to the natural world. Perhaps nothing challenges our faith or so provokes our need for God as a loved one who was born with or acquires a disability. It can be an occasion for great loss or great gain spiritually. Many individuals demonstrate that the path, though filled with challenges, yields spiritual maturity for many who have disabilities and for those who love them.

While every situation differs, the principles upon which the kingdom of God is built stand strong and offer Godly guidance for ministering to all those affected. We offer 10 such Christian Biblical principles. Ultimately ministry requires us not only to pray but also to act in a supportive vibrant Christian community like that of the early church. Throughout this chapter we are assuming that *ministers* are primarily made up of the Christian lay community, for example, family, friends, educators, psychologists, doctors, nurses, as well as sometimes ordained ministers.

Created in the Image of God: Our Primary Identity

No matter the degree of our limitations, we are all created in the image of God. Being in the image of God, all who love God and confess Jesus will ultimately see him and know themselves as God knows them (1Corinthians 13:12, *English Standard Version*, Crossway). Whether we choose to know God or not, this is the primary identity of us all; we are first and foremost human beings made in the image of God our Creator. Many documents have been written testifying to this truth for example the Papal writings of Popes Paul VI 1971; John Paul II 1984; Benedict, 2009. This challenges us to know first the true identity of the person with disabilities prior to our addressing the symptoms of his/her disability (Bogdan and Taylor 1989).

We are also created to be eternal beings—our spirits will live on. While suffering may last for the night, we are promised that joy does come in the morning. Whether that is tomorrow morning or at the end of our earthly physical existence we will all be freed of our physical limitations—limitations with which we all ultimately must live before physical death even if only for a few moments.

Parents and others can help their children know God and confess Christ through dedication, baptism, instruction and prayer. God does not hold children accountable in the same way he does adults; he did not even number children under the age of 20 (Exodus 30:14). Parents and ministers can use the authority Jesus has given them to claim their children for the kingdom of God. God desires that none should perish. He is no respecter of persons; he does not prefer the able bodied or highly intelligent as the world does. We can be certain that people with disabilities have the same access to God (Horning 2011). He knows us better than we know ourselves, even to having numbered the hairs on our heads. He has known us all from before the womb and there we were fearfully and wonderfully made. Even people with very severe disabilities have bodies made to heal and circumvent disease and souls to contribute in some way. People with disabilities who paint beautiful pictures by holding the paintbrush with their feet or mouth encourage us, as do those who simply encourage us with their smiles.

According to the Westminister Confession we are all created with an innate ability to glorify God and to enjoy Him forever. As ministers and parents our task is to stir up this promise as faith is not uniquely connected to cognitive or physical abilities (Gaventa 2005) and methods for children to meditate on Scripture, such as those developed by a protégé of Montessori, Sofia Cavaletti (1992) offer great resources for churches. In a local church the most extravagant worshipper is a forty-year-old man with Down syndrome. He cannot verbally tell you about God, theology or the four spiritual laws but it is evident to even the casual observer that he knows God and enjoys Him! We wonder if God loves his expression of worship more than the most perfect worship leader; like Jesus who preferred the poor widow's mite to all the contributions of the rich.

We All Fall Short of the Glory of God: We All Have Disabilities

Though we bear this imago dei, we all bear it imperfectly. This is demonstrated throughout the Bible, sometimes even in terms of what we now call disabilities—Moses stuttered, Jacob walked with a limp, Jonathan's son was crippled, not to mention the many who struggled to believe and/or be obedient to God, even among the greatest—Jonah, Moses, and Peter. Alas, this list rightly includes us all. Philosopher, Alasdair MacIntyre (1999) suggests that the concept of disabled and non-disabled are flawed, "There is a scale of disability on which we all find ourselves. Disability is a matter of more or less, both with respect to degree of disability and in respect to the time periods in which we are disabled."

Jean Vanier, philosopher, theologian and founder of the L'Arche Communities (begun as Catholic communities) established homes where adults with disabilities and those not considered by the world as disabled live, work, and grow together in community. Vanier (1979, 1992, 1995, 1997, 1998, 2004) teaches that the recognition of our own brokenness gives us the truth, humility and understanding we need to live in community and to minister to one another.

Possibly the greatest advantage of Christianity over all other religions is the very real possibility of increasingly achieving self-knowledge in the hands of a loving God who accepts us where we are and, with our consent and desire, moves us toward more wholeness and sanctity (Moltman 1989). It is in only in the presence of self-knowledge that we can see the truth of what inside us lies behind our avoidance of those with disabilities, e.g., the averting of eyes and disinclination to engage. As one parent told Sharon Rogers (1999), "They treat [our daughter] like she's a rock and act as if she is not there." Self-knowledge helps us confront our own fears and frailties, our sense of powerlessness, and our own disabilities so that we can minister more effectively.

Though others may not identify our own disabilities, we can know them and take them to God who has made provision both for our forgiveness and for healing. As promised *if we confess our sins, he is faithful and just to forgive us our sins and to cleanse us from all unrighteousness* (1 John 1:9). So we are not only able to see our own failures, we are promised that once seen and confessed, God begins to heal them for our good and the good of others.

The Least in the Body of Christ: Not Like the World

One of the most profound principles of Christianity is the composition of the body of Christ on the earth. The body of Christ on earth is made of all those who have accepted him as their savior. Like cells in a physical body, each of us serves some purpose in building up the body of Christ. This body is the mystical and practical expression of Jesus in the physical world and is empowered by the Holy Spirit. Those with disabilities are no exception. While society often looks at those with disabilities as the least, in God's kingdom the least are essential to the body of Christ; we belong together. This passage in Paul's first letter to the Corinthian church makes it clear how we work together for good. Christ is the only provision God has given us to create unity out of diversity.

> For just as the body is one and has many members, and all the members of the body, though many, are one body, so it is with Christ. For in one Spirit we were all baptized into one body—Jews or Greeks, slaves or free—and all were made to drink of one Spirit. For the body does not consist of one member but of many. If the foot should say, "Because I am not a hand, I do not belong to the body," that would not make it any less a part of the body. And if the ear should say, "Because I am not an eye, I do not belong to the body," that would not make it any less a part of the body. If the whole body were an eye, where would be the sense of hearing? If the whole body were an ear, where would be the sense of smell? But as it is, God arranged the members in the body, each one of them, as he chose. If all were a single member, where would the body be? As it is, there are many parts, yet one body. The eye cannot say to the hand, "I have no need of you," nor again the head to the feet, "I have no need of you." On the contrary, the parts of the body that seem to be weaker are indispensable, and on those parts of the body that we think less honorable we bestow the greater honor, and our unpresentable parts are treated with greater modesty, which our more presentable parts do not require. But God has so composed the body, giving greater honor to the part that lacked it, that there may be no division in the body, but that the members may have the same care for one another. If one member suffers, all suffer together; if one member is honored, all rejoice together. (I Corinthians 12:12–26).

Rather than today's new eugenics seeking to rid the world of those with disabilities by scientifically detecting disabilities before birth and advising parents to abort (Britt et al. 1999). or assisting in suicides, this passage clearly indicates that the most indispensable parts of the body are those that seem weakest to the world. These parts of Christ's body may very well be the very substance that holds us together—*that there may be no division*. When they suffer, we all suffer; when they are honored, we are all honored. Martin Luther King (1998) summarized the whole passage—*For some strange reason I can never be what I ought to be until you are what you ought to be. And you can never be what you ought to be until I am what I ought to be. That is the way God's universe is made.* In fact, the kingdom is so made that only those who can become like children will be able to enter the kingdom of God. Those with disabilities may have the advantage on the rest of us. We are blessed when we bless one another.

That My House May Be Filled: Inviting Them into the House

There are two passages where Jesus clearly prefers to fill his house with those with disabilities; both appear in Luke 14. The first is the parable where a master of a house is giving a wedding feast and many of those first invited are simply too busy to come to him. Jesus tells us, *when the master of the house became angry and said to his servant, 'Go out quickly to the streets and lanes of the city, and bring in the poor and crippled and blind and lame.' And the servant said, 'Sir, what you commanded has been done, and still there is room.' And the master said to the servant, 'Go out to the highways and hedges and compel people to come in, that my house may be filled'* (Luke 14: 21–23). Jesus also advised a man who had invited him to dinner, *When you give a dinner or a banquet, do not invite your friends or your brothers or your relatives or rich neighbors, lest they also invite you in return and you be repaid. But when you give a feast, invite the poor, the crippled, the lame, the blind, and you will be blessed, because they cannot repay you. For you will be repaid at the resurrection of the just* (Luke 14: 12–14).

One of the most serious issues faced by those with disabilities is loneliness. This is clearly an issue with which the church and ministries can respond faithfully. At a recent disability summit offered for persons who minister to those with disabilities, participants consistently pointed out the lack of provision inside most churches to include those with disabilities (LaRocque and Eigenbrood 2005; Mansfield et al. 1999). One church ministry shared their mission statement: *To identify and break down barriers that keep people with disabilities and their families from being able to fully participate in the body life of the church.*

Pastor Harold Wilke (1992), , born without arms, writes of the need for "religious communities to proclaim that people with disabilities are welcome and needed in the House of God." Thornburg (1992) shares, "If there are barriers of attitude, communication or architecture for anyone, the foundation of the House of God is weakened for everyone. Rather than being a burden, shared need and vulnerability should be recognized as the 'glue' of a supportive community." It is estimated that close to 20 % of the world's population is disabled (U.S. Census Bureau 1992; Kessler Foundation 2010). Brown and Strawn (2010) write regarding our need for supportive communities:

> Persons with disability provide an important case-in-point. Persons who are disabled (physically, cognitively, and/or emotionally) by definition have some form and degree of difficulty flourishing on their own outside of a community that has an imagination for ways to help them thrive. However if we believe that the primary concern of the church is the inner life of each individual Christian, it is easy to disregard the role of the church community in the flourishing of those who are disabled. We may smile at a person who is depressed or open the door for the person in a wheelchair, but more consistent, long-term, and deep involvement is too often not seen as having a claim on us as spiritual persons or as a church community (p. 22).

Many churches have members who have lost communication skills due to strokes or communication problems that accompany other disabilities. These can exacerbate loneliness. Holland (2007) in her book on a wellness approach to communication disorders discuses the application of the "Eden alternative principles" to the field of communication disorders as she sketches a wellness approach to helping those who are disabled. These principles address the "three plagues of loneliness, helplessness and boredom [that] account for the bulk of the suffering among elders." These principles apply to building a church or community for anyone with disabilities. A few of the principles for creating a community include creating opportunities to give as well as receive care, to imbue daily life with variety and spontaneity, and to honor them. Worrall (2006) points out the critical role in balancing hope and honesty and suggests that effective work in communication disorders requires hope, recognition of the impact on the family system, and services directed toward encouraging a meaningful life. Clearly Jesus wants his house to be filled with everyone working together toward a more abundant life.

Candace Vickers (2008, 2010) is a Christian speech and language therapist who has worked for years to develop a process she calls Communication Recovery for stroke victims. In this process healing is accomplished in a small communities, something like families or cell groups, by pairing communication partners with people working to regain communication skills. The development of these small communities could be done within a church or ministry setting. The National Association of Christians in Special Education also asserts that the Christian community has a unique role to play in the lives of individuals with disabilities.

You Did It for Me—Serving Jesus Practically

When anyone visited Mother Teresa's ministry it was very likely that she would quote the Scripture in Matthew 25 where Jesus tells his disciples *I was hungry and you gave me food, I was thirsty and you gave me drink, I was a stranger and you welcomed me, I was naked and you clothed me, I was sick and you visited me, I was in prison and you came to me.* His disciples asked him when they had seen him in such condition and he replied, *Truly, I say to you, as you did it to one of the least of these my brothers, you did it to me.* At that, Mother Teresa would take her hand or yours and on each finger say a word—*you-did-it-for-me*. For this reason, Mother Teresa insisted that every person they touched was simply *Jesus in the distressing disguise of the poor* (Poplin 2008). This is the essence of true ministry; to minister to one another we minister to Christ who also took on real wounds. To leave members without the help they need is to hurt his entire body.

Many of the needs of families are quite practical and relatively easily met within a community such as a church. This practical help can involve procuring mechanical aids that assist in communicating with others. These aids become more sophisticated and more user friendly every year. They can help children and adults who cannot speak contribute to conversations, use email and text, compose, and even participate in prayer groups. Churches are ideal places to organize groups of communication partners.

At other times what is needed is to visit those who are lonely or sick, and bring them into a community that cares about them. Mother Teresa used to tell the story of man whose house the sisters and she cleaned (Poplin 2008). They found under years of dirt a beautiful lamp. They cleaned the light and asked if he ever used it. He said there was no need for it, as no one ever came to his home. Mother asked him if the sisters came to visit (sometimes that is all they do) would he light the lamp? They did and he did. He later wrote to her saying that *the lamp they lit in his heart was still shining.*

Sadly, parents of children with serious disabilities have a higher than average incidence of divorce (Reynolds 2010; Colson and Colson 2010; Seltzer et al. 2001). Respite care is one of the most critical needs so that parents can enjoy normal times alone and with one another. Tending to the care of the member with disabilities provides times of refreshing for parents and families. Church ministries can easily take on the task of aiding families with babysitting and respites. To pray and offer spiritual guidance is a good thing but as James suggests it is also essential to act. *What good is it, my brothers, if someone says he has faith but does not have works? Can that faith save him? If a brother or sister is poorly clothed and lacking in daily food, and one of you says to them, "Go in peace, be warmed and filled," without giving them the things needed for the body, what good is that? So also faith by itself, if it does not have works, is dead (James: 2:14–17).*

See My Hands, Put Your Hand in My Side—Jesus Experienced Our Suffering

After Jesus' resurrection, he appeared to his disciples and showed them his wounds (Luke 24: 39–40). Using liberation theology, Nancy Eiesland (1984) argued that God showed his unity with the disabled by becoming disabled as he suffered on earth. While Biblically it is difficult to support her ideas of God as disabled, it is not difficult to see that Christ, the incarnated word of God did submit himself to all kinds of wounds as he took on flesh and was tortured for our sake. During her life, Eisland campaigned for various reforms on behalf of the disabled. She was known to add humor to her work, calling those without disabilities the *temporarily able-bodied.*

Because of his taking on human flesh, the author of Hebrews tells us *Therefore he had to be made like his brothers in every respect, so that he might become a merciful and faithful high priest in the service of God, to make propitiation for the sins of the people. For we do not have a high priest who is unable to sympathize with our weaknesses, but one who in every respect has been tempted as we are, yet without sin (Hebrews 2:17, 4:15)*. Christ clearly experienced all we can experience and thus he is able to understand us, have mercy, and work in our lives.

All Creation Groans for His Return: The Problem of Evil, Suffering and Pain

Ed Silvoso (1994) wrote that *why* is the favorite question of the evil one because on this side of heaven we will not know the specific answer to these questions of why suffering strikes one and not another. The problem of evil, pain and suffering has been a persistent question in the mankind for as long as recorded history. Christians understand all suffering to be a result of the fall, a fall that affected all of creation. C. S. Lewis (1962) and Gregory Boyd (2003) each come to similar conclusions about the existence of pain and suffering. God created us as creatures for mutual love; God loves us and desires for us to love Him. His desire for us to love Him is not for His sake but for ours, for in this divine relationship He is free to grant us spiritual gifts and revelation as a loving parent gives gifts to the child he loves. In order for us to love another person, that person must have freedom to choose to love us; God gave us free will. Otherwise God would have had to make us like the men in the fictional town of Stepford *remade* their wives.

Through extensive Scriptural references, Boyd adds the fact that God describes our condition in the fall before the return of Christ as a spiritual war, with suffering. This fall has placed us in a war between good and evil while we exist on this earth. C.S. Lewis reminds us of the fact that "the sufferings of this present time are not worthy to be compared with the glory that shall be revealed to us. If this is so, a book on suffering which says nothing of heaven, is leaving out almost the whole of one side of the account (p. 144)."

In a fallen world, people make decisions to drink and drive, place chemical plants and dumps near people's homes, injure one another physically and psychologically. Jesus tells us that evil cannot create but rather comes to *kill, steal and destroy (John 10:10)*. The effects of evil are not limited to human beings, but Paul tells us that all creation is under the effects of the fall, the earth, trees and animals—that *all creation groans for his (Jesus) return (Romans 8:22)*. Jesus told us to preach the gospel to all *creation* not just to all people. Scripture suggests that disabilities: may demonstrate the glory of God, be a consequence of sin—individual, ancestral, communal and national, or even the result of direct the interference of Satan in the world. However, Scripture reminds us that for those who love God, all things will work together for good (Romans 8:28).

A good resource for ministry for those who struggle with blaming God and continue asking *why* is Boyd's more popular book, *Is God to Blame?* Here Boyd presents the problem of evil and suffering through a case of Melanie who loses a child at birth. He ends the book with a summary:

> I believe that this truth is extremely important to remember when we are experiencing the painful arbitrariness of life. We are in a war zone, and everything hangs on our being able to identify who is fighting against us and who is fighting for us. The ultimate criteria for deciding what is and is not from God is Jesus Christ. If the one who died on the cross wouldn't have done it, you have every reason to assume an event is not from God or part of his will. Living with this Christ-centered perspective, we are freed from asking the unanswerable question of why life unfolds the particular way it does, and we are empowered to do something about it… And neither this nor any other theological perspective can fully take away the pain of [Melanie's] loss. But by her accepting the ambiguity of a war-torn creation and the clarity of God's beauty revealed in Christ, Melanie was able to rekindle her love for God and her passion for life. The painful ambiguity of life cannot crush one whose eyes are fixed on Jesus Christ (p. 196–7).

The ministry of Joni Eareckson Tada (1997, 2007, 2009) and others (e.g., Carter 2007; Presbyterian Church 1989, 2006; United Methodist 2010; Orthodox Church 2009; Thornburg 1992) provide valuable resources for churches and ministers to those who live in the midst of suffering. Tada shares that in her weakness and vulnerability, Jesus' time on the cross redeems her and grants her the strength of salvation. One of the most mystifying and glorifying truths of Christianity is that God uses our suffering for good.

The Plans I Have for You: The Contributions of Those with Disabilities

The prophet Jeremiah assures us that God has a good plan for everyone: *For I know the plans I have for you, declares the LORD, plans for welfare and not for evil, to give you a future and a hope. Then you will call upon me and come and pray to me, and I will hear you. You will seek me and find me, when you seek me with all your heart.* (Jeremiah 29:11–13) Often in disability ministries and particularly in special education, there is so much emphasis on the disability that the destiny and contributions of the child or adult with a disability is overlooked.

Sharon Rogers (1999) studied seven families of youngsters unable to speak and with limited movement. She discovered that inside the families these children were precious and important part of the family. In fact, she found that while the school was often struggling with the teaching the mechanics of communication and thought the children were not communicating, parents and siblings inside their homes had established simple ways of communicating significant personal messages of affection and needs, and that these children were making profound contributions to family life. Dorel's mother told Sharon, "These children are dear to us even if we do not always understand them because they teach us the wonder of life and the joy of achievement. They take over our lives and hearts and teach us endless patience and perseverance, even as they fill us with doubt and puzzlement. They do not give up and neither can we." Joelle's mother said she "is a beacon of light, hope, strength and courage. She is my sunshine." And Lisa Joy's father said of her daughter "She wants to do things for others. Everyone wants to do something for someone else."

In classrooms all across the country, children without obvious disabilities befriend and are befriended by those with disabilities. The effect is that children learn about compassion, friendship, and humility and about the essence of living in an imperfect world. Many people with handicaps have blessed the world a great deal, such as Helen Keller, Steve Hawking, Joni Eareckson Tada, Nick Vujicic, Itzhak Perlman, Andrea Bocelli, and Temple Grandin.

In Mother Teresa's ministry, Jacqueline De Decker, a Belgium social worker had wanted to become a missionary but became seriously ill and could not. Instead she founded the Sick and Suffering Co-workers of the Missionaries of Charity, a group that prays for the poor and suffering and for the active Missionaries, thus turning their own suffering into good for others. The Missionaries each pray for their prayer partner in return.

In every ministry with those who have disabilities an exhaustive search of the contributions of the disabled person should be made. L'Arche communities are excellent examples of how this principle works and their founder, Jean Vanier's books are a good resource. Harvard theologian, Henri Nouwen lived the later years of his life in an L'Arche community in Toronto serving and being served by Adam, a man with severe disabilities. When Adam passed away, only a short time before Nouwen passed, he wrote:

> Here is the man who more than anyone connected me with my inner self, my community, and my God. Here is the man I was asked to care for, but who took me into his life and into his heart in such an incredibly deep way. Yes, I had cared for him during my first year at Daybreak and had come to love him so much, but he has been such an invaluable gift to me. Here is my counselor, my teacher, and my guide, who could never say a word to me but taught me more than any book, professor, or spiritual director. Here is Adam, my friend, my beloved friend, the most vulnerable person I have ever known and at the same time the most powerful… He has returned to the heart of God from which he came (1997, p. 104).

This seems to us the ultimate task of ministering with families with members who have disabilities. To find and focus on the gifts in them that can be shared with the family and larger community and to focus those with disabilities on sharpening this gift and sharing it. True relationships are reciprocal and true life involves participation and choice in the activities of life that enjoy God's creation.

Father, Forgive Them for They Know Not What They Do—Radical Forgiveness

One of the most damaging emotions to any of us, including those who are disabled is unforgiveness. This is particularly difficult for those involved in accidents caused by others or those who blame God. We have heard it said that unforgiveness is like drinking poison and hoping the other person dies. Jesus taught and showed us the truth of forgiveness; it frees us. Here we have the most radical example—a man who went about doing good, is falsely accused, tortured by crucifixion and yet on the cross he asks *Father forgive them for they know not what they do (Luke 23:24).* No one had asked for forgiveness or even realized their need for it.

With God's help we can do the same. Those ministering can aid the family and individual in the work of forgiveness and in so doing move into deeper levels of forgiveness themselves (Smedes 1984; Kendall 2007). Otherwise, to the limitations imposed by the disability will be added the extra burden of living with unforgiveness. Not only are we called to forgive but also to be forgiven. When we confess, God forgives and we are set free. There are many times in any family when members need to be reconciled to one another. In a family with the additional stress of coping with disabilities, the importance of forgiving quickly is heightened thus the reward of regular reconciliation greater. As those who minister with families we also must confess our own weaknesses and inaction on part of the disabled and seek forgiveness.

Be Ye Transformed: Spiritual Maturity

> Now the Lord is the Spirit, and where the Spirit of the Lord is, there is freedom. And we all, with unveiled face, beholding the glory of the Lord, are being transformed into the same image from one degree of glory to another. For this comes from the Lord who is the Spirit (2 Corinthians 3:17–19).

The goal of all ministries is to help others become increasingly transformed into Christ's image. With the help of the Holy Spirit this transformation brings us closer to fulfilling our unique destinies. In helping others transform, we are also changed, ministers, families and caregivers grow alongside children and adults with disabilities. As the passage above makes clear this is a work of the Holy Spirit and we cannot be truly successful without God.

The gifts of those who are disabled stretch us, cause us to realize our dependence on God and disabilities, to come closer for his wisdom, to look more carefully at the person before us, to understand more about God's love, and to know ourselves better. Ministry with those with disabilities involves an expansion of our capacity to work alongside Christ to meet others' needs. True transformation enriches marriages, families, and community binding them together in common and uncommon needs and gifts. For those who live with disabilities it is a call for them to use their freedom to explore and contribute their abilities, gifts and desires.

As Henri Nouwen (1990, 1997) expressed so well, the best person to minister is a wounded healer. It is the healer who knows his/her own wounds to whom is given the power to assist our Lord in healing. Nouwen suggests that the one who ministers is (1) the articulator of the inner events, (2) the authority in compassion, and (3) the contemplative who watches vigilantly for signs of hope.

Jesus never dealt in abstractions; his teaching and his actions were always both spiritual and practical. Since each person differs, the practical needs, benefits and outcomes will differ and we reiterate that this involves both ministering with the families in the spiritual realm and in the practical world.

God loves all of his creation; he created every person to be unique. His Son, the incarnated word of God, came to earth and died for the salvation and freedom of every one. God's Holy Spirit has no limits, knows no boundaries and is present always. It is in God's hands, we place our desires to minister with those who are disabled and it is in His power we can build a welcoming community.

Audrey Holland (2007) begins her book with a story of the great violinist, Itzhak Perlman's performance in New York in 1995. He appears on the stage walking laboriously in his metal braces to the chair, he sits down and unfastens the clasps on his leg braces. Just as he began to play the first few bars, one of his strings broke with a loud noise. Everyone expected a pause for a new instrument, but instead he closed his eyes and signaled the conductor to continue. He played with great passion and power, almost recomposing the music. The audience cheered. He later said to the reporter, Jack Reimer of the Houston Chronicle, "You know, sometimes it is the artist's task to find out how much music you can still make with what you have left." That is our task, all of us, and with God's help it is possible.

Summary of Practical Guidelines

First and foremost, those with disabilities often suffer because of loneliness and exclusion; we often speak to their families as though they are not present. So in all ministry situations we must situate ourselves to be able to establish eye contact with the entire family and speak to them with their families, sometimes this requires nothing more than to remember to pull up a few chairs around a wheelchair. Spending the time and energy it takes to begin to understand a member's speech and respond is critical as well, as they are often unnecessarily silent. We often need to listen more and talk less, even to gestures that stand in for words.

I remember a pastor who had been removed from his church and was almost despondent for years as he pursued other things told the story that he was in a church when a young adult man with Down's syndrome came up to him and gave him a life changing prophetic message. The young man in his late 20s just walked back to where he was standing waiting on his wife and told him, "The Lord says you are supposed to be his preacher. What are you doing here?" God's gifts go so far beyond our understanding and focusing constantly on one's disabilities will cause us to miss them and to leave their gifts undeveloped.

Secondly, we must remember that whether people with disabilities are children or adults, they have the same desires and needs as any other human beings. They also love baseball games, dances, concerts, movies, going out for ice cream or to other favorite places, being read to, playing board or card games, in short, being included and acknowledged—not with a pat on the head, as though they are perpetual children, but a pat on the back or shake of the hand or any gesture that would be age appropriate.

Jesus taught very deep things with stories that drew even young children; he is not a theologian who teaches only in the synagogue or church, he is the very present

God of all—young and old. Sofia Cavalletti (1992), following the methods of her predecessor, Maria Montessori, developed a method whereby children could reflect deeply on Scripture. They simply wrote His stories into small books and arranged a box with the necessary props and characters (e.g., sheep, fence pieces and the Shepherd). As the teacher read aloud the Scripture book, selected by the child, the child (in her case) moved the wooden characters and props around. Sometimes the teacher would read it several times and then back away as the child began to work with the figures. Cavalletti refused to call this "play"; she said children work just like adults. The deep thought children would move into during these times, she said was "prayer." We can do the same for the disabled.

Respite opportunities for parents are critical and relatively easy to arrange by either taking the family member with disabilities on an outing with our families, into our own homes, or going to their homes for a few hours or even a weekend or longer. Helping families find and access needed services and even physical resources such as the latest walkers, chairs, hearing devices, visual aids, speech generating programs, and other advanced technology will be a great ministry to families.

Churches can develop committees to work on accessibility, communication needs and other services that will make the church and its ministries far more welcoming. Many people with disabilities can participate in church activities from which they are often excluded—passing out bulletins, taking up the offering, and some even reading the Scriptures. Depending on their own strengths many can be involved in prayer groups and chains, confirmation classes, baptism, church or school committees. The church and its various groups can emphasize "belonging" in so many ways as Carter (2007) have more fully developed.

There are no limits on what a faith community can do to support their members with disabilities, whether they are children or adults. And in turn there is no limit to what God can add to these efforts. It is clearly one of the most blessed of all opportunities to serve God's beloved. His ways are not our ways….

"The eye cannot say to the hand, "I have no need of you," nor again the head to the feet, "I have no need of you." On the contrary, the parts of the body that seem to be weaker are indispensable, and on those parts of the body that we think less honorable we bestow the greater honor, and our unpresentable parts are treated with greater modesty, which our more presentable parts do not require. But God has so composed the body, giving greater honor to the part that lacked it, that there may be no division in the body, but that the members may have the same care for one another. If one member suffers, all suffer together; if one member is honored, all rejoice together (I Corinthians 12: 21–26)."

References

Bogdan, R., & Taylor, S. (1989). Relationships with severely disabled people: The social constructions of humanness. *Social Problems, 36*(2), 135–148.

Boyd, G. (2003). *Is God to blame?* Downers Grove: InterVarsity Press.

Britt, D., Risinger, S., Miller, V., Mans, M., Krivchenia, E., & Evans, M. (1999). Determinants of parental decisions after the prenatal diagnosis of Down syndrome: Bringing in context. *American Journal of Medical Genetics, 93*(5), 410–416.

Brown, W., & Strawn, B. (2010, Spring). Spiritual flourishing and embodied life, *Theology News and Notes, 57*(1), 21–23.

Carter, E. (2007). *Including people with disabilities in faith communities: A guide for service providers, families & congregations*. Baltimore: Paul H Brookes Publishing Co.

Cavaletti, S. (1992). *The religious potential of the child* (trans: P. & J. Coulter). Chicago: Liturgy Training Publications.

Colson, E., & Colson, C. (2010). *Dancing with Max*. Grand Rapids: Zondervan Publishers.

Eiesland, N. (1984). *The disabled God: Toward a liberation theology of disability*. Baltimore: Abington Press.

Gaventa, B. (2005). Celebrating the sacred in shared meals: Grace and blessing. In K. M. Schwier & E.S. Stewart (Eds.), *Breaking bread, nourishing connections: People with and without disabilities together at mealtime* (p. 115). Baltimore: Paul H. Brookes Publishing Co.

Guggenbühl, L. (1858). *Atlantic Monthly, 1*(4), 41.

Holland, A. (2007). *Counseling in communication disorders*. San Diego: Plural Publishing.

Horning, K. (2011). *Just the way I am: God's good design in disability*. Bernidji: Christian Focus.

Kendall, R. T. (2007). *Total forgiveness*. Lake Mary: Charisma House.

Kessler Foundation & National Organization on Disability. (2010). The ADA, 20 years later: Survey of Americans with disabilities. http://www.nod.org. Accessed 8 Sept 2010.

King M. L., Jr., Carson C., & Halloran P. (Eds.). (1998). *A knock at midnight*. New York: Grand Central Publishing.

King M. L. (1998). *The autobiography of Martin Luther King*. New York: Warner Books.

LaRocque, M., & Eigenbrood, R. (2005). Community access: A survey of congregational accessibility for people with disabilities. *Journal of Religion, Disability, & Health, 9*, 55–66.

Lewis, C. S. (1962). *The problem of pain*. New York: Macmillan.

MacIntyre, A. (1999). *Dependent rational animals: Why human beings need the virtues*. Chicago: Open Court.

Mansfield, C., Hopfer, S., Martineau, T. (1999). Termination rates after prenatal diagnosis of Down syndrome, spina bifida, anencephaly, and Turner and Klinefelter syndromes: A systematic literature review. *Prenatal Diagnosis, 19*(9), 808–812.

Moltman, J. (1989). Liberate yourselves by accepting one another. In N. Eiesland & D. Saliers (Eds.), *Human disability and the service of God: Reassessing religious practice* (pp. 105–122). Nashville: Abingdon Press.

Nouwen, H. (1989). Sermon 3301: Journey to L'Arche. http://www.csec.org/csec/sermon/nouwen_3301.htm. Accessed 22 Sept 2010.

Nouwen, H. (1990). *The wounded healer*. New York: Image Books.

Nouwen, H. (1997). *Adam, God's beloved*. Maryknoll: Orbis Books.

Nouwen, H. (2002). *The life of the beloved*. New York: Crossroad Publishing Company.

Orthodox Church of America. (2009). Standing Conference of the Canonical Orthodox Bishops of America (OCA). Disability and communion. Orthodox Church of America at http://www.oca.org/RHPrint.asp?ID=268. Accessed 8 Sept 2010. (Orthodox Christian Disability Resources. (2009). http://ocdresources.files.wordpress.com. Accessed 22 Sept 2010).

Pope Benedict XVI. (2009). *Caritas in Veritate*. Rome: The Vatican.

Pope John Paul II (1984). *Salvifici Doloris*. Rome: The Vatican.

Pope Paul VI (1971). *Rerun Novarum*. Rome: The Vatican.

Poplin, M. (2008). *Finding Calcutta: What Mother Teresa taught me about meaningful work and service*. Downers Grove: InterVarsity Press.

Presbyterian Church (U.S.A.). (1989). *Celebration of that all may enter: Responding to disability concerns*. Louisville: Office of General Assembly & The Education and Congregational Nurture Ministry Unit.

Presbyterian Church (U.S.A.). (2006). *Living into the body of Christ: Toward full inclusion of people with disabilities*. Louisville: Office of General Assembly & The Advisory Committee on Social Witness Policy of the General Assembly Council.

Reynolds, D. (2010). Parents of autistic children no more likely to divorce than other parents. http://www.emaxhealth.com/1506/parents-autistic-children-no-more-likely-divorce-other-parents.html. Accessed 22 Sept 2010.
Rogers, S. (1999). *Hearing them into voice: The hermeneutics of listening to children who do not speak*. Unpublished doctoral dissertation, Claremont Graduate University. Claremont.
Rogers, S., & Mayne, L. (In press). *I-Communicate*. Baltimore: Brookes Publishing.
Seguin, E. (1907). *Idiocy: It's treatment by the physiological method*. New York: Teacher's College, Columbia University.
Seltzer, M., Greenberg, J.S., Floyd, F. J., Pettee, Y., & Hong, J. (2001). Life course impacts of parenting a child with a disability. *American Journal of Mental Retardation, 106*(3), 265–286.
Silvoso, E. (1994). *That none should perish*. Ventura: Regal Books.
Smedes, L. (1984). *Forgive*. New York: Pocket Books.
Smith, J. D. (1998). Histories of special education: Stories from our past, insights for our future. *Remedial and Special Education, 19*(4), 196–200.
Tada, J. E. (1997). *When God weeps: Why our sufferings matter to Almighty*. Grand Rapids, MI: Zondervan.
Tada, J. E. (2007). *Hope: The best of things*. Wheaton: Crossway Books.
Tada, J. E. (2009). *A lifetime of wisdom: Embracing the way God heals you*. Grand Rapids: Zondervan.
Tada, J. E. & Estes, S. (1997). *When God weeps: Why sufferings matter to the almighty*. Grand Rapids: Zondervan.
The Westminster Shorter Catechism 7.001. (2007). *The Constitution of the Presbyterian Church (U.S.A.) Part I, Book of Confessions (2007)*. Louisville: Office of the General Assembly, 175.
Thornburgh, G. (Ed.). (1992). *That all may worship: An interfaith welcome to people with disabilities*. Washington, DC: National Organization on Disability.
United Methodist Committee on Relief. (2010). Making your church accessible. http://new.gbgmumc.org/umcor/work/health/disc/churchaccessible/. Accessed 18 Sept 2010.
U.S. Census Bureau. (1992). http://www.census.gov/population/www/pop-profile/disabil.html. Accessed 18 Sept 2010.
Vanier, J. (1979). *Community and growth*. London: Darton, Longman & Todd.
Vanier, J. (1992). *From brokenness to community*. Mahwah: Paulist Press.
Vanier, J. (1995). *An ark for the poor: The story of L'Arche*. Toronto: Novalis.
Vanier, J. (1997). *Our journey home*. Toronto: Novalis.
Vanier, J. (1998). *Becoming human*. Mahwah: Paulist Press.
Vanier, J. (2004). *Drawn into the mystery of Jesus through the gospel of John*. New York: Paulist Press.
Vickers, C. (2008). *Social networks after the onset of aphasia: The impact of communication recovery groups*. Unpublished doctoral dissertation, Claremont Graduate University, Claremont.
Vickers, C. (2010). Social networks after the onset of aphasia: The impact of aphasia group attendance. *Aphasiology, 24*(6–8), 902–913.
Wilke, H. (1992). Creating the caring congregation. In G. Thornburgh (Ed.), *That all may worship: An interfaith welcome to people with disabilities*. Washington, DC: National Organization on Disability.
Worrall, L. (2006). Professionalism and functional outcomes. *Journal of Communication Disorders, 39*(4), 320–327.

Mary Poplin is a professor of education, and former Dean of Education at Claremont Graduate University. She has written widely in the areas of special education, highly effective teachers in low-performing urban poor schools, as well as about her experience working with Mother Teresa (Finding Calcutta, 2008) and in the area of worldviews and Judeo-Christian principles (Is Reality Secular, 2014).

Laying a Strong Foundation in the Family: The Power of Storytelling

Roger Friend

Abstract The author asserts that spiritual counselors and leaders can strengthen families if they are able to convey various spiritual truths regarding the family and character via storytelling. The author states that one can reach family members of all ages, particularly children, using this technique. The chapter gives a variety of examples of teaching spiritual truths via this vast, relatively underutilized, means of communicating truth. The author shares that storytelling is essential to help children develop a conscience and gives examples regarding how storytelling can have an efficacious impact.

Keywords Family · Children · Youth · Storytelling · Parents · Parenting · Ministry

A Resurrection in the Awareness of the Value of Storytelling

It was really William Bennett's (1995, 1996, 1997a) writings that recently reawakened the Christian world to the practice of storytelling as a means of building childhood character. His writings reveal that children, in particular, need moral examples presented via storytelling that include both real life heroes and fictional stories that can provide a "moral compass" (1997b, 1998, 2008). Moreover, Bennett has made it clear that character lessons via storytelling are not only valuable for youth, but also for people of all ages (Bennett 2011). They can also benefit the recipient and the storyteller alike (Bennett 2008, 2011).

William Bennett reminded many people of the long tradition of character building storytelling that has been practiced for countless centuries dating back to the days of the Bible (e.g., Deuteronomy, *Holy Bible*, NIV, 1979; Jeynes 2010a). William Bennett's books are particularly designed to be a tool for teachers in the public schools (Bennett 1995, 1996). Nevertheless, historically the church and family have served as the primary conveyors of character education through storytelling

R. Friend (✉)
Vista Christian Fellowship, 820 Williamston St., Vista, CA 92084, USA
e-mail: Roger_friend@hotmail.com

W. Jeynes, E. Martinez (eds.), *Ministering Spiritually to Families*,
DOI 10.1007/978-3-319-13302-7_11

(Cremin 1970; Eavey 1964; Jeynes 2007). Over the course of the history of the West, whether it was the parents, the churches, or the schools that train children in the ways of character, storytelling played a prominent role (Cremin 1980; Cubberley 1920; Fraser 2001). Noah Webster recognized this principle, as did other prominent educators in the 1700s such as Benjamin Rush (Cubberley 1920; Marshall and Manuel 1977; Unger 1998). The founder of the kindergarten, Friedrich Froebel (1782–1852) also valued the salience of storytelling, even in song (Doherty 1977; Downs 1978; Jeynes 2006). Horace Mann and other early founders of the public schools recognized the place of storytelling to such an extent that they even sought after and found a schoolbook writer who could masterfully write stories, both factual and fiction, in order to explicate via storytelling some of the most important virtues that one could have (Gatto 2001; Mann 1840, 1844, 1907; Messerli 1972). His name was William McGuffey (Westerhoff 1982).

Not only is storytelling worthy of merit, based on historical precedent and success, but also research indicates that reading stories with children is one of the most morally and academically beneficial activities academically that parents can engage in with their children (Jeynes 2010b). In fact, studies indicate that many parents prefer to send their children to schools that will recognize the character building benefits of education (Jeynes, 2000, 2012).

Pastoral Ministry and Storytelling

Like any other Sunday, I called forward the children of the church, including our four children, to share a children's message. Typically, I picked illustrations from old books of children's stories, Aesop's Fables and the Classics … anything that would support sound Biblical teaching. For those who recoil at the proposition that anything of truth can be taught through imaginary storylines, let us not forget some of our most meaningful Biblical stories that "stick" with us are the most extreme in nature … a donkey talking (Numbers 22:22–35, *Holy Bible*, NIV, 1979); or a man with a boat full of animals, escaping the judgment of God (Genesis 7:7–9, *Holy Bible*, NIV, 1979) and a man named Jonah, swallowed by a big fish for disobeying God (Jonah 1:11–17, *Holy Bible*, NIV, 1979). Yes, but these Biblical stories are true we exclaim. Yes, but Jesus Himself drove home moral truths in a similar manner; e.g. planting within the listener's mind the picture of flowers spinning around in an attempt to enhance their beauty (Matthew 6:28, *Holy Bible*, NIV, 1979). Certainly the prospect of a naked king who believed he sported the finest of regal ware is far-fetched, but it certainly offers a vivid and true picture of man's pride (Elliot 1909–1914). Can Jesus' statement concerning the futility of man's storing up riches on earth (Matthew 6:14, 20) be better illustrated than Tolstoy's encounter between Pahom and the Bashkirs in "*How Much Land Does a Man Need*"? (Tolstoy 1907).

One of the advantages of serving as Senior Pastor of the same church for thirty-five years is the continual contact with people reaching adulthood that you ministered to in their childhood (Dobson 2007). Now in their adult years, you find out what they remember from years before (Hetzendorfer 2009). Additionally, our four children grew up in our home and church from the beginning of our ministry, thus a practical sub-group is afforded from which to draw conclusions. Our children are now 34, 32, 28 and 26 years old.

Over the past 35 years of facing breakdown within the family unit, the recurring challenge affecting both dysfunctional and strong families is the period when children traverse the period between adolescence and adulthood (Jeynes, 2002, 2005). "My parents just don't understand," "I don't believe what my parents believe," or "I can make my own choices," are familiar responses from the emerging young adult. Each of these responses is symptomatic of the lack of a prior action plan to promote an easier transition during this inevitable part of family life. Not addressing this issue early leads to a "showdown" between the family members. The "because I say so" approach of the 1950's will no longer work in a computerized world with TV, computer and smart/cell phones in every home (Ehrensaft 1997; Kindlon 2001). And throwing them out is challenged by a culture that has not thrown out theirs. How then is the best way to plan for this volatile "line drawn in the sand" experience short of buying ones own island or choosing a monastery for a permanent home?

In some cultures, the mother weans the child from the breast by taking solid foods, softening the food in the mouth and then feeding the child small portions of the moistened food. This is similar to how Jesus taught in the ancient Israelite culture. Instead of teaching in abstract theological terms, Jesus spoke almost exclusively in simple, easily digested snapshots (Griggs 1981). These pictures demanded a response and were met by either total rejection or acceptance of the listening parties. Jesus' word pictures (the sower and his seeds; the son who squandered his inheritance etc.) "stick" with the interested hearer. Jesus' stories or parables were only to be understood by those who were looking for truth and not coming to Him with minds already made up. Jesus demanded this open-minded attitude for entrance into His Father's kingdom and defined it as the mind or heart of a child, (Mark 10:13–15, *Holy Bible*, NIV, 1979). Coincidentally, Jesus' Father demanded the children of Israel teach the stories and commands all day long (Deuteronomy 6:7; 11:19, *Holy Bible*, NIV, 1979). Each time the Israelites walked by a certain mound of stones and their children asked the meaning of the stones, they were to repeat the miraculous history of God's deliverance. Thus, when the child became an adult, emblazoned on his mind was the story which he would remember each time he walked past the rocks. The visual picture was the catalyst for remembrance (Joshua 4:19–24, *Holy Bible*, NIV, 1979).

Storytelling accomplishes three things. First, it produces snapshots that "stick" in our memories. Second, storytelling opens the door to the process of critical thinking. Finally, storytelling is vital for development of a conscience. Unfortunately, much of today's teaching is abstract and didactic both at school and in the home. Is this the best way for a child to learn morals and values? Why did Jesus take the time to speak in simple pictures? Perhaps it is time for a revival of the snapshot or story approach, which will teach the children morals and values while at the same time enabling them to think through and evaluate the relative merit of the choices themselves. This storytelling approach also generates warmth that can endear the listener to the storyteller, which goes a lot farther in gaining respect than the "my way or the highway" approach (Griggs 1981). I have seen too many adults lose their children because this approach eventually creates a box canyon which leaves the adult with only one way out and that is to fight with the one who stands in the way of their escape.

The ability to talk about an issue from a pictorial starting point is far superior to the didactic; "Because I told you so," approach. In *Developing Literacy Skills through Storytelling*, Linda Fredericks states, "Stories are not just incidental to the development of literacy in young people—they are essential. They are a powerful and indispensable tool to teaching literacy and critical thinking skills to students." (Fredericks 1997, p. 2). M. K. Zabel in *Preventing School Failure* echoes this conclusion, noting, "Critical thinking skills, vocabulary, and language patterns are enhanced through use of stories" (in Koki 1998, p. 2). Fredericks continues, noting the work of author and educator Joseph Chilton Pearce who asserts, "the repeated exposure to stories and the subsequent triggering of mental images stimulates appropriate neural development in the brain. It is the reason that children will insist on hearing the same story again and again—the hearing of a story causes neural pathways to form and strengthen within the brain, and the strengthened connections between the different parts of the brain allow the child to more easily incorporate additional learning" (Fredericks 1997, p. 2). These observations are extremely important when we entertain the thought of the best approach to inculcating moral and Biblical truth in our children.

Snapshots that Stick

The movie Citizen Kane is still considered one of the top, if not the best, motion pictures of all time (Ebert 2002; Gievett and Spiegal 2007). The movie begins with a snow globe falling from an old man's hand and the single uttered word, "Rosebud." The remainder of the movie focuses on a reporter's pursuit of the meaning of Kane's final word. The journalist traces Citizen Kane's life from childhood to his death in search of the answer (Gievett and Spiegal 2007). The viewer's journey includes Kane's simple childhood in Midwestern poverty to newspaper magnate and world traveler. His seemingly endless purchases of the world's finest treasures eventually find their home in Kane's mansion … Zanadu. As the movie concludes, the closing scene views the countless crates stored in the seemingly endless aisles of Kane's warehouses. Then, the viewer looks into the mouth of a giant furnace where the least valuable items are simply being thrown into the fire. The camera zooms in and focuses on a little boy's sled melting under the blast of the ferocious furnace. As it is consumed, the inscribed word "Rosebud" is seen crackling and melting on the surface of the sled. Kane spent his life amassing a fortune and then spending it on the world's priceless treasures. But, it took his entire life to come to the conclusion that living in poverty, with a real family with his own inexpensive sled "Rosebud," were the happiest moments of his life (Gievett and Spiegal 2007).

Citizen Kane offers a snapshot of the importance of relationships and little things vs. the shallowness of the pursuit of riches and the owning all the earth offers (Gievett and Spiegal 2007). It is a portrait of everyman's journey and the choices we make concerning what Jesus warned as the futility of "storing up treasures on earth" (Matthew 6:19, *Holy Bible*, NIV, 1979). Truly, what does it "profit a man if he gains the entire world and loses his soul?" (Mark 8:36, *Holy Bible*, NIV, 1979). We have the option of simply telling our children they should be concerned more with spiritual things and not pursue the world's treasures in pursuit of happiness, or acquainting the maturing child with a story, which leaves an indelible photo in a child's mind. Of course this is only one of many of life's messages that need to be taught, but the principle is the same for all.

Snapshots continually bombard our teenagers. Yes, they bombard children too, but the mix of life's snapshots and puberty offer an emotional/prurient cocktail that is unequalled in terms of the threat of the wrong sticky portraits on children's souls. Television, movies, internet and peer example offer the values and morals of the culture and persuasions that often run counter to the morals and values a family holds dear (Ehrensaft 1997; Kindlon 2001). Perhaps this is why the Israelites were told to destroy all pictures they encountered upon their arrival into the Promised Land (Numbers 33:52, *Holy Bible*, NIV, 1979). Pictures affect our choices. The nude body of Bathsheba, bathing on a roof, overcame David. The seemingly endless, fertile land of the Bashkirs overcame Pahom. And it was not until Kane's final breath that he discovered true happiness was not found in the aimless increase of life's stuff.

What is it about picture stories that work? First, they break down the complex and make it simple (Griggs 1981; Stolpe 2007). Each year the largest television sports viewing event is the Super Bowl. Next to the game itself, anticipation is high for the paid advertisements. Outstanding advertisements are able to break down and communicate, through snapshots and storytelling, messages that will stick with the viewer. To this day, the Coca Cola ad involving a little boy and Hall of Famer Mean Joe Green remains at the top of all-time great Super Bowl advertisements. This one-minute commercial features a young boy offering the exhausted Hall of Famer a cola as he walks through the tunnel back to the team room. Mean Joe turns the young admirer down. When Mean Joe sees the letdown he has caused the little boy, he acquiesces and gulps down the soft drink. As the lad walks away, Green calls out, "Hey Kid," and throws the boy his game-worn jersey. This simple act of kindness and the look on the little boy's face leave an indelible print on our minds how kindness begets kindness, far superior to story-less commands to be kind we make on a routine basis.

Opening the Door to the Process of Critical Thinking

Keeping with the subject of life's journey, Leo Tolstoy's (1907) classic short story, "How much Land does a Man Need?" focuses on what Alexis de Tocqueville described as a character flaw imbedded in the American spirit. In his analysis, de Tocqueville (1945, pp. 136–137) summarized,

It is odd to watch with what feverish ardor Americans pursue prosperity. Ever tormented by the shadowy suspicion that they may not have chosen the shortest route to get it. They cleave to the things of this world as if assured that they will never die, and yet rush to snatch any that comes within their reach as if they expected to stop living before they had relished them. Death steps in, in the end, and stops them before they have grown tired of this futile pursuit of that complete felicity which always escapes them.

Tolstoy (1907) presents the universal nature of de Tocqueville's observations in the form of a short story. Written in 1886, Tolstoy crafts a parable of contentment vs. the inexhaustible nature of greed. The story begins with a visit to a peasant family by the elder sister of the peasant farmer's wife. During the visit, the two women get into an argument about whether the city or the peasant lifestyle is preferable. The elder sister suggests that city life boasts better clothes, good things to eat and drink, and various entertainments. The younger sister replies that although peasant life may be hard, she and her husband are happy, will always have enough to eat, and are free from the temptation of worldly affairs.

The peasant woman's husband is Pahom, who believes the answer to all his struggles is the purchase of more land. The story focuses on his repeated purchases of land, culminating in a surreal encounter with the seemingly simpleminded people known as the Bashkirs. They offer Pahom as much land as he can walk in a day in trade for a thousand rubles. If, however, he does not return to the starting point of his land grabbing by sunset, he loses the land and his money. The night before his quest, Pahom dreams, seeing himself lying dead before the devil. This portent signals his approaching doom. The next day, Pahom finds himself walking farther and farther from his starting point marking off more and more land. Over each ridge is even better land. Finally, Pahom notices he is far from the starting point with little time to return. He begins to run as the sun is setting. The final hill proves too much for Pahom and he drops dead in front of the chief of the Bashkirs. The chief's servants bury him in a six foot grave, thus answering the question, "How much land does a man need?" The answer concludes the story … "six feet from his head to his heels was all he needed." (Tolstoy 1907, scene ix).

The reader finds himself entangled in the universal nature of this temptation. From the beginning, Pahom's tragic flaw is evident in his exclamation that if he only had more land his struggles would end and he "shouldn't fear the Devil himself!" (Tolstoy 1907, scene i). Little does he know, the devil is listening and decides to give Pahom the opportunity to obtain that for which he wished as Pahom struggles to finish his quest, the observer feels the strain of his exhausted body and the futility of his mission. At the conclusion, the wide-eyed reader finds himself in front of life's mirror with the question, "how many material possessions will I need to bring happiness into my life?"

The appreciation for storytelling is universal (Griggs 1981; Stolpe 2007). In the business sector, storytelling in sales is presently one of the "hot" areas of focus. In her book "Slide:ology," Nancy Duarte (2008) helps the presenter value becoming a visual communicator. In her subsequent offering, "Resonate" she "breaks the code" as she puts it, bringing to the presentation format what storytellers crafted for centuries. As she puts it, "Language and power are inextricably linked … Great communication is similar to telling a story. As a story unfolds it builds in anticipation, you lean forward, your heart races, the audience is informed and entertained at the same time because stories naturally create a human connection" (Duarte 2010). To Ms. Duarte, this is a must in a VUCA world (vulnerable, uncertain, complex and ambiguous). Corporate presenters must learn from the storytellers if they are to "resonate" with their potential clients.

Storytelling is not a shortcut. One has to familiarize themselves with great stories and life lessons that need, once again to be presented to children (Griggs 1981; Stolpe 2007). In the process, the learner and the presenter both grow. But, it is not just about learning. It is also about developing the ability to think like the great storytellers think ... in other words, to analyze subjects and critically discern the importance of both large subjects and the constituent parts. It is not just the great stories of the world that are of importance in the adventure of storytelling. It is your personal story that has the ability to "stick" at the deepest level with your child. As one teacher remarked, "Storytelling is an act of love. Sharing stories connects us to each other. When I tell my story, it connects to your story" (McElroy 1997).

Storytelling is Vital for Development of a Conscience

Recently, a couple I had not seen in over twenty years approached me at a funeral. After sharing cordialities, the wife shared how their grown son had called her that week and used a phrase from one of the children's stories he had heard in his youth to describe what was presently happening in his own life. Then she asked me to tell her husband the story of the Stinky Camel. This is one example of the many times people will testify how memories that were produced from storytelling have impacted their lives.

The story of the Stinky Camel begins in a far away land, many centuries ago, where a Bedouin herdsman lived in a little thatched hut in the middle of the desert. One very cold winter evening the herdsman was trying to keep warm, when he hears a rustling noise from outside his hut. Then, hearing a scratching noise coming from his roll-up parchment window, he proceeds to raise up the parchment and to his surprise, he is staring into the face of a shivering, rather smelly camel. Then, to his utter chagrin, the camel proceeds to address him in pleading tones, saying, "Oh please, I am so cold ... I do not know how much longer I can survive ... but, if you would be so kind, if I could but for the briefest moment stick my head in your window ... I believe it would warm me enough to brave the rest of the night." After a moments thought, the Bedouin responds, "Yes, for the briefest of moments you may stick your head in my window." With that the stinky camel sticks his head inside. As the herdsman retreats to the far side of the hut and buries his head in his tunic to escape the cold ... and the camel's stench ... the Bedouin hears a crash from the direction of the window. Peering from beneath his tunic, he is greeted with the sight of not only the camel's head, but also his two front legs in his hut. "What are you doing," the herdsman exclaims, as he demands the camel leave. "Oh please," the camel begs, "if you will let me remain for just a brief moment, I will leave a most thankful and encouraged friend for life." "All right, but just for the briefest of moments," the man answers, retreating once again to the other side of his hut. Here, he again buries his face in his tunic to avoid the extreme cold … and the camel's odor. A few moments later, the Bedouin is startled by the sound of another crashing noise. To his surprise, standing right in front of him is the stinky camel. "You have taken advantage of my trust," cries the livid host. "Now, out of my house. You are untrustworthy and have taken advantage of my most innocent and generous disposition. Out, now!" But, the camel does not move. Instead, he stands still, and with a circular chewing motion the stinky camel spits in the man's face and responds, "No, I have now become accustomed to this place and must say I like it very much. I have decided to make your acquaintance and this place my permanent home."

And so it is today, with many unsuspecting Bedouins along life's journey. We negotiate with small temptations, allowing them into our lives. They evolve from the smallest and often most innocent of intentions, yet all too often we find the foul new guest gradually moving in until the stinky visitor finally rules our lives.

Over the years, many have greeted me with the remembrance of this story and how it reminds them of the power of temptation. To my chagrin, on more than one occasion my own family members have warned this unsuspecting Bedouin that I was allowing unprofitable distractions into my life, robbing valuable time from my already full schedule.

The power of storytelling and its effect upon maturing young adults cannot be overstated (Griggs 1981; Stolpe 2007). Fredericks (1997) tells the story of a substitute teacher's experiences with troubled youth. These students had been removed from their regular classes due to disruptive behavior and she was the fourth teacher in four weeks enlisted to lead the class.

"'Now,' she declared proudly, 'we have order in the classroom, those students are learning their subjects, and they're really interested in their studies. 'You know why?' She paused for a moment while all the other teachers, eager to hear her explanation, nodded their heads and leaned towards her. 'The reason,' she said, 'is that I begin every day by telling them a story. The stories help the students to focus their attention and calm down. After they hear each story, we have a brief discussion about the content. After that, we move on to English, math, and history and they're ready to learn.'"

Storytelling in the home offers a foundation upon which the family can navigate the complex twenty-first century world of bits, bites and endless flow of details and facts. This is essential to establishing direction and fostering critical thinking and can enhance the depths of one's Christian commitment, which yields a copious number of benefits (Jeynes 1999). Yes, it takes time. But, consider Proverbs 6:6 (*Holy Bible*, God's Word translation, 1995), "Consider the ant, you lazy bum. Watch its ways, and become wise."

Our new age of an endless flow of information and its offspring: an ever-increasing nation of multitaskers has generated research into the long-term effects of modern technology and gadgets on adults and children. In "*Your Brain on Computers: Hooked on Gadgets, and Paying a Mental Price*," (Nass 2010). preliminary observations are alarming (Nass 2010). Clifford Nass, (p. 1) a communications professor at Stanford remarks, "While many people say multitasking makes them more productive, research shows otherwise. Heavy multitaskers actually have more trouble focusing and shutting out irrelevant information, scientists say, and they experience more stress." And even more alarming, Nass (p. 1) notes, "And scientists are discovering that even after the multitasking ends, fractured thinking and lack of focus persist." In other words, the number of children suffering from attention disorders well could be on the rise as a result of the growing 21st century multitasking, gadget driven lifestyles.

The resulting effect on the home could prove disastrous. Nass (2010, p. 1) states that new studies are important "because they show multitasking's lingering effects." Continuing, he says, "The scary part is, they can't shut off their multitasking tendencies when they're not multitasking." Finally, Nass concludes, "the ultimate risk of heavy technology use is that it diminishes empathy by limiting how much people engage with one another, even in the same room. The way we become more human is by paying attention to each other," he said. "It shows how much you care." "That empathy, Mr. Nass said, is essential to the human condition." "We are at an inflection point … A significant fraction of people's experiences are now fragmented." (Nass, p. 1).

The Promise of a Land "Overflowing with Milk and Honey"

Juxtaposed to this new societal wave is the age-old art of storytelling. The family, business and leadership development are each responding to the fragmentation experienced in their given disciplines. Leadership and business coach Leta A. Beam in *The Lost Art of Storytelling,* details six common features or functions associated with good storytelling. They:

Conjure up vivid mental images that are relatable
Provide just the right amount of detail while leaving something to the imagination
Captivate and engage almost everyone
Are believable, even if there is a stretch
Flow and it is easy to be swept up by them
Are intentional. The point is very clear and most everyone gets it.

Probably no one understands this better than one of the emerging voices affecting the church today … Margaret Feinberg (2009). In her book, *Scouting the Divine,* she offers a powerful example of the stickiness of stories that the casual reader may miss without the presence of a great storyteller. As Feinberg asks, "How does a shepherd understand the twenty-third Psalm? How does a farmer view the last verses of Matthew 9? How does a beekeeper interpret the meaning of a land overflowing with honey? How does a vintner read John 15?" (Feinberg, 2009, pp. 12–13).

In talking with a beekeeper she discovered that the obvious is often overlooked. The promise of a land "overflowing with milk and honey," necessitates bees. Her time with the beekeeper brought out this simple fact. "Speaking just as a beekeeper, a land overflowing with honey is naturally bountiful, a land that's got everything you need and then some" (Feinberg 2009, p. 143). The beekeeper went on to explain that a hive of bees will collectively travel as far as "55,000 miles and tap more that two million flowers to make one pound of honey. A productive hive can make up to two pounds of honey in a single day. Many natural factors affect the bees' ability to make honey, including the amount of seasonal rain, the variety and abundance of vegetation, and the type and frequency of weather patterns. To Gary (the beekeeper) the mention of honey meant all these things had to be in place, a perfect gathering of good things in the land …This was a land functioning in its proper, God-designed rhythms. The result was natural abundance. The description "overflowing with honey," offers a glimpse into what God desires and promise us all—an invitation for us to taste and see that the Lord is good." (Feinberg 2009, pp. 143–144).

Feinberg immersed herself in these divergent worlds, much like others who have lived with lions and baboons, to understand the depth of meaning of these classic Biblical stories. What she discovered was a richness and depth of understanding that moved her from the position of Bible reader to that of Biblical expositor and transmitter of stories that accomplish the functions distilled by Beam.

Granted, few people can spend years or even months living amongst beekeepers and vintners. But, we as parents can turn off the television, wean ourselves from over-indulging our favorite pastime and read a book (or listen to an audio book). Classics, such as *Gulliver's Travels*, the *Emperor's New Clothes*, *Great Expectations* and the *Gift of the Magi* offer poignant moral statements. Additionally, simply typing in a subject on Google can easily access on-line stories, driving home morals, virtues, integrity and honor.

Dr. Ben Carson (2013), head of Pediatric Neurosurgery of John Hopkins University, recently spoke at the National Day of Prayer Breakfast. He spoke about growing up in abject poverty and being raised by a mother who could not read. Those ingredients, he noted, were a recipe for continued poverty. But, she made her sons read two books a week. At first Dr. Carson did not like being cooped up in the house reading, but after awhile he became accustomed to this regimen. Looking back, Dr. Carson reminisced, "Between the covers of those books I could go anywhere, I could be anybody, I could do anything. I began to read about people of great accomplishment and as I read those stories, I began to see a connecting thread. I began to see that the person who has the most to do with you and what happens to you in life is you. You make decisions. You decide how much energy you want to put behind that decision and I came to understand that I had control of my own destiny." Dr. Carson gives an excellent example of how the power of success stories helped him rise from poverty to become a leading contributor in our society.

Conclusion

Storytelling offers both valuable understanding and an invitation to travel outside the walls of the conventional home. Storytelling opens up and pushes the family unit into the world of exploration with meaningful field trips and life experiences that will stick with and form the maturing child's understanding of who they are in relationship to the world in which they live and the moral choices associated with living with others.

The choice is simple. Many of us find ourselves in the position of the weathered traveler. On his walk the sojourner comes to the intersection of two roads. One road climbs up the face of a large hill. It appears to be infrequently traveled. The path is not well marked and appears to be a somewhat difficult climb. On the other hand, the road to the left has been well traveled, is flat and offers little resistance. As the traveler examines his options, he is overcome with the sense he has been at this junction before. He senses he has walked this flat road to the left many times. Then, he begins to question what is over the top of the hill. Yes, it will necessitate effort, but who knows what "aha" moment may be his at the summit!

I propose that you; the reader may well be the wayfarer of this story. You have attempted to bring order and direction to your family in a manner that would produce a strong unit and also inculcate critical thinking that would produce the choice of your Biblical morals, but you lack confidence in the ultimate outcome. I encourage you to go up the hill. To do so, you may have to empty your pockets of stinky camels and your backpack of some aimless pursuits, but once you reach the summit, the view is extraordinary. Once there, you will be able to clearly see the land before you. It is fruitful and overflowing with milk and honey. It is the land of the storyteller.

References

Beam, L. A. (2013). *The lost art of storytelling.* www.vantageinter.com/downloads/Storytelling.pdf. Accessed 12 Dec 2013.

Bennett, W. J. (1995). *The children's book of virtues.* New York: Simon & Schuster.

Bennett, W. J. (1996). *The book of virtues.* New York: Simon & Schuster.

Bennett, W. J. (1997a). *The book of virtues for young people.* New York: Simon & Schuster.

Bennett, W. J. (1997b). *The children's book of heroes.* New York: Simon & Schuster.

Bennett, W. J. (1998). *The children's book of America.* New York: Simon & Schuster.

Bennett, W. J. (2008). *The moral compass: Stories for a life's journey.* New York: Simon & Schuster.

Bennett, W. J. (2011). *The book of man: Readings on the path to* manhood. Nashville: Thomas Nelson.

Carson, B. (2013). http://www.maggiesnotebook.com/2013/02/benjamin-carson-national-day-of-prayer-nov-7–2013-transcript-video/. Accessed 12 Dec 2013.

Cremin, L. (1970). *American education: The colonial experience, 1607–1783.* New York: Harper & Row.

Cremin, L. (1980). *American education. The national experience, 1783–1876.* New York: Harper & Row.

Cubberley, E. (1920). *The history of education.* Boston: Houghton Mifflin.

Dobson, J. C. (2007). *Life on the edge: The next generation's guide to a meaningful future.* Carol Stream: Tyndale House.

Doherty, C. H. (1977). *Kindergarten and early schooling.* New York: Prentice Hall.

Downs, R. B. (1978). *Friedrich Froebel.* Boston: Twayne.

Duarte, N. (2008). *Slide:ology: The art and science of creating great presentations.* Beijing: O'Reilly Media.

Duarte, N. (2010). Blog Webinar, Sept. 28, 2010.

Eavey, C. B. (1964). *History of christian education*. Chicago: Moody Press.

Ebert, R. (2002). *The great movies*. New York: Broadway Books.

Ehrensaft, D. (1997). *Spoiling childhood: How well-meaning parents are giving children too much- but not what they need*. New York: Guilford Press.

Elliot, C. (1909–1914). The emperor's new clothes in *tales by Hans Christian Andersen, The Harvard Classics* Vol. 17. New York: Collier & Son.

Feinberg, M. (2009). *Scouting the DIVINE*. Grand Rapids: Zondervan.

Fraser, J. W. (2001). *The school in the United States*. Boston: McGraw Hill.

Fredericks, L. (1997). *The Resource Connection, 2*(4), 1–4.

Gatto, J. T. (2001). *The underground history of American schooling*. New York: Oxford Village Press.

Gievett, R. D., & Spiegal, J. S. (2007). *Faith, film, and philosophy: Big ideas on the Big screen*. Downers Grove: IVP Academic.

Griggs, P. (1981). *Using storytelling in Christian education*. Nashville: Abington.

Hetzendorfer, R. (2009). *The pastoral counseling handbook*. Nashville: Beacon Hill Press.

Holy Bible (1995). *Holy Bible, God's word translation*. Grand Rapids: Baker.

Holy Bible (1979). *Holy Bible, New international version*. Nashville: Thomas Nelson.

Jeynes, W. (1999). The effects of religious commitment on the academic achievement of black and Hispanic children. *Urban Education, 34*(4), 458–479.

Jeynes, W. (2000). Assessing school choice: A balanced perspective. *Cambridge Journal of Education, 30*(2), 223–241.

Jeynes, W. (2002). The relationship between the consumption of various drugs by adolescents and their academic achievement. *The American Journal of Drug and Alcohol Abuse, 28*(1), 1–21.

Jeynes, W. (2005). Effects of parental involvement and family structure on the academic achievement of adolescents. *Marriage and Family Review*, *37*(3), 99–117.

Jeynes, W. (2006). Standardized tests and the true meaning of kindergarten and preschool. *Teachers College Record, 108*(10), 1937–1959.

Jeynes, W. (2007). *American educational history: School, society, and the common good*. Thousand Oaks: Sage.

Jeynes, W. (2010a). *A call for character education and prayer in the schools*. Westport: Praeger.

Jeynes, W. (2010b). The salience of the subtle aspects of parental involvement and encouraging that involvement: Implications for school-based programs. *Teachers College Record, 112*(3), 747–774.

Jeynes, W. (2012). A meta-analysis on the effects and contributions of public, public charter, and religious schools on student outcomes. *Peabody Journal of Education, 87*(3), 305–335.

Kindlon, D. (2001). *Too much of a good thing: Raising children of character in an indulgent age*. New York: Hyperion.

Koki, S. (1998). *Storytelling: The heart and soul of education*. Honolulu: Pacific Resources for Educational Learning.

Mann, H. (1840). *Third annual report*. Dutton & Wentworth.

Mann, H. (1844). *Seventh annual report*. Dutton & Wentworth.

Mann, M. P. (ed.) (1907). *Life of Horace Mann*. Washington DC: National Education Association.

Marshall, P. & Manuel, D. (1977). *The light and the glory*. Grand Rapids: F Fleming Revell.

McElroy, N. (1997). *The Resource Connection, 2*(4), 1–4.

Messerli, J. (1972). *Horace Mann: A biography*. New York: Knopf.

Nass, C. (2010). *Your Brain on Computers: Hooked on Gadgets, and Paying a Mental Price. New York Times Business Day*, Technology section, June 6, p. 1.

Stolpe, A. (2007). *10 steps to effective storytelling*. Boston: Berlee Press.

Tocqueville, A. (1945). *Democracy in America*. New York: Alfred A Knopf.

Tolstoy, L. (1907). *How Much Land Does a Man Need?* London: Penguin.

Unger, H. G. (1998). *Noah Webster: The life and times of an American patriot*. New York: Wiley.

Westerhoff, J. H. (1982). *McGuffey and his readers: Piety, morality, and education in nineteenth-century America*. Nashville: Abingdon.

Index

W. Jeynes, E. Martinez (eds.), *Ministering Spiritually to Families*,
DOI 10.1007/978-3-319-13302-7

W

Y

CPSIA information can be obtained at www.ICGtesting.com
Printed in the USA
LVOW04*1223270115

424536LV00011B/342/P

9 783319 133010